LIVING THE HALACHIC PROCESS

QUESTIONS AND ANSWERS FOR THE MODERN JEW

INCLUDING AN OVERVIEW OF THE
HISTORY AND PROCESS OF HALACHA

Answers to Queries Sent to the
ERETZ HEMDAH INSTITUTE

Headed by
Rabbi Yosef Carmel   Rabbi Moshe Ehrenreich

Edited by
Rabbi Daniel Mann

DEVORA
PUBLISHING
JERUSALEM ◆ NEW YORK

Living the Halachic Process
Published by Devora Publishing Company
Text Copyright © 2007 by Eretz Hemdah Institute

A companion CD to this book containing source sheets for the questions in
the book is available. Contact Eretz Hemdah at:
5 HaMem Gimmel St.
POB 36236 Jerusalem, 91360 Israel
Tel. (972-2) 537-1485
Fax. (972-2) 537-9626
WEB SITE: www.eretzhemdah.org
E-MAIL: info@eretzhemdah.org

COVER DESIGN: Michelle Levy, Jerusalem Typesetting
TYPESETTING & BOOK DESIGN: Raphaël Freeman, Jerusalem Typesetting
COPY EDITORS: Robert Cohen & Sybil Ehrlich
EDITORIAL & PRODUCTION MANAGER: Daniella Barak

ISBN Hard: 978-1-932687-88-0

E-MAIL: sales@devorapublishing.com
WEB SITE: www.devorapublishing.com

Printed in Israel

Dedicated to the memory of

Leah and Rabbi Jacob Mann
הרב יעקב ולאה מן ז"ל
Quincy, Mass.

Miriam and Abraham Roseman
אברהם אייזיק ומרים רוזמן ז"ל
Kew Gardens Hills, New York

In Honor of My Dear Wife
Jinny

Jerry Pinsky

This Sefer is Dedicated in Memory
of our Beloved Fathers

Leonard Naider
יוסף אריה בן אברהם צבי

Joseph Serle
ישראל בן משה נחום

Who taught us leadership, menschlichkeit
and love of Yiddishkeit and Eretz Yisrael

May their memory be an inspiration
to their children, grandchildren,
and great-grandchildren
whom they both loved dearly,
and may they be a source of consolation
and blessing for their wives

Molly Naider and **Belle Serle**,
together with whom they instilled
their future generations
with true Jewish values.

Anita and Fred Naider

Tel: 548-4765

YOUNG ISRAEL OF RIVERDALE
4502 HENRY HUDSON PARKWAY EAST
RIVERDALE, NEW YORK 10471

Mordechai Willig, Rabbi

בס"ד אור ל' ח'

[handwritten Hebrew text]

11 Iyar 5766

The Eretz Hemdah *Kollel* (Institute) publishes weekly the pamphlet "Hemdat Yamim." The *Kollel*, headed by Rabbis Yosef Carmel and Moshe Ehrenreich *shlita*, answers the questions of individuals and institutions throughout the four corners of the world. Some of the answers appear weekly in the column "Ask the Rabbi," which is edited by my dear and prominent friend and student, Rabbi Daniel Mann *shlita*. The answers were written with quotations of sources and logical explanations, and it is proper that the *Kollel* should publish a full book that gathers the answers for the benefit of the community. May all who are involved in this *mitzva* be blessed to sanctify His Name publicly for many healthy and productive years to come.

Mordechai Willig

Contents

How to Use This Book

We have tried to make this book as clear and "user-friendly" as possible. Following are several things to be aware of, which will enable you to make the most efficient use of the book.

The book's sections (alphabetized from A to K) are organized roughly according to the order of the Shulchan Aruch, followed by questions of *hashkafa* (Jewish philosophy). Within most sections, the questions and answers start with the most simple and those of interest even to those with limited background and progress to the more difficult and those that appeal to the more advanced learner. The exceptions are Mo'adim (Section D – Festivals), which follows the order of the year (from Rosh Hashana), and Berachot (Section B – Blessings), which is difficult throughout.

Almost all Hebrew and Yiddish words are italicized, but only the first time in each question (and in the Introduction). Names of books and their authors can be used interchangeably. When the intention is to the author, the words are not italicized; when it is to the book or section of the book, they are italicized.

When a source is simply cited at the end of a statement (usually in the footnote), the statement can be found clearly in the source. However, when the citation says "See…" the source *may* not say precisely what the statement does. Rather, it may be arguable whether that is what the source indicates, or the source may be a good place to find information on the issue at hand. (Occasionally "see…" is used because the cited work may not be considered authoritative enough to be a full halachic source.)

A unique CD that accompanies *Living the Halachic Process* is available. It is comprised of source sheets, corresponding to the questions of the book, which contain major sources related to the answers. This enables the advanced learner to come to his or her own conclusion and/or deepen his or her understanding of the topics. It is particularly valuable for one who wants to present a class based on the questions in the book in a text-based format. The next page contains a sample source sheet. Those who are interested in the CD should contact us at 972-2-537-1485, fax to 972-2-537-9626 or e-mail us at info@eretzhemdah.org.

The extensive glossary also serves as an index (questions are referred to by the letter of the section, followed by the number within the section). All Hebrew words that are found in the Table of Contents are found in the Glossary, even if they were explained in the body of the book.

Much time was spent on preparing a significant introduction, outlining and highlighting the "History and Process of Halacha." We encourage both beginner and more advanced learner to make use of it, albeit with different focuses and at different stages in their use of the book. The first three chapters are basic. The fourth is bibliographically focused (most will want to only skim through it). The fifth (how a rabbi arrives at a decision) may be of interest for all levels.

Enjoy learning *Living the Halachic Process*!

Sample Source Sheet From Companion Compact Disc

Rushing to Eat *Afikoman*

Q It seems that every year we have a conflict between those who want to rush to eat the *afikoman* by *chatzot* (astronomical midnight) and those who want to allow the *seder* to advance at its own pace. What should we do?

1. רש"י, פסחים דף קיט עמוד ב

אין מפטירין אחר מצה אפיקומן - שצריך לאכול מצה בגמר הסעודה זכר למצה הנאכלת עם הפסח, וזו היא מצה הבצועה שאנו אוכלין באחרונה לשם חובת מצה אותה שלאחר אכילה, ועל כרחינו אנו מברכין על אכילת מצה בראשונה, (הואיל ובאה) [אף על פי שאינה באה] לשם חובה, כדאמר רב חסדא לעיל (קטו, א) גבי מרור דלאחר שמילא כריסו הימנו היאך חוזר ומברך עליו, הכי נמי גבי מצה, הלכך תרוייהו מברך ברישא, והדר אכיל מצה באחרונה בלא ברכה, אבל לא מרור דלאו חובה הוא.

2. רא"ש, פסחים פרק י' סימן לד

פירש רשב"ם שצריך לאכול מצה בגמר סעודה זכר למצה הנאכלת עם הפסח בכריכה, וזו היא מצה הבצועה שאנו אוכלין באחרונה לשם חובה, ועל כן אנו מברכין על אכילת מצה בראשונה אע"ג שאינה עליו לשם חובה, מדאמר רב חסדא לעיל גבי מרור, דלאחר שמילא כריסו היאך חוזר ומברך עליו, הלכך מברך אתרווייהו ברישא והדר אכיל מצה של מצוה באחרונה, ואחר אותה מצה אין נפטרים ממנה באכילת דבר אחר, שלא לשכח הטעם ע"כ. ולפי זה, היה נראה שצריך לאכול עמה מרור וחרוסת, כיון שהיא זכר למצה הנאכלת עם הפסח בכריכה, ועליהן היה ראוי לברך [על] אכילת מצה אלא שכבר כריסו מילא כריסו ממנה, ואי"כ צריך לעשות כמו בזמן המקדש, שהיו אוכלין הכל ביחד הלל וסייעתו, ואף לרבנן מצה לאכול ביחד. אמנם תמיהני: למה עושין כריכה בתחילה, ויפסיק בכריכה אחרונה זכר למקדש הלכך נראה לי, דאותה מצה אינה לשם חובה, אלא אוכלין אותה זכר שהיה נאכל על השובע באחרונה, ולפי שהוא זכר לפסח, יש ליתן לה דין הפסח שלא לאכול אחריה, וא"צ עמה מרור וחרוסת.

3. גמרא, פסחים דף קכ עמוד ב

... דתניא: (שמות יב) ואכלו את הבשר בלילה הזה, רבי אלעזר בן עזריה אומר: נאמר כאן בלילה הזה ונאמר להלן (שמות יב) ועברתי בארץ מצרים בלילה הזה מה להלן עד חצות. אף כאן עד חצות. - אמר לו רבי עקיבא: והלא נאמר חפזון - עד שעת חפזון. אם כן מה תלמוד לומר בלילה - כול יהא נאכל כקדשים ביום - תלמוד לומר בלילה - בלילה הוא נאכל, ואינו נאכל ביום. אמר רבא. אכל מצה בזמן הזה אחר חצות, לרבי אלעזר בן עזריה לא יצא ידי חובתו. - פשיטא, דכיון דאיתקש לפסח - כפסח דמי! - מהו דתימא: הא אפקיה קרא מהיקישא, קמשמע לן, דכי אהדריה קרא - למילתא קמייתא אהדריה.

4. רמב"ם הל' חמץ ומצה פרק ו הל' א

מצות עשה מן התורה לאכול מצה בליל חמשה עשר שנאמר (שמות י"ב) בערב תאכלו מצות, בכל מקום ובכל זמן, ולא תלה אכילה זו בקרבן הפסח אלא זו מצוה בפני עצמה ומצותה כל הלילה... ומשאכל כזית יצא ידי חובתו.

5. שולחן ערוך אורח חיים סי' תעז סע' א

לאחר גמר כל הסעודה אוכלים ממצה השמורה תחת המפה כזית כל אחד, זכר לפסח הנאכל על השובע, ויאכלנו בהסיבה ולא יברך עליו, ויהא זהיר לאכלו קודם חצות. (ויקדים עצמו שגם ההלל יקרא קודם חצות) (ר"ן פ' ע"פ וסוף פי"ב דמגילה).

משנה ברורה סימן תעז ס"ק ו

ויהא זהיר וכו' - שכיון שהוא זכר לפסח, צריך לאכלו בזמן פסח, והפסח אינו נאכל אלא עד חצות. וכי"ש כזית הראשון שמברכים עליו על אכילת מצה שצריך ליזהר מאד לאכלו לאחרונה עד חצות, ובדיעבד אם אחר, מסתפקים הראשונים אם יצא ידי חובתו, וע"כ יאכלנו ולא יברך עליו עד חצות, וגם מרור, אף שהוא מדרבנן, יזהר לאכלו קודם חצות, ואם אחר, יאכלנו בלא ברכה. ואם החשיך לו קודם אמירת הגדה עד סמוך לחצות, יקדש וישתה כוס ראשון ויטול ידיו ויברך המוציא ועל אכילת מצה ויאכל, וגם יברך על המרור תיכף קודם חצות, ואח"כ יאמר הגדה ויסעוד סעודתו [אחרונים].

6. רמ"א אורח חיים סי' תעו סע' א

הגה: לא יאכל ולא ישתה הרבה יותר מדאי, שלא יאכל האפיקומן על אכילה גסה או ישתכר ויישן מיד (מהרי"ל).

משנה ברורה סי' תעו ס"ק ו

אכילה גסה - דהיינו שאינו מתאוה כלל לאכול, שאז אינו עושה מצוה מן המובחר, שאף שאפיקומן הוא זכר לפסח, והפסח נאכל על השובע, דהיינו שהוא שבע כבר, ולכן אוכלין האפיקומן אחר גמר הסעודה, דהיינו שיהא צריך שיהא לו קצת תאוה לאכול, ואם לאו אין זה מן המובחר. ואם נפשו קצה באכילה מרוב שובע, אף שדוחק עצמו לאכול, אינו יוצא ידי חובתו כלל במצוה זו, שאכילה גסה כזו אינה נקראת אכילה כלל. כתבו הפוסקים אל יהיה אכילת אפיקומן עליו לטורח, דעי"ז אין מתקיים המצוה מן המובחר:

Foreword

Prominent among the community services that Eretz Hemdah Institute happily provides for the broad Jewish community are the fax and internet "Ask the Rabbi" services, both for rabbis around the world and for the general public. The project was begun by the instruction of our president and spiritual leader, *Haga'on HaRav* Shaul Yisraeli, *zt"l*, and under his direct guidance. We have continued according to the principles he set out for us. In this framework, we have published six volumes of the BeMareh HaBazak series, comprised of answers in Hebrew to the queries of rabbis throughout the world. We are proud to present the first volume of *Living the Halachic Process*, a collection of responsa in English. This gives an opportunity for English-speakers to enjoy the fruits of Eretz Hemdah (which literally means, the desired Land).

We want to take this opportunity to praise our student and friend, Rabbi Daniel Mann, a graduate of Eretz Hemdah, upon whom we bestowed the "crown of *Yadin Yadin*" (ordination as a rabbinical judge) and who serves on our rabbinical court, "Mishpat V'Halacha B'Yisrael." Rabbi Mann has worked with dedication to have this book published, working hard on the details of each answer in order to present the public with "clean flour" (a polished product). If only there were more like him amongst Israel.

We thank the heads of the Orthodox Union (OU), our partner in the Ask the Rabbi project. Our thanks also to Devora Publishing for their professional work on the book.

With Torah blessings,

Rabbi Yosef Carmel   Rabbi Moshe Ehrenreich

Preface

When approaching a project such as the publishing of a Torah book, one should ask himself what he is providing that is of value and need to the community of potential readers. A plethora of fine books on topics of halacha exists not only in "Rabbinic Hebrew" but also in the English mother tongue of so many of our Jewish brethren. Those who are fluent in intricate halachic literature have access to many different styles of halachic works, whether they are based upon Talmudic passages, written as codes by topic, or perhaps in the most exciting of genres, as responsa. What is uncommon is a book of responsa that is written in English in a scholarly sound yet simplified and personal manner.

In order to understand this hybrid format, it is important to understand what responsa do (see also Introduction to the History and Process of Halacha, 4D). Responsa literature is a compilation of answers to questions sent to leading halachic authorities (*poskim*), usually regarding specific cases that arose. Historically, they were usually sent by local rabbis who wanted to enlist the expertise of a recognized *posek*. Therefore, these answers of rabbis to rabbis tend to be complicated discourses, which jump from source to source and from topic to topic and include a myriad of questions, theses, proofs, and arguments. The need for simplicity and digestible presentations gives way to the need for the responding rabbi to prove his point to the colleague who asked the question or to centuries of rabbis who might analyze and apply it to parallel cases.

We at Eretz Hemdah have offered for close to two decades, in collaboration with the Jewish Agency's Department for Religious

Services for the Diaspora, a responsa service designed for rabbis from isolated communities. To date, we have published six Hebrew volumes of *BeMareh HaBazak*, containing complied responsa from this forum. We employed much of the classical approach, while "updating" it with a more modern, academic style of writing and format, along with modern forms of communication, such as fax and e-mail.

Living the Halachic Process, Questions and Answers for the Modern Jew utilizes a new genre to present a small sampling of more than 10,000 questions that we have answered in the second stage of our "Ask the Rabbi" service. The questions are sent to us from throughout the world via the internet by Jews (and even non-Jews) with widely varied levels of Jewish knowledge and of observance.

The idea to launch an Internet "Ask the Rabbi" site arose over a decade ago, partially in cooperation with the Orthodox Union (ou) in New York. We were enthused by the opportunity it presented to Jews who need access to rabbinic rulings or advice, who want to access Eretz Hemdah's expertise, or who want the anonymity that the internet provides. Yet, we were aware of certain complications. Responses in most of our respondents' native Hebrew or even learned answers using complicated rabbinic style would be of little use to many queriers. We have tried to make peace between the rabbinic urge to be halachically thorough and the practical need to keep things as short and straightforward as possible. The result is the style you will see in the responsa in this book. (Of course, depending on the level of the question and the apparent knowledge base of the querier, the style and sophistication of the answers also varies.)

Another issue we must deal with is that we are answering directly to an interested party whom we do not know. This is different from classical responsa, where the local rabbi receives the responsum from the posek and then proceeds to explain it and apply it to the specific case of the congregant whom he knows. We have to play the role of both the posek and the local rabbi and try to ascertain or intuit the background behind the personal question of someone we "meet" briefly within cyberspace.

The next question arose with regard to sharing the accumulated information with the public. On one level, we are in the midst of making as many questions and answers as possible available on our internet site, after removing identifying information and censoring sensitive subject matter. However, we also want to highlight to a broader audience certain representative issues in a manner that would do more than just an answer a question. Rather, we want to further the knowledge, appreciation, and sophistication of those with an interest in the "why"s and "how do we know"s of halacha. We view this project as a tool to serve as a window to the fascinating world of responsa literature. In addition to the weekly "Ask the Rabbi" column that we have published in our "Hemdat Yamim" leaflet and the ou Israel Center's "Torah Tidbits" (under the title "The Vebbe Rebbe"), we believe that book form allows for a serious study and learning experience. Thus arose the idea for this book, *Living the Halachic Process.*

What we mean by a *window* to responsa literature is that the presentations herein do not conform to the complete style of responsa. We do explain the basis for our rulings. However, for sake of brevity and simplicity, we withstand the temptation to elaborate on every nuance, proof, derivation, equivocation, etc. that go into our analysis of the sources referenced and the issues involved in arriving at an answer. We provide the skeleton; with all their flesh, most answers would be 5–10 times longer and much more textual and exacting than they are presented in this forum.

At the same time, we often find it important to hint at some of the practical, moral, or educational issues that affected our approach to the answer, which extend beyond the Talmudic and halachic analysis. This is often important for the querier and/or for the public to be aware of.

In order for the learning experience to be more complete, we are concurrently preparing a cd of source sheets to accompany the responsa in the book. This allows the more advanced learner to conveniently look up some of the sources behind our rulings and compare and contrast them with his understanding of the matter. For technical reasons, this could not be distributed along with the book. In the "How to Use this Book" page, there are instructions on how to obtain them. As always, those with questions and comments on the subject matter can turn to us through our website and continue the learning process.

Let us now discuss briefly our approach to the content of the halachic rulings that we render. In a word, that which we strive for, first and foremost, is balance. As we explain in the Introduction to the History and Process of Halacha, there are different approaches to various elements of rendering halachic rulings. From our perspective, it is crucial for the posek to arrive at a healthy balance in most regards, along the lines of the basic Maimonidean concept of "the golden path." Let us mention a few areas where this is true.

We feel that it is important to be willing to look for significant leniency on many halachic issues. However, we do not feel that the general public should embrace tenuous leniency as a matter of course. Rather, cases of great need, which can take many forms, are the more appropriate time for applying unusually lenient rulings. We respect those who go out of their way to follow halacha stringently in their personal lives, by trying to ensure that their actions are acceptable according to even fringe opinions. However, we do not feel that this is the correct approach to be taken in general or those who make use of our "Ask the Rabbi" services.

We are of the opinion that *minhag* (custom), whether it be that of a family or of a community, should play a strong role in deciding halacha. Of course, our queriers, as well as the readership of our columns and this book, come from diverse communities with varied minhagim. However, the general orientation of the community that we come from and that we serve is what is called in Israel "*Dati Leumi*" and, in the Diaspora, "Centrist Orthodox" or "Modern Orthodox." Members of these communities are likely to have direct or indirect affiliation with such institutions as Yeshivot Hesder, Bnei Akiva, Mizrachi, Yeshiva University, Young Israel, etc. While we love and respect other "groupings" and their halachic approaches, our responses are as tailored to our natural "constituency" as possible. This too is a relatively unique element of this book.

We also believe that it is positive to present our querier and our readership with a picture of the "halachic landscape" on a specific question. It is often inappropriate to give the impression that there is one clear ruling that is right in a specific case or for a specific person. Let one know that which is clearly permitted, that which is definitely forbidden, and that which is not clear and may depend on a person's leanings or the dynamics of his circumstances, which may be beyond our capabilities to discern from a distance (see more in Question H-6).

We do not believe that our published works, our online services, or those of others are a substitute for a close relationship with a local rabbi. Such a rabbi should hopefully be the primary guide with regard to both halachic and personal matters. However, we are aware that in this "information age," people do not want to be limited to a single source of information. Just as one may check the internet before or after going to his family doctor, she expects the freedom to become educated on certain issues in places other than at her rabbi's doorstep. The interest in deeper and broader Torah knowledge is something that, after all, is a very healthy one. We hope that our efforts to be one of many providers of this broadening of people's knowledge and understanding will continue to be blessed with Divine Assistance. We hope that this book, in particular, will provide a new appreciation of the world of studying and applying halacha in a responsible and sensitive manner.

Hopefully, the reader will discern these approaches and find them balanced and fair, but, of course, everything is relative and depends on the eyes of the beholder. What might seem balanced to us might seem extreme to someone else. If people on different sides of certain issues find us extreme in opposite directions, that may be an indication that we are somewhat balanced after all.

It is now my distinct pleasure to thank some of the people who enabled this book to see the light of day in its present form. Like all projects of Eretz Hemdah, this project was guided by our *rashei kollel* (deans), Rav Yosef Carmel and Rav Moshe Ehrenreich. Their continual dreaming and implementation of the idea of training serious scholars as rabbinic leaders for the Religious Zionist community and beyond has enjoyed great success. Likewise, they have been the driving force behind the many additional projects Eretz Hemdah has undertaken to aid the worldwide Jewish community. These include but are not limited to: providing a respected address for halachic responses; training, enriching, and energizing the education of emerging and established rabbis; a variety of publications on subjects of the day; founding a rabbinical court for monetary matters that is dedicated to professionalism and responsiveness to the realities of the modern economic climate. All these successes can also be credited to our founding president, mentor, and spiritual guide, *HaGaon HaRav* Shaul Yisraeli, whose accomplishments extended to every aspect of rabbinic endeavor. His involvement during the Institute's first decade and his memory over the last decade since his death have shaped our course.

The English language "Ask the Rabbi" service, from which the questions before you are primarily taken, has been guided by Rav Carmel with great dedication and expertise. It is he who approves answers, written by the young rabbis of the *Kollel* (advanced institute) and a group of volunteers, including distinguished retired rabbis, which are sent out to queriers. Because much editorial work has gone into the preparation of the answers that are published and since the deans and fellows of Eretz Hemdah are not native English speakers, I must take responsibility for the final word and wording of the material within. Keeping this responsibility in mind, I researched and wrote the great majority of the responsa in this book. As always, everything was done with the approach of Eretz Hemdah in mind as much as possible. Many of the halachic rulings and their presentation were discussed at length with our deans.

To bring the literary quality of this book up to the standard we strive for, I enlisted the help of *avi mori* (my father/teacher), Rabbi Dr. Jonah Mann. He went over the texts with great dedication, making many important corrections and comments, with some further assistance from *imi morati* (my mother/teacher), Tirtza Mann. To complete the family effort, my oldest daughter, Aviva, compiled the texts for the accompanying CD. Riki Freudenstein has been proofreading "Hemdat Yamim," the feeder to this book, for many years. The office staff at Eretz Hemdah, led by Yafa Rozenhak, has been of inestimable help in all of the Institute's endeavors, including this one. My sincere thanks to all of them. Thank you to the staff at Devora Publishing, led by Yaacov Peterseil and Daniella Barak, including Eli Cohen, Sybil Erlich and Rahel Jaskow for their professionalism and friendship.

Teachers, colleagues, friends, and students helped both in researching the answers and in reviewing portions of the text of the book. Those who have helped in researching and crafting answers include: from Eretz Hemdah – Rabbi Menachem Jacobowitz, Rabbi Dr. Menachem Epstein, Rabbi Amotz Kohen, and Rabbi Natanel Chayat; from Yeshiva University – my *rebbe* and senior colleague, Rabbi Dovid Miller, and Rabbi Assaf Bednarsh. Regarding reviewing parts of the end product, I would like to thank: Rabbi Menachem Jacobowitz, Rabbi Dovid Miller, Rabbi Dr. Aharon Rakeffet, Rabbi Dr. Adam Ferziger, and Rabbi Shmuel Goldin, who made suggestions that have been implemented, and other friends, colleagues, and students who have reviewed sections and/or given encouragement. I want to express my very special thanks to my rebbe, Rabbi Mordechai Willig. In addition to helping me in so many ways over the years, he went over all of the responsa in this book and offered many valuable insights in their regard. Another special thanks goes to my wife, Natanya, not only for her support, but for her *rebbetzin*'s instincts and insights that also are imprinted on this project. May we be blessed to continue to educate our children in the ways of Torah, *yir'ah*, and *middot tovot* and continue to see *nachas* from them.

Finally and above all, I personally – and we at Eretz Hemdah – thank HaShem not only for life and health but also for His help in enabling us to be involved in the beloved endeavor of teaching His Torah to His people from His Holy Land. May we all be blessed to continue to do so.

Rabbi Daniel Mann
Shevat 5767 (February 2007)

Introduction

The History and Process of Halacha

In the next several pages, we will try to provide a very basic history of the way halacha developed and the rudiments of how it works. We do not intend to present innovative discoveries or to provide a rigorous academic thesis on these topics. Rather, we want to simply and clearly present facts and explain phenomena that are prerequisites to putting the responsa in this book and, indeed, the serious study of any realm of halacha in perspective. This can enable the novice to navigate the ensuing halachic discussions, as well as help the "halachically experienced," who may have overlooked some information or under-appreciated certain phenomena, to achieve a deeper understanding of this field. Each of the topics upon which we will touch is the subject of volumes of research literature. We hope that, in this condensed form, the information will be more appropriate for our purposes.

1. Halacha – A Basic Definition

We will start with a basic working definition of the Hebrew word halacha. This noun comes from the verb root for walking or going. As we go through life, we need a path to follow in order to safely reach our intended destination. In the spiritual realm, it is insufficient simply to *desire* to serve HaShem (God) and to bring ourselves to a high spiritual level and to closeness to Him. We need to know what practical steps we must take in order to reach the destination. For the most part, HaShem gave us instructions how to reach this lofty goal. These specific instructions are the basis of halacha. (Note: often in rabbinic jargon, including in this work, halacha also refers to the opinion that is accepted as normative practice.)

Halacha tells us what we are supposed to do and from what we are supposed to refrain. In most cases, these instructions take the form of binding commandments, both positive and negative, that we call *mitzvot*. Some of the positive mitzvot apply constantly (e.g., loving HaShem). Some are time-related, including daily (e.g., putting on *tefillin*), weekly (e.g., reciting *Kiddush* on Shabbat) and yearly (e.g., eating matza on Passover). Some are situational (e.g., blessing HaShem after completing a meal). Most negative commandments apply constantly (e.g., never killing, stealing, or eating non-kosher food). Some are time-related (e.g., not eating on Yom Kippur) and some are situational (e.g., not withholding the pay owed to a worker). Halacha is a major part of the body of Jewish teachings broadly called Torah (which comes from the root to teach). (Torah can also refer to more specific elements of Jewish teachings, such as *The Five Books of Moses* or laws of Divine, rather than of rabbinic, origin. We apologize for any confusion that this variety of meanings may cause in the chapters that follow.)

2. Torah – Written and Oral

HaShem presented the Torah to us in two complementary forms: written (*Torah shebichtav*) and oral (*Torah shebe'al peh*). The written form (the Written Law) is contained in *Tanach* (the *Holy Scriptures*). *Tanach* (or *Tanakh*) is an acronym for *Torah* or *Chumash* (*The Five Books of Moses* or *Pentateuch*), *Nevi'im* (*The Prophets*), and *Ketuvim* (The Writings). HaShem dictated the words of the *Chumash* to *Moshe Rabbeinu* (Moses) and instructed him to write them in Torah scrolls, which have been scrupulously copied since the day of his death. Many sections of the *Chumash* contain very few commandments. Examples are *Bereishit* (*Genesis*), the first parts of *Shemot* (*Exodus*) and *Bamidbar* (*Numbers*), and the first and last parts of *Devarim* (*Deuteronomy*). One might call these "historical" sections, but that, to a great extent, would miss the point. Far more than a national history, the less halachic sections are the source of much of the beliefs, philosophy and ethics of the Torah.

The 613 mitzvot are found in the *Chumash*; no one can add to or subtract from this set, not even the prophets. In fact, the other two parts of *Tanach* (known as *Nach*) do not teach us any mitzvot. In the realm of halacha, *Nach* can serve only to imply how HaShem expects us to implement the mitzvot of the Torah or to introduce a protection or implementation of a Torah law (see Chapter 3).

As anyone who seriously studies both the *Chumash* and halacha is aware, it is impossible to know precisely how to fulfill a commandment based on the Written Law's cryptic instructions alone. Thus, through Moshe, HaShem presented to the Jewish people an Oral Law, which we are to use as a tool to expound the Written Law and determine how to implement the mitzvot of the Torah. This Oral Law has several elements.

One important, but somewhat limited, element is known as *halacha l'Moshe miSinai*. Halacha l'Moshe miSinai refers to HaShem's oral, halachic communications to Moshe at Sinai, which, in many cases, provide details related to the mitzvot found in the written text of the Torah. An example is that, although HaShem commanded in writing not to eat certain foods, the minimum amount that constitutes a full violation of the prohibition (usually, the size of an olive) was transmitted orally to Moshe.

Another element of the Oral Law, which is more commonly found in Torah scholarship (but also is more complex), is the *middot shehaTorah nidreshet bahen* (hermeneutics). These are the analytical techniques that HaShem instructed Moshe to use in order to expound upon the halachic sections of the Torah. *Chazal* (the Rabbis of Talmudic times, see Chapter 4, Sections A and B) applied these rules to derive laws related to the mitzvot – laws that have the same authority as those that were explicitly stated in the Torah. Rabbi Yishmael had a list of thirteen such rules. In the post-Talmudic period, we no longer derive laws using this system. Rather, we study the laws that Chazal obtained with this method and try to understand the laws' parameters. Even understanding hermeneutics on this level is very complex, and few people in recent generations have had the confidence to expound upon it. Thus, most post-Talmudic halachic analysis is aimed at uncovering what the Talmudic texts mean and applying them, rather than trying to analyze the laws from their source in the Written Law.

3. Rabbinic Law

In addition to the authority given to the Rabbis to extrapolate Torah laws, the Torah also authorized the Rabbis to create a set of rabbinic laws. These rabbinic laws "encase" the Torah laws with extra provisions, whose stated purpose is to protect the existing Torah laws. In other words, if one would be allowed to do x, which the Torah permits, he might go a step further and do y, which the Torah forbids. Therefore, the Rabbis forbade us to do x. The rabbinic parlance for this practice is "making a fence" around the Torah. These rabbinic laws broaden the scope of halacha tremendously. For example, the Torah forbids cooking in milk only of meat from some mammals. The Rabbis extended the prohibition to poultry. Even though birds do not produce milk, their meat has similarities to beef. Therefore, the Rabbis were concerned that if one would eat chicken cooked in milk, he might eat beef cooked in milk (see Question E-1).

Chazal also had the authority to make *takanot* (singular: *takana*). Takanot are institutions made in order to alleviate problems or to meet new challenges within society, from either a religious or even a social or economic perspective. Some examples are the takana not to marry more than one wife and the altering of the rules of business transactions to prevent abuse of the Torah's legal system.

Chazal also created rabbinic positive mitzvot, particularly when they viewed them as logical extensions of Torah principles. For example, the holiday of Chanuka, with all of its laws, is rabbinic in origin. The Rabbis took the existing principles of showing thanks to HaShem and performing acts to perpetuate the memory of His miracles and applied them to miracles that occurred in their days. Also, although the Torah mentions blessing HaShem for food only after it has been consumed, Chazal determined that it is proper to do so before eating it as well.

There are differences in severity and in regard to certain details between Torah laws and rabbinic ones. However, observant Jews treat the two as equally binding except in circumstances where halacha distinguishes between them. The major differences between the two categories regard punishment (which we do not administer in our days) and where there is doubt whether something is forbidden.

4. Rabbinic Historical Periods and Bibliographical Notes

The Oral Law was intended to remain in oral form, as it did for more than a millennium. However, nearly 2,000 years ago, the Rabbis foresaw that if they did not start recording Torah ideas and rulings, much would be lost. This was due to difficulties that prevented the scholars of the time from reaching the levels of their predecessors. Therefore, they decided to "bend the rules" and allow the Oral Law to be written. Once this change was implemented, a new scholastic phenomenon arose that revolutionized the nature of Torah study and brought about the Jewish bookshelf. We will now briefly review different types of halachic literature, according to their time-periods, and explain the function of each.

Note: For a variety of reasons, we refer to the periods using approximate, rounded dates.

A. *Tanna'im* (1 CE–200 CE)

The post-Biblical period began about twenty-four centuries ago with an assembly of scholars known as *Anshei K'nesset HaGedola* and continued with pairs of leading scholars known as the *Zugot*. However, major records of rabbinic literature begin just over 2,000 years ago in *Eretz Yisrael* (the Land of Israel) with the scholars called the *Tanna'im*. Some of the most famous earlier Tanna'im include Hillel and Shammai and their academies, R. (= Rabbi) Akiva, R. Gamliel, and R. Yehoshua. The later Tanna'im, among whom R. Akiva's students were particularly prominent, include R. Yehuda, R. Meir, R. Shimon, R. Yossi, and, finally, R. Yehuda HaNasi (approximately 200 CE). R. Yehuda HaNasi has particular importance in our context. He selected the most authoritative formulations of Tanna'ic discussions and decisions from among the tens of thousands that circulated throughout the various academies. These passages were called *mishnayot* (singular, *mishna*), which, roughly, means learnings. R. Yehuda HaNasi organized the mishnayot in a way that addresses the gamut of halachic issues.

The mishnayot were compiled into six sections or *sedarim*. These sedarim, collectively, are known as *Shas* (the acronym of the Hebrew *shisha sedarim* – six sections). The sedarim were broken down further into *massechtot* (tractates). An overview of the content of the sedarim is found in section B. A generation later, Rav (Rabbi) Chiya and Rav Oshaya compiled other Tanna'ic statements into *toseftot*, which accompany the mishnayot according to the order of *Shas*. The Tanna'ic statements that were not included in either compilation are called *baraitot*. They are often cited by the *gemara* as proof in cases where they give more details on particular topics than do the mishnayot.

B. *Amora'im* (200–500 CE)

After the compilation of the mishnayot by R. Yehudah HaNasi, there was a general acceptance that future generations of scholars would not argue with the Tanna'im. The rationale for this practice, which would be repeated in a similar manner later in halachic history, was as follows. Moshe, who was taught by HaShem, was the source of all Torah scholarship, which he possessed at the highest attainable level. He passed down all that was humanly possible to his disciple, Yehoshua (Joshua), thereby starting an uninterrupted chain of transmission. The accepted assumption is that the closer one is to the beginning of the chain, the higher is his authority. At different points in history, there was a consensus that a clear demarcation between the scholars of different eras had passed. These demarcations were often accompanied by monumental halachic works that summarized the scholarship of the era that was concluding. Under those circumstances, it was decided, formally and/or popularly, that scholars would never again be able to reach the heights of scholarship of their predecessors and that they should, therefore, not argue with them.

Following the period of the Tanna'im was the period of the Amora'im, which lasted for approximately 300 years. The Amora'im made a monumental contribution to the Torah world by discussing the mishnayot, determining the reasons behind them, and applying the general principles that they derived to cases where there was no recorded ruling by the Tanna'im. Moreover, in cases of dispute (*machloket*), the Amora'im were faced with the task of deciding which opinions of the Tanna'im to accept as halacha. In this regard, they formulated several rules. For example, we accept the opinion of the majority over that of the minority. We accept an anonymous opinion in a mishna over an opinion that is found elsewhere in the name of a specific scholar. We accept the opinions of the Academy of Hillel over those of the Academy of Shammai. There are many other rules and notable exceptions to the rules.

At the time of the Amora'im, there were two major Jewish communities and Torah centers in the world: Eretz Yisrael and *Bavel* (Babylonia). Despite the geographical distance between these centers, scholars, students, and scholarly information moved from one to the other. During this period, due in great part to oppression and poverty in Eretz Yisrael, the Babylonian center became the dominant one. Before its scholarship dwindled, in the midst of the Amora'ic period, significant portions of the scholarship in Eretz Yisrael's centers were redacted and compiled to form a work that we call the *Talmud Yerushalmi* (The Learning of Jerusalem).

Although serious scholarship existed throughout Bavel, two major centers arose in Sura and Nehardea (and, later, in Pumbidita). Each had its own academy and academy head (see more in the section on *Ge'onim*). The work that summarized the scholarship of the Amora'im, which was organized by Ravina and Rav Ashi in around 500 CE, is called the *Talmud Bavli* (The Learning of Babylonia). Of the two Talmuds, the *Talmud Bavli* is studied far more. Several factors contribute to this phenomenon: the *Talmud Yerushalmi* is written in difficult language and syntax; it has more variant texts; it covers a period that ended earlier than the period covered by the *Talmud Bavli*; and it has shorter discussions on the topics that are still applicable on a daily basis when Jews live out of Israel and are without the Temple. When a Talmudic scholar, in citing a source, gives the name of a massechet (a book of Talmud) and a page number, he is referring to the page of the *Talmud Bavli*, in the standard editions. Each page number refers to two sides of a page, and we distinguish between the sides – referring to "a" and "b."

The basic structure of the Talmud, both for the Bavli and for the Yerushalmi, is as follows. Generally, the mishnayot that comprise a tractate are cited one at a time. After each one, there is a section of corresponding *gemara*, which is the analysis of the text of the mishna and the ensuing discussion. It is noteworthy that it is not unusual for the gemara to discuss matters that are quite tangential to the mishna's contents. The organizers of the Talmud had an agenda to find a place for a wide variety of wisdom in the fields of halacha, philosophy, Biblical exegesis, ethics, medicine, and even social and financial advice. When the matters were directly related to the discussion of a mishna, it was included in that mishna's gemara; when the wisdom was not related directly to a mishna, there were other ways to find a place for it.

With the completion of the *Talmud Bavli* (modern scholars

disagree about how long the editing continued), another period of scholarship ended. Again, there was a general acceptance that no one after that point could argue against the halachic conclusions that were stated in or even implied by the Talmud. Later generations, to this day, look for proof of their opinions, first and foremost, in the Talmud.

We will now give an overview of the topics covered by *Shas*, according to the sedarim, including a partial list of massechtot:

a. *Zera'im* – This deals primarily with agricultural laws, many of which apply only in Eretz Yisrael. They include the mitzva of giving tithes of different types and the prohibition of crossbreeding. *Talmud Yerushalmi* has discussion on all of the *seder* (singular of sedarim), but *Talmud Bavli* contains only the first massechet, *Berachot*, which deals with daily prayers and blessings on food. References to laws that are related to *Zera'im* are interspersed throughout the *Talmud Bavli* as tangential points to its discussions.

b. *Mo'ed* – This seder deals with the laws of the special days on the calendar, starting with Shabbat and including the various holidays and fasts. There is almost a complete complement of Talmud for this seder. Tractates include *Shabbat*, *Eruvin* (carrying and traveling on Shabbat), *Pesachim* (Passover), *Yoma* (Yom Kippur), *Beitza* (general laws of festivals), *Rosh Hashana*, *Sukka* (the laws of Tabernacles), *Megilla* (Purim), and more.

c. *Nashim* – This seder deals with family law, and it has a full complement of Talmud. Massechtot include *Kiddushin* (marriage), *Gittin* (divorce), *Ketubot* (monetary laws between husband and wife), *Yevamot* (levirate marriage), *Nedarim* (oaths), and *Sota* (adultery).

d. *Nezikin* – Although the word *nezikin* literally refers to damages, this seder discusses the entire range of monetary law and some additional topics. The main topic of monetary law is broken into three massechtot known as "gates," *Bava Kama*,

Bava Metzia, and *Bava Batra*. *Sanhedrin* and *Makkot* discuss the workings of courts, including the administration, when warranted, of punishments. This seder also includes massechtot that deal with a variety of important ancillary topics, such as *Avoda Zara* (idolatry) and *Avot* (general ethics). There are Talmudic tractates on the great majority of the seder.

e. *Kodashim* – The word *kodashim* means sacred items. This seder deals with the Temple (*Middot*), the sacrifices that were brought there for a variety of purposes (*Zevachim, Menachot, K'ritot, Tamid, Bechorot, Kinim*), donations to the Temple (*Arachin*), and their misuse (*Me'ila*). *Chulin* deals primarily with the *kashrut* of animals. There are tractates of *Talmud Bavli* on most of the seder, and most of the tractates are relatively short. Other than kashrut topics of *Massechet Chulin*, these topics come up rarely in our book, which generally deals with modern, day-to-day questions. However, as anyone who has studied Talmud knows, concepts and precedents learned in one place can apply to another in surprising ways. Thus, in addition to its inherent value as Torah, Kodashim also teaches us concepts that are relevant to modern-day halacha.

f. *Taharaot* – This seder discusses the laws of purity and impurity. This is perhaps the most difficult section of *Shas*. It is also one that has relatively few daily applications and on which there is no massechet of *Talmud Bavli* other than its last massechet, *Nidda*, which deals with the laws of family purity. Its longest massechet, *Keilim*, is concerned with the impurity of vessels, and the subject of *Ohalot* is the impurity associated with being in a covered area with a corpse.

c. *Ge'onim* (500–1000 CE)

We have relatively little literature from and information about this period of approximately 500 years. The world's rabbinic scholarship was concentrated in the academies of Bavel, which survived throughout the periods of the Amora'im and the *Ge'onim*. In fact, the term *ga'on* (the singular of ge'onim) was the title of the head and leading scholar of each of the academies. The academy heads were world Jewry's religious leaders. They interacted (sometimes harmoniously and sometimes less so) with the political leader of Babylonian Jewry, the *Reish Galuta* (the Exilarch). The Reish Galuta, who was always a descendant of the monarchal family of David, had strong and official status as the political head of the Jewish community of Bavel.

Some of the rulings of the Ge'onim have survived in responsa literature or in citations by their successors from the period of the *Rishonim*. However, of the periods we have mentioned, this one has had by far the least impact on modern halachic scholarship. The period of the Ge'onim ended with the decline of the Babylonian Jewish community and the close of the *yeshivot* of Sura and Pumbedita after so many hundreds of years. At that point, Talmudic and halachic scholarship arose in a variety of different places.

D. *Rishonim* (Early Scholars, 1000–1500 CE)

The *Rishonim* "opened up" the Talmud and halacha, in general, enabling their coherent and organized study on a variety of levels. The early Rishonim were particularly crucial in this regard.

Some 950 years ago, Rashi (R. Shlomo ben Yitzchak) wrote one of the first, and still the most used, running commentaries to almost all of *Talmud Bavli*. Somewhat later, a group of scholars from the general area of France-Germany, who spanned more than a 100-year period, wrote a further commentary, *Tosafot*. *Tosafot* critiques and complements Rashi's work. The commentaries of Rashi and Tosafot frame the gemara in the standard editions of the Talmud. *Tosafot* is not a running commentary, but it discusses, often in depth, individual aspects of the gemara, which *Tosafot*'s authors felt Rashi had erred about or left room for further development.

Some of the other Rishonim who followed *Tosafot*'s style include (in chronological order) the Ramban, Rashba, Ran, and

Ritva (to whom we refer according to their acronyms, Rabbi *X* son of *Y*). Unlike Rashi and Tosafot, these scholars lived in Spain, whose Jewish community was enjoying a "golden age" during much of the period in which these scholars wrote (the 13th through 15th centuries). While serving primarily as commentaries to help people understand the Talmud, their works – known as *Chidushei* (the novel ideas of) *HaRamban, HaRashba* etc. – also influence the process of determining practical halacha. Firstly, in the course or in the summary of their discussions, the authors often state what they feel should be done in a given case not discussed in the Talmud or which of the Talmud's opinions should be accepted. Furthermore, we accept even the Talmud's implied opinions. Therefore, when one knows how to correctly understand the cases that the Talmud discusses and the logic behind the rulings, he can determine the Talmud's view on questions that are not explicitly addressed in the Talmud or even in the Rishonim.

Nevertheless, the Rishonim's more direct and profound impact on the world of halacha was brought about by summarizers and codifiers, not commentators. One of the first Rishonim, the Rif (of Morocco), the leading halachist of his time, wrote a work that modeled after the gemara, but removed much of the debate and replaced it with his rulings as to which opinions among those presented in the Talmud should be accepted. Some 300 years later, the Rosh (one of the Tosafot scholars, from Germany) wrote a similar work in a slightly expanded form, which dealt with more applications of the Talmud's rulings.

Probably the greatest scholar and personality of the period of the Rishonim, the Rambam (R. Moses Maimonides, latter part of the 12th century), wrote the most important halachic code of this era. The Rambam called this code *Yad HaChazaka* or *Mishneh Torah* (in rabbinical parlance and bibliographical citations, it is common to simply refer to the book as the *Rambam*). This code made it possible to learn halacha systematically, independently of the Talmud. One must understand that Talmudic discussions jump from topic to topic in an attempt to derive halachic concepts from precedents found in diverse areas of halacha. The Rambam gathered the conclusions of the various gemarot, reworded them into extremely clear and precise Hebrew paragraphs and organized them by topic into fourteen sections and close to 100 subsections that encompass all of the laws (and some basic philosophy) that can be derived from the Talmud. Although this is only a code that summarizes conclusions and decides between Talmudic opinions, there is no post-Talmudic work whose language is studied as much for nuance and attempted application as the *Rambam*. To this day, the *Rambam* is at the core of many, if not most, high-level Talmudic *shiurim* (lectures) delivered in the leading *yeshivot* (rabbinical seminaries). Another important code that is organized by topic is the *Arba'ah Turim* (usually called the *Tur*), a four-section work written by Rav Yaakov, the son of the Rosh.

The third major source of halacha from the period of the Rishonim is responsa literature. As practical questions arose throughout Jewish communities the world over, a local rabbi would at times feel it necessary to enlist the advice of one of his region's greatest authorities. In those times, it was rarely practical to send a letter to another part of the world. In fact, it was not usually necessary, as most countries had at least one outstanding, recognized halachic authority (*posek*).

The responsa, known in Hebrew as *shut*, an acronym for *she'eilot u'teshuvot* (questions and answers), are fascinating to study as they reveal the thought process of the posek and often provide a historical and human perspective. However, the application to halacha is, in some ways, more difficult in the case of responsa than in the case of either of the other two major sources of halacha from the Rishonim. The commentaries and codes deal primarily with general cases concerning a single issue under normal circumstances. Likewise, the main purpose of the section in the code is to determine the "generic" halacha on a given issue. Responsa literature deals primarily with real-life questions that were so complicated or serious that the local authority did not want to rely upon his own understanding. Several issues may interplay in one case. (See Chapter 5, Stage 4 for greater perspective.) Often the ruling is based on multiple doubts. For example, we can be lenient in a certain case because of a combination of several, related or independent, possible reasons for leniency. The combination of reasons can allow for leniency even if each individual reason is not convincing. The level of need of the person on whose behalf the question is asked (by his rabbi) may play a major role. In many cases, a posek will lean toward a strict ruling, yet will be lenient in the event of great need. In other cases, he may lean toward leniency but suggest stringency for those who have easy alternatives. It is, thus, often difficult to identify the posek's halachic opinion in a generic case. Nevertheless, the study of responsa is crucial for determining halacha, both despite and because of its special nature. Most of the published responsa are written in an in-depth and clear manner that makes the author's view of the general issues quite apparent. Furthermore, because the responsa are concerned with specific circumstances, a posek can study how centuries of predecessors applied Talmudic principles to complex and touchy real-life situations.

We will list a sample of the major authors of responsa, categorizing them by period and region, distinguishing between Sephardic and Ashkenazic and, very roughly, between early and late. Please note that, in the context of Rishonim, the term "Sephardic," which literally means, "from Spain," refers to any Jew whose origins are from the region of Spain, which includes Provence and North Africa. Likewise, the term, "Ashkenazic," which literally means, "from Germany," also includes France. Middle Eastern and East European Jews are classified as Sephardic and Ashkenazic, respectively, but their communities were small, and, for the most part, they did not leave records of comparable scholarship in the period of the Rishonim.

Early Sephardic – Rif, Ri MiGash, Rambam, Ra'avad, Rashba (voluminous).

Early Ashkenazic – Maharam MiRutenburg, Rosh, Maharach Ohr Zarua.

Late Sephardic – Ran, Rivash, Tashbetz, Radbaz.

Late Ashkenazic – Terumat HaDeshen, Maharil, Mahari Weil.

E. *Acharonim (*Later Scholars, 1500–present*)*

In broad terms, one could say that the periods of the Rishonim and *Acharonim* were separated by one historical event and by the works of one scholar. The event, which caused the destruction of the most prominent Jewish community of its time and the dispersion of its inhabitants, was the Spanish Inquisition. The scholar was Rav Yosef Karo, born in Spain a few years before the Inquisition, who eventually settled in Safed in Eretz Yisrael.

As we have seen, the main centers of Jewish life and scholarship in the period of the Rishonim were Spain (and the neighboring regions) and France/Germany. After the expulsion from Spain, the Sephardic communities initially settled in North Africa, Turkey, Holland, and Eretz Yisrael. Of the communities that formed in these areas, only the one in North Africa remained stable until modern times. During the period of the Acharonim, the Ashkenazic communities moved slowly eastward. In the beginning, Poland emerged as an important Torah community. As time progressed, Lithuania, Ukraine, Russia, and Hungary were added to the list of countries that produced major halachic works.

Rav Yosef Karo wrote a commentary, the *Beit Yosef,* on the code of the *Tur.* Not only did he explain the *Tur,* but he also used the opportunity to survey and discuss the major opinions among the Rishonim on the questions at hand. Subsequently, Rav Moshe Isserles (Rama) of Cracow, Poland authored the *Darchei Moshe,* in which he comments on both the *Tur* and the *Beit Yosef.* In these notes, Rav Isserles stressed the opinions of the later Ashkenazic *poskim* (plural of *posek*) and the practices of the Ashkenazic communities. Rav Yosef Karo used the *Beit Yosef* as the basis for his famous work, the *Shulchan Aruch.*

The *Shulchan Aruch* has been the most authoritative code of halacha, from soon after its publication until today, and it is the main source of practical mitzva observance for Sephardic Jewry. It consists of the same four sections and (approximately) 1500 *simanim* (chapters) as does the *Tur*. To understand the source and rationale for the *Shulchan Aruch's* rulings, one can refer to the *Beit Yosef* and, usually, see the explanation in the author's own words. The Rama inserted glosses into the text of the *Shulchan Aruch* that reflect how Ashkenazic rulings differ from those of the Shulchan Aruch. Where the Rama does not comment, the *Shulchan Aruch's* ruling is assumed to be binding, unless proven otherwise, for the Ashkenazic communities as well. The *Shulchan Aruch*, as modified by the Rama's glosses, is still the most important authority for Ashkenazic communities the world over.

The four sections of the *Tur/Shulchan Aruch* are:

ORACH CHAYIM: This name means "the way of life." The first third of this section deals with daily rituals chronologically from the time one wakes up in the morning until he goes to sleep at night. It includes the laws related to hygiene, wearing *tzitzit*, donning tefillin, the prayers, and the blessings before and after eating foods. The weekly laws of Shabbat and the brief laws of the new month are contained in the next third of *Orach Chayim*, and the annual festivals are covered in the final third.

YOREH DEAH: This section deals, in general, with ritual law that is not time-based. The first third is concerned with the kosher status of various foods. The rest of *Yoreh Deah* is comprised of smaller sections. They include the laws of idolatry, usury, family purity, oaths, relationships with parents and teachers, charity, sacred scrolls, circumcision, agricultural laws, burial, and mourning.

EVEN HAEZER: This section contains the laws that pertain to marriage. Starting, logically, with the mitzva to marry, it progresses to the laws of whom one may marry, the laws of the wedding ceremony, and to the monetary and other obligations that take effect after marriage. The last parts of *Even HaEzer* discuss the dissolution of marriage. Here, one finds the laws of *gittin* (divorce), *yibbum/chalitza* (the processes that a woman needs her brother-in-law to perform if her husband dies without children), and suspicion of adultery.

CHOSHEN MISHPAT: This last section of the *Tur/Shulchan Aruch* is concerned with monetary law. It begins with the laws of a Jewish court and of testimony given before it. It then discusses the relative strength of different types of claims and the administration of an oath in order to decide between the claims of the litigants. Other areas of monetary law discussed are worker/employer relations, contracts and transactions, damages, watchmen, etc.

As the *Shulchan Aruch* emerged as the basis of halachic practice, much of the halachic writing of the Acharonim began focusing on that work. Every page of the standard editions of the *Shulchan Aruch* is bordered by several commentaries, which differ somewhat from section to section and from edition to edition. The commentaries, sometimes called *nosei keilim* (literally, those who carry the weapons), differ from each other in style and purpose. However, generally their functions are to explain the source and logic of the *Shulchan Aruch/Rama*, discuss cases not addressed explicitly within, and point out the few places where the custom is not to follow the *Shulchan Aruch*. In these ways the commentaries, while primarily "serving" the *Shulchan Aruch*, are often, themselves, the most important tool for determining practical halacha.

Other commentaries, which were not included in the standard *Shulchan Aruch* editions, were published independently. (In many cases, a commentary was first published independently, and, when it proved to be popular, it was incorporated into a standard edition.) Still other works are codes in their own right, but they follow the order of the *Shulchan Aruch* and base themselves closely on its content. Often, they reword the *Shulchan Aruch* and edit it according to their opinions.

Let us now mention some of the most important commentaries on the *Shulchan Aruch*, most of which are cited extensively throughout *Living the Halachic Process*. Most of them are found in one or more of the four sections of the *Shulchan Aruch*, but not in all. We will thus present them section-by-section. [Note that the identity of halachic authors and their *sefarim* (books) are often interchangeable. A work may be referred to by the name of its author (e.g., the Gra, the Rambam); other times, the author is identified by the name of one of his famous works (e.g., the Chafetz Chayim, the Chazon Ish).] It is accepted parlance, when referring to the book or the author, to speak about them in the present tense, even though the work is centuries old.

ORACH CHAYIM: The primary commentators are the Magen Avraham and the Taz, both of whom lived in Eastern Europe in the 17th century. The *Magen Avraham* is considered, by most, somewhat more authoritative than the *Taz*. There are a few works written on these two commentaries that appear on the page or in the back of the standard editions of the *Shulchan Aruch*. Prominent among them are the Pri Megadim, who has a separate commentary on each of the two, and the Machatzit Hashekel, who has an enlightening running commentary on the Magen Avraham. The Gra (the Ga'on of Vilna, 18th century) provides cryptic but highly regarded notes on the passages of the *Shulchan Aruch*. Important Sephardic commentaries include the *Pri Chadash* (late 17th century) and the *Birkei Yosef* (18th century), both of which were written in Eretz Yisrael.

Among the more recent halachic contributions, the most prominent was written by Rabbi Yisrael Meir HaKohen (Kagan) of Radin, Poland, known best by the name of his early publication, the Chafetz Chayim. His commentary to *Orach Chayim* has three components. Each component is named, but the work, as a whole, is referred to by the name of the primary component, the *Mishna Berura*. The *Mishna Berura* explains the *Shulchan Aruch* and *Rama*, summarizes the opinions of the major authorities up to its time (the turn of the 20th century) and presents its own conclusions. The second component, the footnotes to the *Mishna Berura*, is called the *Sha'ar HaTziyun*. The third component, the author's more in-depth analysis of specific issues of interest, in which he often discusses the topics from their roots in the gemara and the Rishonim, is called the *Bi'ur Halacha*.

We will now discuss the special role of the *Mishna Berura*. Once that role has been clearly defined, we will understand why the *Mishna Berura* is so regularly cited in this and other works and why his opinion seems to carry so much halachic weight. However, in order to put things in perspective, we need to digress to a more general topic.

It is important to point out the relationship of the Acharonim to the *Shulchan Aruch* and the Rishonim. We saw above that those who came after the Tanna'im and the Amora'im, respectively, would/could not disagree with scholars of the previous period. They interpreted their predecessors' statements, applied them to new circumstances, and, by necessity, had to choose which of their opinions to follow when no clear consensus existed. In contrast, there was no formal decision made that Acharonim may not argue on Rishonim. Admittedly, Acharonim do not generally do so. However, it is not uncommon for early Acharonim to argue on late Rishonim. The same is true regarding the Shulchan Aruch and his counterpart, the Rama. Even though their combined *Shulchan Aruch* was, for the most part, accepted as the final word in halacha, it is common to find the opinions of early Acharonim that argue with them. These Acharonim were specifically "emboldened" to do so when the local practice was different from the Shulchan Aruch's or when, in their opinion, the majority of the Rishonim differed with the Shulchan Aruch's ruling. Later Acharonim rarely reject a given ruling of the Shulchan Aruch unless earlier Acharonim had already done so.

As early as the time of the Talmud, the following paradoxical concept had been formulated. Although we revere the earlier authorities as greater and as having a stronger Sinaitic tie than their successors, we are more likely to accept the views of the later generations (*hilchata k'batra'i*). The reason is as follows. The later authorities accepted the primacy of their predecessors. Therefore, if, in spite of this, they took issue with their predecessors, it was only after studying their arguments and carefully deciding against them. In contrast, the earlier authorities were not privy to the later authorities' opinions and logic. Therefore, we have to consider the possibility that if the earlier authorities had seen their successors' arguments, they would have conceded the point. Thus, if an Acharon cites the opinion of a Rishon or the Shulchan Aruch and says that we do not accept a particular ruling, we are likely to follow the Acharon. (Of course, often various Acharonim debate whether we should accept or reject a ruling of the Shulchan Aruch.)

Having the above in mind, we can say that, at our point in history, the *Mishna Berura* is considered the most authoritative work on daily, practical halacha. To a certain extent, the Mishna Berura himself has at times been "outdated" by more recent authorities. Scholars such as the Chazon Ish, Rav Moshe Feinstein and Rav Shlomo Zalman Orbach, to name a few prominent 20th century poskim, on occasion disagree with the Mishna Berura's conclusions. Many, especially among their closer following, will abide by the decisions of more recent poskim rather than those of the Mishna Berura. However, the Mishna Berura still stands as the modern Ashkenazic world's chief authority of halacha, whose status is approaching the status that the Shulchan Aruch has enjoyed throughout the period of the Acharonim until this day.

The Sephardic communities use the *Mishna Berura* as a book for study and as a major halachic authority. However, they do not accept it as an almost "automatic bottom line," as do Ashkenazim, for the following reasons.

Firstly, in a case of a dispute between the Shulchan Aruch and the Rama, even though the Mishna Berura will explain both opinions, he will generally accept the Rama's ruling, whereas Sephardim will accept the Shulchan Aruch's ruling. Secondly, although a community will acknowledge the greatness of the halachic authorities of other Jewish communities and may study their writings, each community has its list of "favorites." Ashkenazic poskim, including the Mishna Berura, rely heavily on the following early or middle Acharonim: Gra, Chatam Sofer, Noda B'Yehudah, and Rav Akiva Eiger. In contrast, the leading Sephardic sages of that period include the Pri Chadash, Chida, Ben Ish Chai, and Rav Chayim Falagi. A halachic work of similar scope to that of the Mishna Berura, from a Sephardic perspective, is the *Kaf HaChayim*, and we cite it not infrequently.

As history unfolds and because Sephardic communities are relatively united in modern-day Israel, a new authority has arisen, namely, former Chief Rabbi Ovadya Yosef. Through his voluminous responsa and the writings of his sons, whose work he oversees, Rav Ovadya, as he is called, has presented a clear and scholarly voice that most Sephardim have accepted.

The third reason that Sephardim do not accept the Mishna Berura broadly is that the Mishna Berura was written for the Ashkenazic community, taking into account the customs of the various sub-communities. At the time, there was little connection between European Jewry and the communities of North Africa and the Middle East. Thus, the Mishna Berura does not address the important element of *minhag* (custom) concerning Sephardim. It is noteworthy that some Sephardim have registered the same complaint about Rav Ovadya Yosef. Rav Ovadya, who hails from Baghdad, does not put as much stress on the customs and approach of North African Jewry as some of the devotees of its customs would like.

After this long digression, let us return to the world of bibliography. There are other independent codes of halacha that follow the order of the *Shulchan Aruch*. They include the *Levush* (late 16th century), *Shulchan Aruch HaRav* (by the first Lubavitcher Rebbe, late 18th and early 19th centuries), and the *Aruch HaShulchan* (late 19th century). Other codes that deal with daily, practical halacha, which do not follow the *Shulchan Aruch*'s order, include the *Chayei Adam* and *Kitzur Shulchan Aruch*.

In the last few decades, there has been tremendous growth

in the publication of code-like books, written in a modern style, each of which is limited to one topic. This phenomenon arguably began with Rav Neuwirth's *Shemirat Shabbat K'Hilchata* on the laws of Shabbat, a sefer that we cite frequently. Other similar works are *Ishei Yisrael* and *Tefilla K'Hilchata* on prayer and *V'Zot HaBeracha* on blessings, to name just a few. We will mention other works that employ a similar style in connection with different sections of the *Shulchan Aruch*.

This new genre is also found in English sefarim (books). Perhaps, the first series of topical books in English was produced by Rav Shimon Eider. This phenomenon continues with an ever-growing series of Artscroll publications, written by different authors. Other individuals and organizations have followed suit. Although serious scholars write these works, they do not always have the scholarly clout that some of the authors of previous generations had. Rather than taking bold stands of his own, the author in the modern genre concentrates on compiling and clearly expressing the views of past and present halachic authorities.

We do not belittle the accomplishment of the aforementioned "modern codifiers." We note that *Living the Halachic Process*, although it uses the different genre of responsa, is also not an attempt to break new ground from a scholarly basis. Instead, our goal is to present matters analyzed with a classical, halachic approach in a format that is novel (see Preface to *Living the Halachic Process*).

Along the line of modern compilers, it is appropriate to mention a new series, *Piskei Teshuvot*, following the order of *Orach Chayim*, which is proving to be very useful and popular. This work, which has been helpful to us in our research, compiles opinions on questions related to the *Shulchan Aruch* and *Mishna Berura*. It puts particular stress on questions that have come to the fore in recent times and refers extensively to the poskim of our time.

YOREH DEAH: The two main commentaries on the *Yoreh Deah* section of the *Shulchan Aruch* are the *Taz* (also on *Orach Chayim*) and the *Shach*. The Taz once again is viewed as slightly less authoritative than his counterpart is. The Shach (Rabbi Shabtai the Kohen, 17th century) may have been the most respected halachic authority during the period of the Acharonim. As was the case in *Orach Chayim*, here in *Yoreh Deah* the Pri Megadim comments upon the two main commentaries and the revered Gra provides his notes (as he does for all four sections of the *Shulchan Aruch*).

Perhaps the most important addition to the pages of the standard edition of Yoreh Deah is the late 19th century work, *Pitchei Teshuva*. This work, which literally means "openings of responsa [literature]," compiles many of the most important related halachic positions of the Acharonim that are not found in the commentaries of the *Shulchan Aruch*. Often these opinions come from responsa literature, as the name implies. The fact that the *Pitchei Teshuva* decides to cite a given position and the way that he treats the opinion are both indications of whether the opinion is accepted halacha. A work, which more voluminously compiles opinions on issues in *Yoreh Deah*, is the early 20th century *Darchei Teshuva*. The Pri Chadash, the Birkei Yosef, and Kaf HaChayim, whom we mentioned above as three of the most important Sephardic commentators on Orach Chayim, write on Yoreh Deah as well. Rabbi Avraham Danzig, the author of the code *Chayei Adam* on *Orach Chayim*, also authored a code on the subject matter of *Yoreh Deah*, known as *Chochmat Adam*. As there is no *Mishna Berura* on *Yoreh Deah*, many consider the *Chochmat Adam*'s rulings as the most authoritative on practical matters of *Yoreh Deah*. Others favor the *Aruch HaShulchan*. Rav Yaakov of Lisa, who is best known for his commentary *Netivot HaMishpat* on *Choshen Mishpat*, wrote the *Chavot Da'at* on much of *Yoreh Deah*. In addition, there are several commentaries on individual topics of *Yoreh Deah*.

As is true for *Orach Chayim*, there is an increasing number of modern-style sefarim, in Hebrew and in English, on the individual areas of halacha covered in *Yoreh Deah*. In fact, there are too many for us to give a meaningful sampling. We will just mention that Rav Yeshaya Bloy has written fine works on the laws of usury, *mezuza*, and charity, each of which we have used in the preparation of this book. Rav Shimon Eider's book on the laws of family purity (a topic that we have avoided in this forum) is, as we mentioned above regarding all of Rav Eider's sefarim, a trailblazer in the phenomenon of high-level halachic works in English.

EVEN HAEZER: Although this is probably the least studied section of the *Shulchan Aruch*, there are very significant, classical commentaries on it. The main commentaries are the *Beit Shmuel* and *Chelkat Mechokek* (17th century, Eastern Europe). Above, regarding the study of *Yoreh Deah*, we discussed the importance of the *Pitchei Teshuva*. On *Even HaEzer*, the *Pitchei Teshuva* writes much more extensively. Additionally, the *Ba'er Heitev*, which in other sections of *Shulchan Aruch* (written by different people) simply summarizes the main commentators, adds many of his own comments to *Even HaEzer*. One of the most eye-opening of the commentaries is the *Avnei Milu'im*, written by the author of the *Ketzot HaChoshen* (see *Choshen Mishpat*).

The most important recent work on a significant part of *Even HaEzer, Otzar HaPoskim*, was actually written by a group of scholars. It contains extensive citations of countless halachic works on *Even HaEzer*'s subject matter and is indispensable for the scholar who needs to rule on these matters.

Although some present-day works on *Even HaEzer* have emerged, the number does not compare to the number of works on either *Orach Chayim* or *Yoreh Deah*. This is because the subject matter of *Even HaEzer* is not very practical on a day-to-day basis. *Even HaEzer* is used primarily in adjudication between spouses, in officiating at the various family-related ceremonies (primarily marriage and divorce), or in dealing with specific, marriage-related halachic problems. These are the domain of knowledgeable rabbis and do not readily lend themselves to popular halachic literature.

CHOSHEN MISHPAT: The main commentaries on the page are the *S'ma* (17th century) and the *Shach*, which we already mentioned. Although the Taz wrote a commentary to *Choshen Mishpat*, his comments here are terser than they are in other sections of the *Shulchan Aruch*. The Gra and *Pitchei Teshuva* serve their usual functions (described above). The most famous *Choshen Mishpat* commentaries from the middle of the period of Acharonim are the *Ketzot HaChoshen* and *Netivot HaMishpat*. The former, usually just called the Ketzos (in the Ashkenazic pronunciation) is often referred to as the father of modern *lamdanut* (Talmudic analysis). Rather than concentrating on detailed textual analysis, the work tends to arrive at broad principles that give new approaches to the questions at hand. The *Netivot HaMishpat*, which was written by a contemporary, Rav Yaakov of Lisa, is largely a critique of the *Ketzot*.

Like *Even HaEzer*, *Choshen Mishpat* is mainly the domain of judges, not of the general public, and it has relatively few practical guides. We note that as business ethics has thankfully become an increasingly popular field, more books and articles have been published on the subject for both expert and layman. There is a wonderful present-day series, serving both the knowledgeable layman and the scholar, with clearly presented analysis of opinions on the topics of *Choshen Mishpat*. It is entitled *Pitchei Choshen* and is authored by Rav Bloy, whom we mentioned previously.

Responsa literature in the period of the Acharonim has many of the same characteristics as in that of the Rishonim. However, partially because of the invention and increased utilization of the printing press, the number of works and the average length of the individual responsa has increased greatly. Jewish and general society and technology have changed greatly in the last two hundred years. Therefore, the manner in which recent responsa literature has dealt with new halachic questions, challenges, and opportunities makes them particularly fascinating and indispensable.

Among the fields where this phenomenon is manifest are medical ethics, conversion, and technology on Shabbat.

We now present a very partial list of authors and works of responsa that, arguably, have had the greatest impact on practical, halachic scholarship today.

Early and middle Acharonim: Maharit, Maharshal, *Sheeilat Yaavetz* (Rav Yaakov Emden), *Noda B'Yehuda*, Chatam Sofer, Rav Akiva Eiger, *Rav Pealim*, *Chayim Shaal* (Chida), Chavot Yair.

Last century and a half: *Shoel U'Meishiv, Melamed Leho'il, Achiezer, Daat Kohen* (Rav A.Y. Kook), *S'ridei Aish, Igrot Moshe* (Rav M. Feinstein), *Yabia Omer* (Rav Ovadya Yosef), *Minchat Yitzchak, Tzitz Eliezer*.

It is interesting to note that, even within the realm of responsa literature, we feel the presence of the *Shulchan Aruch*. Firstly, when one can cite or infer from a ruling of the Shulchan Aruch and/or Rama what their opinion is on the matter at hand, the final ruling is all but decided. Even regarding organization, many of the responsa are divided into volumes according to the section of the *Shulchan Aruch* to which the subject matter relates. Within each volume, the order of topics often follows the order of the subtopics within the *Shulchan Aruch*. We mention parenthetically that we have also roughly employed a *Shulchan Aruch*-based organization in *Living the Halachic Process*.

5. The Process of Halacha – Approaches Toward Rendering Halachic Rulings

Rabbis who render halachic rulings must go through several steps. In most cases, various rabbis will do so in a similar fashion and will come to the same or at least a similar ruling. Yet because of training, orientation, and circumstances, there will at times be significant differences in their approaches to solving the issues. As a result, different rabbis may come to very different rulings and/or practical guidance on the same question. In order to give some appreciation of the complexity of the halachic process, we will go through the stages and elements of the process and explain how styles differ.

This study will also enable the reader to put in perspective our orientation, as it finds expression in *Living the Halachic Process* and in Eretz Hemdah's other venues for rendering halachic opinions. We will discuss our approach to halacha and to the type of responses that appear in this book in the Preface, which we urge the reader to read thoughtfully.

STAGE 1 – *Absorbing the details of the question and its background*

The first task of the posek regarding a specific question raised by an individual (as opposed to writing a code or a general article) is to understand the details, both technical and personal, of the case. Two cases that may sound identical to the layman may turn out to be dissimilar in terms of crucial nuances and, thereby, have different rulings. We will concentrate on the personal elements of a case later in this analysis. The rabbi should realize that the real question might not be limited to what the inquirer thinks the issue is. Therefore, he may need to request additional information that might be relevant to the decision-making process as it evolves.

STAGE 2 – *Identifying the halachic issues*

The next step is to analyze the case in order to identify the different halachic issues that need to be addressed. Even a simple case may hinge on several complicated halachic disputes among authorities, whereas a complicated case may boil down to a single clear-cut halachic precedent. This analysis should be done before one even opens a book to research an issue. It is also one of the hardest things for a developing, young rabbi to learn since the question of what needs to be researched can itself not be easily researched. Rather, one must know how to identify the issues using logic, creativity and intuition, which, ultimately, is based upon deep-rooted halachic and Talmudic experience.

STAGE 3 – *Research and appraisal of the halachic issues*

The third part of the process is to research the specific issues that have been identified. Nowadays, there are several series of books and CDs that make a plethora of works and opinions available and relatively easy to find. Often, the challenge is not finding the information but finding the time and possessing the organizational skills necessary to sift through it.

There are two basic approaches to deciding how to deal with the available halachic information. (One can also use a combination of the two or vary his approach depending upon the nature of the question and upon other factors.) One approach can be called the *iyun* (in-depth analysis) approach and the other can be called the *beki'ut* (breadth of material) approach. We will illustrate these approaches by comparing the styles of two of our time's most prominent poskim.

Rav Moshe Feinstein (1897–1986), author of the Igrot Moshe, was the most respected posek in the history of American Jewry. Without formally announcing his intention to do so, he took the iyun approach. Rav Moshe had a highly unusual mastery of the classical sources, many of which we have mentioned in the bibliographical sections of this introduction. By classical sources, we mean the most central and respected works of previous centuries. In every generation, after all, dozens of halachic works are written and only a handful are placed in the highest tier of scholarship that all scholars of future generations will study. This includes the *Talmud Bavli*, the writings of the major Rishonim, the *Shulchan Aruch* and its major commentaries, and a few prominent works of responsa from the period of the Acharonim. Besides these works, Rav Feinstein cites only a handful of others with any regularity.

The approach to *p'sak* (rendering rulings) that Rav Feinstein was taught and/or developed was to analyze the classical sources carefully in order to uncover their principles and logical underpinnings. One then applies those principles to a myriad of permutations of related questions. Rav Feinstein also used his own logic, grounded in a mastery of the workings of halacha, to discover and to apply new ideas that are not found in the classical sources. If Torah-based logic indicates a certain halachic direction, it is acceptable to follow it in the absence of explicit classical sources, whether supportive or not. This intellectual independence is a phenomenon that is more typical of the Rishonim than of many of the Acharonim. Among the Acharonim it depends greatly on the style of learning taught in a certain region, with Rav Feinstein being a mildly extreme example of the Lithuanian approach.

To rule responsibly on a topic without the concurrence of "colleagues" from the period of later Acharonim, one must be certain that his mastery of the classical sources is indeed rock-solid. Without boasting about it to others, Rav Moshe Feinstein had the confidence that he could base his decisions almost entirely on classical sources, as only a handful of people in a generation can do. Indeed, due to Rav Feinstein's expertise, one can almost never find a ruling of his that can be refuted by an explicit passage from a classical source or even by an indisputable inference from one.

The approach that is almost diametrically opposed to Rav Moshe's is that of Rav Ovadya Yosef (born in 1920, may he live to 120), author of Yabia Omer, Yechaveh Da'at, and other *sefarim*. Rav Ovadya is blessed with a memory that is beyond astounding. (It is told that as a young and poor yeshiva student, Rav Ovadya would pay a local bookstore a small fee to allow him to peruse entire books. He would climb a ladder in order to reach a book and, while standing on the ladder, would commit its contents to memory.) In addition to a mastery of the classical sources, Rav Ovadya probably knows more books verbatim, spanning many centuries of rabbinic scholarship, than the average rabbi has ever heard of.

On almost any conceivable question, he can and does cite dozens of previous rulings and halachic discussions. It is almost senseless for him to arrive independently at a new piece of logic. After all, anything that has not been mentioned by any of centuries of authors is unlikely to be correct. It is interesting that Rav Ovadya will often quote works of living authors who are much younger and less prominent than he. His biggest task in arriving at a general halachic conclusion is to assess the weight of the different opinions and arguments that he has compiled. The "weighing process" is based both on the prominence of the different poskim and the perceived cogency of their arguments.

Most poskim employ some combination of these two extreme approaches. Few have the standing and confidence to take Rav Moshe Feinstein's approach. Few have the vast knowledge to use Rav Ovadya Yosef's approach. (We note again that technological advances and other factors have vastly improved the accessibility of halachic material. Therefore, on many issues, one may have sufficient source material to use Rav Yosef's approach.)

A rabbi's style of brainstorming, collecting sources, and analyzing them does not depend that much upon his orientation, halachic philosophy or circumstances. It depends more upon the system of analysis that he was taught, his skills, his resources and, occasionally, time constraints.

STAGE 4 – *Translating the halachic indications into a ruling*

The final stage of the process of rendering a ruling is to turn the information and indications of what the halacha appears to be into an actual decision. It is at this stage that a rabbi's halachic philosophy and various other factors, objective and subjective, play a major role. Frequently, the ruling is clear: the matter is clearly permitted, is clearly forbidden, or the steps one needs to take are *x*, *y*, and *z*. However, in many of the cases for which one needs a rabbi to research, there are reasonable indications in each direction. The rabbi will often find that according to some authorities, the practice is permitted and according to others, it is forbidden. How is he to rule? Following are some considerations in which different poskim have notably different approaches.

1. Chumra (stringency) vs. kula (leniency)

There are communities where the normal procedure in a borderline case is to be stringent (*machmir*). After all, they reason, if you were given a potion that might be tasty but might be poisonous, would you drink it? Others correctly point out that HaShem did not intend that we should be forbidden in everything until proven permitted. Taking this to the other extreme, some feel: "If it is clearly forbidden, we are willing to refrain from it. If it is unclear, then we have enough restrictions and need not be concerned about doubtful ones." Actually, although there are theoretical grounds for such extreme philosophical approaches, several rules exist that should, and to an extent do, help us arrive at a more balanced approach.

Let us mention just two in a highly oversimplified manner. One rule is that when there is doubt concerning a matter of Torah law, we rule strictly; when there is doubt in a rabbinic matter, we rule leniently. A second rule is that majority opinions prevail over minority ones. In spite of the presence of such rules, for a variety of reasons, to which we cannot do justice to in this overview, they only *help* us decide. They do not preclude different approaches in general and in specific cases. Some poskim have a clear tendency toward *kula* and others toward *chumra*. Usually, the tendencies are quite modest, allowing for occasional novel leniencies and novel stringencies but mainly moderate, balanced rulings.

2. She'at hadechak (extenuating circumstances) and b'di'eved (after the fact) [see also question D-7]

These are factors that, in general, make any posek more likely to rule leniently. The concept of *she'at hadechak* mandates that in the face of extenuating circumstances, one has greater license to rely upon lenient, even minority, opinions. For example, one's refusal to eat at someone's home would be Insulting to the host, and the food that is served is permitted according to a minority of opinions. A rabbi might rule that under these circumstances, one can rely upon the lenient opinion. A classic example of *b'di'eved* is when one unknowingly added to a dish that he was preparing an ingredient that is forbidden according to many opinions. The rabbi would have told him not to use the ingredient, but the question arose after it was already added. May he eat the food? Is the pot still kosher? These are questions of b'di'eved.

There is a famous halachic phrase that the ruling in a case of she'at hadechak is similar to that in a case of b'di'eved. In both cases there is more reason to be lenient than in the case of l'chatchila (under normal circumstances, where one must decide whether to do the matter in question in the first place). Some rabbis weigh these factors of leniency more strongly than others do. Furthermore, at times, there can be a difference of opinion concerning whether a given situation is really a she'at hadechak. For example, let us revisit the host above who, arguably, is lax on kashrut standards. Some might say that it is proper to rely on lenient opinions to avoid embarrassing the host. Others might have a different outlook, contending that embarrassment should not be a factor in this type of halachic decision and that the host should be taught that his or her standards are unacceptable. Of course, the individual personalities and the relationship of the parties involved are considerations that might need to be taken into account.

There are certain cases that are often raised by the classical poskim as she'at hadechak. Prominent among them are a significant loss of money, questions that arise about food before or on Shabbat, and the need to provide food for guests.

3. Minhag (accepted practice) [See also question D-22]

Another factor in determining the halacha is *minhag*, the accepted practice regarding the matter involved. In other words, even if the rabbi's analysis of the classical sources makes him lean toward a certain conclusion, if the accepted practice is to act differently, he might recommend the accepted practice rather than his halachic inclination. There are areas of halacha where the minhag is surprisingly lenient; there are areas where it is surprisingly strict and even increasingly so over the generations. Yet, many consider minhag, whether it be one of worldwide Jewry or restricted to a given community, a relatively compelling factor. We refer in this context to the minhag in a community of God-fearing people who are dedicated to the adherence to halacha. This community must also have been under the leadership of capable rabbis during the time the minhag was initiated.

Why do we attribute to minhag such prominence? One of the main reasons is the belief that if HaShem allowed a well-intentioned community to act in a certain way, it is likely to be an appropriate approach. Furthermore, if a practice was adopted by a community and continued for some time, it is probable that the rabbinic leadership approved of it.

From a pragmatic perspective, changing a minhag can be detrimental for a few reasons. First of all, since much of religious practice is based on following family and community tradition, if one questions the significance of one tradition, he endangers people's resolve to continue conforming in other areas of religious practice. In addition, any deviation from accepted practice is likely to elicit angry reactions, and we strive to avoid disputes. Finally, if the minhag was a voluntary stringency that the community accepted, it can take on the status of a vow that the community members must keep (see question H-12). Thus, unless one is convinced that the minhag is incorrect, the rabbi should leave it intact.

One of the factors that shapes a community's minhag is the idea that it is normally bound to follow the rulings of its communal rabbi(s). This concept sometimes extends beyond the community to a region or to a broader ethnic subgroup. There have been many instances throughout Jewish history when a certain rabbi was so respected by other rabbis and/or the lay community of the region that they decided to follow his rulings even when it contradicted an existing minhag or the consensus among poskim. As we have seen, the Shulchan Aruch and Rama had such standing in the Sephardic and Ashkenazic regional ethnic groups, respectively. We should note that both of these poskim made an effort to follow existing practice, not to overrule it based on their own inclinations. Poskim who shaped practice in given communities even when they contradicted existing minhagim include the Rambam among Yemenite Jews and the Gra among certain elements of the Lithuanian community.

Among the poskim who take minhag most seriously are two Moshes: Rav Moshe Isserles (the Rama) and Rav Moshe Feinstein. Among those who seem to give it relatively little weight is the Chazon Ish.

4. Tzeruf shitot (combining opinions) [see also question c-7]

An important, general method of p'sak is called *tzeruf shitot*. It could happen that no one factor can justify leniency, e.g., when a majority of poskim reject any such individual idea. However, several weaker indications may exist, which, when considered together, could justify leniency. Consequently, what one idea standing alone cannot do, the convergence of many such ideas conceivably can. Some poskim are more likely than others to use this approach. Rav Ovadya Yosef, for one, uses it extensively.

Note that tzeruf shitot may yield a strict decision. Specifically, if a certain practice is potentially objectionable for a few reasons, a rabbi may forbid it even though no individual potential problem is sufficiently compelling on its own.

5. Considering the inquirer's attitude toward halacha

It is important, at this point, to emphasize that a lenient decision is not necessarily a compromise of halachic standards and a stringent one is not necessarily beyond the letter of the law. As we wrote earlier, if the ruling is clear-cut, i.e., the matter is forbidden or is permitted without question, the posek has no problem. The difficulty arises within the large gray area that is between these extremes. (See question h-6.) When a question falls into this area, one of the factors that a rabbi must consider is the effect that the p'sak will have on those for whom it is intended. A factor that plays a crucial role is the mind-set of the rabbi's congregation or of the individual asking the question. To what extent are they interested or willing to accept strict rulings? How "sure" do they want to be that in no way possible are they doing something improper?

One group may go so far as to want its rabbi to permit something only when he can do so with nearly absolute certainty. The rabbi will usually accommodate and will issue strict decisions quite freely even when the doubt is small. In another community, the rabbi may feel that his members have difficulty abstaining from even that which is clearly forbidden or doing that which is clearly required. He may fear that if he forbids any more than the absolute minimum, they are likely to react negatively. This communal attitude could take the form of becoming generally unwilling to follow the rabbi's instructions even in areas where there is no room for leniency.

Even under less severe circumstances, a person may not have the discipline to comply with the p'sak. It might then have been preferable for the rabbi to have given the person the latitude to take the lenient path that he eventually did take rather than to cause him to violate his rabbi's instructions. Even if the person or people do immediately abide by the p'sak, if they are "turned off," their willingness to follow halacha in general might be compromised, causing damage "down the road." Under such circumstances, the rabbi may legitimately decide that his mandate is to try to find and to implement leniencies as if the situation were an objective she'at hadechak even when it is not.

Often a community that is generally receptive to stringencies, or at least that is not demanding leniencies, may react differently concerning certain specific issues where they perceive a compelling reason and/or are accustomed to follow an unusually lenient opinion. The rabbi is likely to explore whether leniency is possible, unless he decides to challenge his community to try to change their "bad habits" in that area. (One notable example: many who usually are very stringent are nevertheless unwilling to accept a p'sak that forbids smoking altogether or even just on *Yom Tov*, where leniency is particularly difficult to defend.)

There are times when a rabbi properly follows a stricter-than-necessary approach for a community that is weak in its observance. This phenomenon, which has clear precedents in the Talmud, is based upon the concern that the members of the community will abuse and overextend a potentially legitimate leniency or misunderstand its application.

A common, touchy situation for a rabbi exists when his community members are diverse in the level of stringency that is appropriate for each of them. Ideally, he would be strict for one and lenient for another. However, can he employ a double standard within one community? (Often, parents have that question regarding behavioral issues of their children.) If not, should he be strict for all or lenient for all? In practice, some rabbis will indeed render opposite rulings privately for different congregants.

Another alternative is for the rabbi not to give a clear-cut ruling but to present the situation as it is. He can say, for example, "That is a good question! There are very significant opinions that permit the matter and likewise those who forbid." The hope would be that the one who is less capable of accepting stringency would understand the statement as giving him permission to do the matter in question, whereas the more cautious individual would refrain because he was not told that it was okay. (Note that some people see a yellow traffic light as essentially red whereas others see it as essentially green.) In addition, the rabbi could continue after making the initial, ambiguous statement by leading each congregant along the path that is appropriate for him. Each rabbi has to learn the technique of explaining halacha to the community and to individual congregants. He has to find an approach that he believes in and to fine-tune it in a manner that is appropriate for the community.

It is interesting to consider the following possibility. Sometimes a particular posek will have a reputation for being lenient and another for being strict. However, part of the tendencies may be a result of the nature of the community for which they are ruling. It is then possible that poskim who are machmir are actually poskim of machmir communities. It should not be automatically assumed that a ruling for one individual is appropriate for another individual or group. In any event, this certainly does not come to deny that certain poskim, because of their personal nature, training or approach, tend more toward leniency or strictness.

Some people direct an accusation toward the rabbinic community: "Where there is a rabbinic will, there is a halachic way." This claim is that whenever the rabbis want to permit something, they will. This statement is patently false. However, it is possible to understand why a person might sometimes feel that it contains an element of truth. After all, if the need is great, a rabbi will be satisfied with a lower level of certainty that the matter is permitted than he normally would. He may expend more time and effort searching for a means to be lenient. In addition, sometimes when one is not able to permit the matter in question, he may be able to use a halachic system to obviate the problem. If leniency was debatable in the first place, it is likely that, in the eyes of many rabbis, the great need will "tip the scale." Thus, there is a relatively high "success rate" in cases where the rabbis feel a great need to find a leniency.

One should realize that often people get the impression that the percentage of lenient rulings in these cases is higher than it really is. The people in need do not always look for a consensus of rabbis who permit the matter but will be satisfied with a small minority. It is not difficult to find a small minority of rabbis who, when the need is great, are willing to permit something that has some basis for leniency. However, we should point out that when the matter is clearly forbidden, even the greatest need will not cause a responsible rabbi to render a lenient ruling.

6. The willingness to rely on creativity

Another matter of halachic approach is the willingness to arrive at and to rely on a novel idea, which, as far as the rabbi knows, is not mentioned by previous poskim. Some poskim will assume that if the idea is not mentioned in halachic literature, it stands to reason that it is not worthy. How could it be that the idea is valid and is not documented? Did it never come up before? (We refer primarily to questions on scenarios that have existed before modern times on a regular basis.) Others take the approach that if it makes sense and/or is consistent with the classical sources, why should the fact that it is not spelled out explicitly preclude it from being correct? Logically, those who generally rely greatly on breadth of knowledge, like Rav Ovadya Yosef, would tend to be more bothered by the lack of supporting positions, which the silence of halachic literature suggests. On the other hand, those who rely on their analysis, like Rav Moshe Feinstein, would not be as reluctant to "go out on their own." One famous, recent posek who espoused many opinions that were unique to him, especially in the direction of stringency, was Rabbi Avraham Yeshaya Karelitz of Vilna and Bnei Brak, known as the Chazon Ish. As opposed to Rav Feinstein, who would even arrive at a leniency based on a novel idea, the Chazon Ish did so more frequently to conclude with a stringency. Thus, for example, his most staunch followers are careful to use a *sukka* with restrictions that previously were unheard of.

Classically, a posek arrives at his position through explicit precedent, textual analysis, or rigorous logic, even if the idea is novel. Those with more confidence are sometimes willing to allow their own halachic *intuition* or that of other respected rabbis to be a major factor in the decision. As in other fields, one with great experience can come to very accurate conclusions based on his intuition. One great rabbi might confide in another: "I am confident that the ruling is as follows, although I cannot yet identify all of the specific grounds for this claim." Other poskim might reason that if one cannot articulate the basis of his ruling or conclusion, he should not rely upon it.

It is interesting to revisit the two poskim whose styles we contrasted in terms of research of the halachic issues, Rav Moshe Feinstein and Rav Ovadya Yosef. How are they similar and do they differ in terms of how they come to their final ruling? Both had a willingness to be lenient; however, in Rav Ovadya's case, it is a deliberate trend, which he has verbalized as an important thing to do. Both took she'at hadechak and minhag very seriously. Rav

Moshe, in particular, would come up with a very novel approach to justify an accepted minhag or a policy that seemed crucial to implement. On the other hand, when he felt that something was improper he was not afraid to forbid it, even when it was difficult for many people to accept. Rav Moshe dealt with many watershed, national Jewish issues. Notably, there were situations that were unique to a people in great flux in a new community (America), as the majority of Jews had turned their backs on conforming to halacha. It is clear from many of those rulings that he understood and took into consideration the religious capabilities of the broader community. He often found leniencies that allowed the broader Jewish community to function with some form of unity and mutual respect. We note, for example, rulings he made regarding giving honors in the synagogue to those whose personal behavior might have precluded them from receiving such privileges. On the other hand, there were other issues in which he felt that a strong, strict stand was the proper way to defend against a continual lowering of standards. On the matter of the height of a *mechitza* in a synagogue, he took a consistent stand, which rejected both the strictest practice and the tendency of some to be particularly lenient. In contrast, Rav Ovadya deals, to a much greater extent, with standard types of questions emanating from and applying to the religious community. Yet, even within that community, he believes in the importance of being lenient when possible.

As we complete this introduction, it is necessary to reiterate that the information and perspective that were discussed are of a basic nature. Yet, understanding the basic history and process of halacha clearly is a prerequisite to appreciating halachic discussion on any reasonable level.

Section A:
Tefilla (Prayer)

A-1: Set Seat in Shul

Question: Please explain the concept of *makom kavua* (a set place) in the synagogue and its origin. My experience has made me question its relative importance compared to respecting others' feelings.

Answer: The *gemara*[1] says: "Whoever sets a place for his prayers, the God of Avraham will help him, and when he dies they will say of him: 'What a humble, righteous man, a student of our father, Avraham.'" Some explain that a set place makes it easier for one to concentrate.[2] Others say it is a sign of humility and trust in *HaShem*, which Avraham demonstrated by *davening* in the same place. Bilam, on the other hand, tried his luck in several places.[3] Others take more mystical approaches.

The commentators explain that the main intent of this halachic preference is to consistently daven in one *shul*. The particular place within the shul is a secondary component.

Practically, what should one do if he finds his set seat occupied? The consensus of the *poskim*, which follows the Magen Avraham's[4] opinion, is that a makom kavua extends four *amot*[5] around one's place.[6] If one can find a free seat within that radius, there is no reason to ask someone to move. Furthermore, one may move from his makom kavua for an important reason.[7] Avoid-

---

1. *Berachot* 6b; see also *Shulchan Aruch, Orach Chayim* 90:19.
2. *Meiri*, ad loc.
3. *Iyun Yaakov*, ad loc.
4. 90:34.
5. Cubits; a total of approximately six feet.
6. Rabbi Mordechai Willig understands that in shuls where the seats are fixed and clearly defined units, even a move of less than four *amot* is significant. However, that may be true in regard to a mourner's change of seat and not necessarily in our context.
7. *Tur, Orach Chayim* 90; *Aruch HaShulchan* 90:23.

ing making others feel uncomfortable is certainly reason enough. ("Students of Avraham" should make *hachnasat orchim*[8] a priority). Additionally, some explanations imply that there is a concern only if one moves of his own accord.

If someone is not very careful about always davening in one shul, coming on time, keeping quiet, and other central laws of *tefilla*, it would be strange to choose makom kavua as his area of piety at the expense of others. Too many Jews have been "turned off" after weeks in a shul, concluding: "The only words anyone ever said to me were, 'You're in my seat.'" Although we must avoid pointing fingers at others for the hurt feelings of some newcomers, we must also deal with the problem.

A legitimate claim one can employ if he wants to remove someone from his seat is ownership of the seat. However, we would suggest that one not make such a claim against a first time, unintentional user of his seat, especially when the owner comes before HaShem asking Him to overlook his imperfections.[9] If one is himself a guest or newcomer, he should avoid sitting in another's seat. He should realize that many people find moving their seats disorienting, and they should be allowed to maximize their tefilla. In general, one should strive to see things from his counterpart's perspective.

It is wise for a shul to have a clear policy regarding members' rights and limitations thereon (e.g., you can ask someone to move until *Barchu*) and to have *gabba'im* greet newcomers and direct them to a safe haven.

---

8. Welcoming guests.
9. See *Yoma* 23a.

A-2: Reading Parasha Sheets During Tefilla

Question: You and others publish *parasha* sheets that are distributed in *shul*. You are probably aware that people read these at various times during *davening*. Is this proper?

Answer: Reading *divrei Torah* (to which we will limit this answer) during davening raises several issues: 1) *hefsek* – an improper interruption in the midst of performing a *mitzva* or reciting a text; 2) lack of concentration on the matter that one is involved with; 3) creating a negative atmosphere or precedent, which may be improperly imitated; 4) *derech eretz*. Let's now analyze each issue.

1) Interruption – One may not speak even divrei Torah in the following places: a) *P'sukei D'Zimra*;[1] b) *Kri'at Shema* and its *berachot*;[2] c) *Shemoneh Esrei*.[3] The rule is that *"hirhur lav k'dibur dami"* (thinking is not like speaking).[4] Therefore, according to most *poskim*, thinking and even reading, while often inappropriate when one should be concentrating on *tefilla*, are not considered formal interruptions.[5]

2,3) Lack of concentration, atmosphere – In the midst of *kri'at haTorah*,[6] *Kaddish*, *Kedusha*, and Shemoneh Esrei, one should not be thinking about other matters. Regarding *chazarat hashatz* (repetition of Shemoneh Esrei), the Magen Avraham[7] cites two opinions regarding whether one who will

---

1. See *Shulchan Aruch, Orach Chayim* 51:4.
2. *Rama, Orach Chayim* 68:1.
3. See *Orach Chayim* 104.
4. See *Berachot* 20b; *Rama, Orach Chayim* 68:1; *Har Tzvi, Orach Chayim* 42.
5. See a fascinating story about the Vilna Ga'on, cited in *Yabia Omer* IV, *Orach Chayim*, 8.
6. *Shulchan Aruch* 146:2; *Bi'ur Halacha*, ad loc.
7. 124:8.

be careful to answer "amen" properly is permitted to learn. The Mishna Berura[8] prefers the strict opinion, out of concern that others will learn to abuse the leniency. The Igrot Moshe[9] points out that at least nine people must be listening to *every word* in order to entertain relying upon the lenient option. One is permitted to learn between *aliyot*, if he is careful to stop as the next *aliya* begins.[10] Before the beginning of chazarat hashatz, most poskim permit silent learning.

4) Since *derech eretz kadma la'torah* (respectful behavior precedes Torah study), it is improper to read during the *d'var Torah* of the rabbi or a fellow congregant.

Although parasha sheets are sometimes read when it is forbidden or questionable to do so, they seem to have replaced a lot of talking and mundane thoughts in many of our shuls. Therefore, on the whole, they seem to have added more to the spirituality of our *batei knesset* than they have detracted.

---

8. 124:17.
9. *Orach Chayim* IV, 19.
10. See *Mishna Berura* 146:6.

A-3: How Long to Wait for a Minyan

Question: We have a *minyan* for *Mincha* at work. Although there is a set time for the minyan, most of the members come from different buildings and tend to be late, in order to avoid having to wait until the minyan forms. As a consequence, the actual formation time of the minyan becomes delayed unpredictably. One solution that has been suggested is to establish a solid deadline of, say, five minutes after the nominal minyan gathering time, after which the minyan would be abandoned for that day. That would pressure people to make it on time. Is it halachically permissible to set such a deadline, or are we required to wait until it is clearly hopeless?

Answer: This is a hard call to make since much of the question is psychological. What will make this group of people come on time, and what will cause it to disband? We cannot judge that without direct contact with the people. There are also pertinent factors that are not clear.

One question is how many people will find a minyan at a different time or place. This is only one factor. It is not against halacha to set a time for the minyan, even if it means that some will miss a minyan altogether. Just as you are not required to wait for a few stragglers after a minyan has arrived, you do not have to wait for ten stragglers. If people cannot "get their act together," then they will have to make personal decisions as to where they will find a minyan. It is also possible, as you suggest, that by canceling the minyan a few times, you will actually enable more people to *daven* with a minyan more consistently.

Regarding the amount of time to expend getting to a minyan and waiting for its formation, it is apparently thirty-six minutes, not including the davening itself.[1] On the other hand, there are

---

1. See *Shulchan Aruch, Orach Chayim* 90:16–17, which can be applied here in different ways.

instances when a person simply cannot afford that much time, which brings us to our next point.

The most prominent variable to consider is whether the time that is wasted by waiting is people's personal time or time that is "borrowed" from work. Certainly, halacha is very strict regarding not wasting an employer's time. In the context of *tefilla*, the Shulchan Aruch[2] says that a hired worker should say a shortened *Shemoneh Esrei* if his employer does not want to extend his break. The Mishna Berura[3] adds that he cannot expend the extra time to daven with a minyan without his employer's tacit permission. Thus, if the time waiting causes people to be missing for more time than they are allotted, it would be wrong to wait unless the time can be made up in a way that is acceptable to each person's employer. One should be extra careful not to contribute to creating an impression that religious Jews have a tendency of disappearing from work for extended periods, which is a serious *chillul HaShem*.

If the waiting time is on free time, then there is more reason to try to be flexible and to be forgiving to stragglers, unless this is counterproductive. Perhaps, one could even think of some worthwhile, creative solutions. One would be to start group learning (of something which lends itself to starting and stopping on short notice), or at least have learning materials available. This way the waiting time can be productive, and, hopefully, it will encourage people to come earlier and/or be less agitated when waiting for stragglers.

If the situation warrants it, you could arrange matters such that if the minyan gets together on time, then you do a full *chazarat hashatz*, and if it is late, then you do a shortened one.[4] This

---

2. Ibid. 110:2.
3. Ad loc.:12.
4. See *Shulchan Aruch* ibid. 124:2.

is a little dangerous if the minyan's longstanding *minhag* is to do the full one and it is phased out because of negligence. We cannot judge from here whether or not the situation warrants the risk.

A-4: Davening by Heart

Question: Should one *daven* from a *siddur* or by heart?

Answer: Halacha is based on certain set rules, beyond which, at times, it realistically takes into account different personal natures and circumstances. Such is the case regarding the issue of where one should look during davening. As a strict rule, one's eyes should be looking nowhere but in a siddur, especially during *Shemoneh Esrei*.[1] Despite this fact, our rabbis knew that we would not always be able to succeed in maintaining tunnel vision. Therefore, one should not daven opposite colorful paintings or the like, which might distract him.[2] It is even proper to have windows (preferably, twelve) around the *shul*[3] so that, prior to davening, in between sections, or if one loses his concentration, he can look through them and be inspired. However, during davening, the proper choices are looking in a siddur and closing one's eyes. Which is better?

In truth, each has advantages. The Sha'arei Teshuva[4] and Mishna Berura[5] cite the Zohar that it is important to have one's eyes closed. Although both are quick to point out that looking in a siddur is also acceptable,[6] it is unclear whether it is as preferable.[7] Moreover, one of the main ideas upon which one should concentrate during davening is picturing himself standing before the *Shechina*.[8] For many people, this is more easily achieved with

---

1. See strong language of *Mishna Berura* 95:5.
2. *Shulchan Aruch, Orach Chayim* 90:23.
3. Ibid.:4.
4. 95:1.
5. 95:5.
6. Ibid.
7. See *Bi'ur Halacha* on 95:2.
8. *Shulchan Aruch, Orach Chayim* 98:1.

closed eyes. One is also usually less susceptible to outside influences with his eyes closed.

Nevertheless, there is also another side of the picture. The Mishna Berura[9] mentions that the Arizal[10] would look in a siddur to help his concentration and to be exact. Looking in a siddur is even more helpful during the repetition of Shemoneh Esrei, when concentration is harder to achieve,[11] and for the *chazan*, who is more susceptible to getting confused.[12] In general, anyone who is susceptible to skipping sections or reciting incorrectly has strong reason to look in a siddur.

The bottom line is that one should use the system that helps his concentration.[13] (Some people employ different "tricks" to maintain focus and meaning in their *tefilla*, most of which are fine halachically). There are, unfortunately, communities where people consider one who davens with his eyes closed a showoff.[14] There is value in avoiding causing people to make such judgments (which in some cases may be correct), but one need not change his practice if he has serious difficulty concentrating with his eyes open even when looking in a siddur.

A factor that seems pertinent to our discussion with respect to *P'sukei D'Zimra* and *Kri'at Shema*, which are composed of *p'sukim*, is the rule that one should not recite p'sukim by heart.[15] However, the Shulchan Aruch justifies the widespread practice of reciting large parts of davening by heart considering that most

9. 93:2.
10. One of the great kabbalists.
11. *Mishna Berura* 96:9.
12. Ibid. 53:87.
13. *Magen Avraham* 93:2; *Mishna Berura* 93:2; *Aruch HaShulchan, Orach Chayim* 93:8.
14. The halachic term is *yohara*.
15. *Gittin* 60b.

people know the words well.[16] [17] On the other hand, it probably wouldn't hurt most people to look at the text during these parts of the tefilla. Consider also that many grammatical mistakes are made during the davening, and careful reading of the text could help rectify some of them.

---

16. *Orach Chayim* 49:1.

17. See additional justifications for the common practice of leniency in *Beit Yosef*, ad loc.

A-5: Taking Time Off From Work to Daven With a Minyan

Question: I am a waiter in a catering hall, and I am often unable to *daven Mincha* or *Ma'ariv* with a *minyan* before or after work, respectively. Should I take time off from my job to go to a local minyan? I fear that I may lose my job if I am caught or, perhaps, even if I demand that I be allowed to go. If my boss allows me to go, I am not sure if my pay will be docked for going.

Answer: There are various important questions that have to do with occasions of conflicting responsibilities to our fellow man and to our Maker. There is no sweeping answer that addresses all of the questions, but there is source material on a variety of cases that can give us guidance.

Tefilla b'tzibbur (davening with a minyan) is very important.[1] Although there are indications that it is just a way to fulfill the *mitzva* of *tefilla* more fully (*b'hidur*), Rav Moshe Feinstein understood tefilla b'tzibbur as an independent obligation.[2] In any case, the *poskim* mention some of the parameters concerning to what extent one must go in order to daven with a minyan.

One must travel up to eighteen minutes in order to attend a minyan.[3] If going to a minyan will *cost* a person money (apparently, beyond small expenses such as paying for a few ounces of gas), he is not required to go. However, if one merely thinks that he can *gain* money by missing minyan, he should attend minyan.[4] If one has a set job from which wages will be deducted for time spent on davening at a minyan, this is considered a monetary loss, and one is not required to go. However, a *ben Torah* who finds that

---

1. See *Berachot* 8a.
2. *Igrot Moshe, Orach Chayim* II, 27.
3. *Shulchan Aruch, Orach Chayim* 90:16; *Mishna Berura*, ad loc.:52.
4. *Mishna Berura* 90:29.

he is in a good financial situation should consider agreeing to a small reduction in pay in order to be able to daven with a minyan. Whenever a person judges whether to accept a job, in addition to considering the salary, he takes "quality of life" factors into account as well. Among the personal and religious factors that are unique to *shomrei mitzvot* and *b'nei Torah* should be the matter of tefilla b'tzibbur.

When one has responsibilities at work, he is required by halacha to take them very seriously. *Berachot* 16a poignantly illustrates how *Chazal* were prepared to lower certain religious obligations (like the optimal manner of davening and *bentching*) to avoid infringing upon the careful fulfillment of one's responsibilities to his employer. Thus, sneaking out is not a halachic option. That same *gemara* mentions that if the employer is not bothered by the employee's normal fulfillment of tefillot and *berachot*, then he should daven and bentch normally.

Therefore, you should raise this matter politely with your boss (without risking your job) and see whether something can be worked out (e.g., you can offer to come in early). You can also investigate whether you can find an early or a late minyan (certainly, if it is within an eighteen-minute radius) in order to obviate the problem.

A-6: Kaddish D'Rabbanan When Parents Are Alive

Question: We had a *minyan* without a mourner, and so we did not say *Kaddish* after *Aleinu*. We subsequently learned some Torah, after which I recited *Kaddish D'Rabbanan*. Some people questioned whether this was right since, *baruch HaShem*, both of my parents are alive. Can/should one with living parents say Kaddish D'Rabbanan?

Answer: There is nothing intrinsic about Kaddish that makes it appropriate only for mourners. *Chazanim* regularly say the Kaddeishim during the *tefilla*. The main issue is regarding the Kaddish following Aleinu at the end of the tefilla (and in a few other places, during *Shacharit*). This was instituted to give mourners who are not able to be the chazan the opportunity to recite at least that Kaddish and to thereby elevate the souls of their departed parents. Thus, *poskim* write that if one whose parents are alive says Kaddish, it may give the impression that a parent has died, and we refrain from this in order that we "not open our mouth to the Satan."[1]

In contrast, Kaddish D'Rabbanan was instituted because of the special impact that it has for the world in general. The *gemara*[2] mentions the saying of *"Y'hei Shmei Rabba"* (the focal point of Kaddish) after learning *aggada* (homiletic portions of the Torah) as one of two things that can keep the world in existence. In theory, and according to the great majority of classical sources,[3] this Kaddish need not be limited to those whose parents have passed away. On the other hand, there is an opinion that only one who

---

1. *Levush HaTechelet* 133:1.
2. *Sota* 49a.
3. See *Shut Chatam Sofer*, IV 132; *Pitchei Teshuva, Yoreh Deah* 376:4.

does not have parents says Kaddish D'Rabbanan.[4] Even though this opinion is rejected, it is hard to deny that the perception of most people is that it is said only by mourners or those without parents.

This perception causes a situation where a parent may be understandably disturbed that his or her child is reciting Kaddish D'Rabbanan. Some authorities[5] contend that, under these circumstances, there is an *element* of "opening the mouth to the Satan." What happens if a parent objects to the saying of Kaddish when it need not be objectionable? There is a major *machloket* among *Rishonim* in a case where a father tells his son not to recite Mourner's Kaddish for his mother (the father's wife, not a divorcee). The Maharam[6] says that the father's objection, which has a logical basis, should be heeded, even though it is unfortunate, as it is important to say Kaddish for the mother. However, the Rama[7] says that we reject the father's objection and instruct the son to say Kaddish for his mother.

The case in question is different from the Rama's in ways that could suggest contrary rulings. On one hand, if the parents and others were more knowledgeable about the background of Kaddish D'Rabbanan, there would be no reason to object. On the other hand, there is less of a requirement to say Kaddish D'Rabbanan, especially after a learning session that is not part of *davening*. It is very common for group learning to end without Kaddish D'Rabbanan (for better or for worse, and that is not our topic now) even if mourners are present. So why create a questionable situation when one can finish the learning without a Kaddish?

We suggest the following approach, which is in line with that of Rav O. Yosef.[8] A parent has the prerogative to object to his son

---

4. *Matei Ephrayim*, cited in *Tzitz Eliezer* VII, 49.
5. See *Yabia Omer* III, *Yoreh Deah* 26.
6. Cited in *Tashbetz* 425.
7. *Yoreh Deah* 376:4.
8. *Yabia Omer*, ibid.

saying Kaddish D'Rabbanan, but the son need not ask permission from his parent in advance. If one wants to ask his parents, he can mention that a son with living parents is permitted to say that Kaddish and hope they do not object. If someone without living parents is present, he should ideally be the one to say Kaddish D'Rabbanan, but if no one is saying the Kaddish D'Rabbanan at the beginning or end of davening, then it is fine for anyone to recite it. (Rav S.Z. Orbach gave such instructions to a colleague of ours with living parents.) In any case, your friends at the minyan have no reason to complain.

A-7: Going to a Place Where a Group Will Miss Torah Reading

Question: I am in charge of a teenage group at a religious camp. Every year the group goes on a five-day camping trip far from camp. We have found that, beyond the trip's recreational value, it is an important experience for our campers, and the atmosphere enables us to make real educational gains. We are unable to bring along a *sefer Torah* and will not be near any *shuls*. There will be regular *minyanim*. May we go on the trip, knowing that we will miss *kri'at haTorah* (Torah reading)?

Answer: We will deal with both halachic and educational issues, starting with the former.

The institution to read the Torah, both on Shabbat and during the week, is an ancient and beloved one initiated by Moshe.[1] There are, though, ample sources in halacha from which it follows that an individual may travel even though it will cause him to miss kri'at haTorah. The Shulchan Aruch, for example, describes the circumstances under which one may embark before Shabbat, for non-*mitzva* purposes, on a voyage by boat that will compromise his ability to properly keep Shabbat.[2] The *poskim* do not raise the issue of kri'at haTorah, and it is not plausible to think that they assumed that a sefer Torah would be available. It seems likely then that missing kri'at haTorah is not sufficiently problematic to warrant avoiding travel. There is also discussion about traveling for non-mitzva purposes in a way that makes one miss a minyan.[3]

In one way, at least, there may be a leniency regarding kri'at haTorah. The *mishna*[4] lists those matters for which a minyan is

---

1. *Bava Kama* 82a.
2. See *Shulchan Aruch, Orach Chayim* 248:1, 4.
3. *Shulchan Aruch, Orach Chayim* 90:16–17 and *Mishna Berura*, ad loc.
4. *Megilla* 23b.

required. Kri'at haTorah is included; *megilla*[5] reading is not. The Ramban[6] explains by noting that the matters listed in that mishna are obligations of only the *tzibbur* (community). Reading the megilla, in contrast, is also an obligation of the individual. If kri'at haTorah is indeed not an obligation of the individual (not everyone agrees[7]), then it is not critical that an *individual* who was forced to miss kri'at haTorah find a minyan to make it up.[8]

The question, though, is how to define a tzibbur. If your minyan of campers is a tzibbur, then it bears the full weight of the obligation. (Great need might outweigh this duty, but the question is still pertinent.) The Yabia Omer[9] cites stories of *talmidei chachamim* who had minyanim in their homes without a sefer Torah and understands that the responsibility of kri'at haTorah was met by the tzibbur in the town's shuls. In your case, the requirement could be satisfied by the rest of the campers, who remain behind. It appears logical that the traveling group does not become a tzibbur until it begins to *daven*. However, that occurs when a sefer Torah is unavailable, and, at that point, they lack the means to carry out the obligation. It is permissible to leave camp and thus create a situation where you will be unable to read the Torah, if you do so at a time when the obligation to read has not begun.

For educational reasons, even beyond halachic requirements, one should consider various options to make kri'at haTorah a possibility. For example, getting access to a sefer Torah at Mincha time is a halachic possibility,[10] especially for Ashkenazim.[11] (Besides technical concerns, it is problematic to have a sefer Torah travel with the group.[12]) The educational message of making an extra

---

5. The Book of Esther.
6. *Milchamot* to *Megilla* 3a of the *Rif*.
7. See *Yabia Omer* IV, *Yoreh Deah* 31.
8. See examples in *Yalkut Yosef* II, p. 23, 27.
9. Ibid.
10. *Mishna Berura* 135:1.
11. See *Yabia Omer* IV, *Orach Chayim* 17.
12. See *Shulchan Aruch, Orach Chayim* 135:14.

effort not to forgo kri'at haTorah can have a positive impact on your campers. Even if you are unable to arrange it, it is educational to let them know how hard you tried and to, perhaps, discuss the issue with them. Many of your campers are from backgrounds where they do not make it to shul every morning. A conversation in which you express how hard it was for you to miss kri'at haTorah even once is likely to be much more effective than preaching or punishing when they miss davening.

A-8: Walking in Front of Someone Who is Davening

Question: One of our columns in Torah Tidbits stated definitively that one may not walk within four *amot* (six to seven feet) of someone during his *Shemoneh Esrei*. Some readers inquired whether this is an absolute rule. What is your opinion?

Answer: We must distinguish between the desirable and the prevalent practice. Under normal circumstances, it is *at least* desirable for people not to walk within four amot of someone in the midst of Shemoneh Esrei[1] (and perhaps *Kri'at Shema*[2] and *Kaddish*[3]). This is the simple reading of the *gemara* and the classical *poskim* and displays good *middot*. However, there are important poskim who provide a *limud z'chut*[4] for less than total fulfillment of the stated halacha. In some cases, stringency is unnecessary or undesirable. We will start with background.

There are two similar *halachot* regarding people who are near a person who is *davening* Shemoneh Esrei: not to sit within his four amot in any direction and not to pass in front of him.[5] The former's main halachic concerns are sitting in a place where the Divine Presence (*Shechina*) is felt and/or appearing not to concur with the content of the *davener's tefilla*. The entire issue of the latter halacha, of passing in front, is, according to almost all *poskim*, the fear of disturbing his concentration.[6] Since this issue is only that of affecting someone else, can he waive his rights? We agree with the column you cited, that one may not allow another

---

1. *Shulchan Aruch, Orach Chayim* 102:4–5.
2. *Eliyahu Rabba* 102:6.
3. *Yabia Omer* v, *Orach Chayim* 9.
4. Justification for an ostensibly incorrect practice.
5. *Shulchan Aruch* ibid.:1.
6. *The Chayei Adam* (26:2) mentions the *Shechina* as well.

to disturb his tefilla, just as he is not allowed to do anything to disrupt his own tefilla.

The poskim have displayed varied approaches regarding flexibility in borderline cases. The Shulchan Aruch[7] rules that one can pass near someone from the side, and the Mishna Berura[8] is inconclusive on the question of whether passing diagonally in front is a problem. He also entertains allowing leniency in specific circumstances where the problem is less severe (e.g., the davener has his face covered by a *tallit*), yet he stops short of permitting it outright.[9] The Aruch HaShulchan[10] is lenient where the two people are separated by furniture that is ten *tefachim* high (roughly waist high), whereas the Mishna Berura[11] is not. None of these sources, though, rationalizes walking directly in front of someone who is blocking access to the aisle.

Some bold ideas of limud z'chut for those who all but ignore the halacha are found in Eshel Avraham (Butchach)[12] and Tzitz Eliezer.[13] The former talks about making an optimistic assumption that, when he wants to pass, the davener has already finished the main part of Shemoneh Esrei or is taking a break in his tefilla. The latter even suggests that since so few people concentrate well anyway,[14] the halacha's full force no longer applies. One should *not* follow these suggestions regularly but can use them to be tolerant of the lenient or in cases of special need.

When one needs to pass in order to fulfill a *mitzva* (e.g., a *kohen* has to *duchen*; he is the *ba'al koreh*) or he has an acute need to use the facilities, most poskim are lenient, as logic seems to

---

7. *Orach Chayim* 102:4.
8. 102:16.
9. *Bi'ur Halacha*, ad loc.
10. 102:13.
11. 102:2.
12. 102.
13. IX, 8.
14. See *Tur, Orach Chayim* 101.

dictate.[15] The Shulchan Aruch[16] says that the requirement to take
the three steps back is insufficient justification to encroach on
another's four amot, even if the latter began davening late. However, when the davener's actions create an *unreasonable* burden on
others (especially on a group) by blocking the door or aisle for an
extended period of time, some poskim draw the line. Da'at Torah,[17]
comparing this case to one who buries the dead in a public thor-
oughfare, says that it is permitted to traverse the area. Consider
also that standing near the davener with an angry face may affect
his concentration more than passing by. Of course, while a slow
or late davener should give thought to his location's effect on others, we should remember that he has feelings, too.

---

15. See cases in *Tefilla K'Hilchata* 12:113–116.
16. *Orach Chayim* 102:5.
17. Ad loc.

A-9: Latest Time to Daven Shacharit

Question: I woke up very late one day. What is the latest one can *daven Shacharit*? Is the davening at that time the same as usual?

Answer: In order to daven Shacharit "at its time," one should finish *Shemoneh Esrei* before the end of four proportional hours of the morning.[1] This is one third of the time between sunrise and sunset (according to some, one third of the time between *alot ha-shachar* and *tzeit hakochavim*, approximately seventy-two minutes before sunrise and after sunset, respectively). However, the *gemara*[2] teaches that one does receive some credit for *tefilla* after "the time" of Shacharit.

The *gemara* compares this late *tefilla* to the concept of *tashlumin*. Tashlumin is making up for a missed tefilla by doubling Shemoneh Esrei at the following tefilla. Because of this comparison and the rules pertaining to tashlumin, some *Rishonim* say that late tefilla applies only if one missed the time by mistake or because of extenuating circumstances.[3] Most say that, until the time of *Mincha*, the late tefilla is not tashlumim and may be recited even by one who was late intentionally. However, *poskim* advise that it is best to have in mind that, in case it is too late, the *davening* should be considered a voluntary one (*tefillat nedava*).[4]

Chatzot, astronomical noon, is the latest of all opinions for the Shemoneh Esrei of Shacharit. (This information is included in some good calendars; be careful to factor in Daylight Savings Time.) In theory, one may daven Mincha then, although, in prac-

---

1. *Shulchan Aruch, Orach Chayim* 89:1.
2. *Berachot* 26a.
3. See *Orach Chayim* 108.
4. *Mishna Berura* 89:6; *Yalkut Yosef, Tefilla* 5.

tice, we wait one half-hour to be on the safe side. At this point, Shacharit is no longer an option except as tashlumin at Mincha.[5]

After chatzot, then, tashlumin at Mincha is applicable, provided that Shacharit was not missed intentionally (*meizid*). When one gets up that late, it is not always clear whether to categorize the lateness as accidental or deliberate. Certainly, if one overslept, tashlumin is allowed. If he woke up earlier and rolled over in bed, aiming to sleep beyond the time, it is presumably meizid. On the other hand, some people are not capable of any serious intent when they roll over in bed. (It is a sign of responsibility when one reaches the point in life when these types of borderline cases stop arising.)

When one davens between the end of "the time" of Shacharit and chatzot, the simple ruling is to omit the *berachot* before and after *Kri'at Shema* (*Yotzer Or* until *Shema* and *Emet V'Yatziv* until *Ga'al Yisrael*).[6] The Bi'ur Halacha[7] raises the possibility that one *might* be justified to include these berachot in the tefilla until chatzot, if he was unable to do so earlier because of extenuating circumstances. However, the average late riser is hard-pressed to make this claim.

---

5. *Rama, Orach Chayim* 89:1; *Magen Avraham* 89:5; the Taz 89:1 argues, see *Mishna Berura* 89:7.
6. *Shulchan Aruch, Orach Chayim* 58:6.
7. Ad loc.

A-10: Number of People Needed to Begin the Repetition of Shemoneh Esrei

Question: When *davening* with a *minyan*, how many people must be finished with their *amida* (silent recitation of *Shemoneh Esrei*) before the *chazan* may begin the repetition?

Answer: It is proper that there be nine men who will listen and respond to *the entire repetition.*[1] How many people need to be finished with their amida in order to assume you have nine *listening*? This is a good question. In any case, the *minhag* is to allow the chazan to start the repetition with nine who have finished the amida, even if we have reason to suspect that some of them are preoccupied with other activities.[2] The Mishna Berura suggests that, in such a case, the chazan should mentally stipulate that if nine aren't concentrating, his *tefilla* should be accepted as a voluntary one.

The Shulchan Aruch,[3] in discussing the requirements for a minyan, says that we may count one person who is davening or sleeping, rather than listening, for the minyan. The Taz[4] wonders how a sleeping person can be included, but, nonetheless, the Shulchan Aruch's ruling stands.

The Mishna Berura[5] suggests that, according to the Shulchan Aruch's approach – that presence without participation is sufficient, even more than one preoccupied person may be included. However, his conclusion is that we may be lenient only with one preoccupied person. The distinction between one and more ema-

---

1. *Shulchan Aruch, Orach Chayim* 124:4.
2. *Mishna Berura* 124:19.
3. *Orach Chayim* 55:6.
4. *Orach Chayim* 55:4.
5. 55:32.

nates from the Hagahot Maimoniot.[6] The *gemara*[7] lists opinions that hold that a minor counts for the tenth man of a minyan. The Hagahot Maimoniot claims that even those who are stringent not to count a minor agree that an adult, who usually *can* count for a minyan, provides the necessary level of *kedusha* for *devarim sheb'kedusha* (matters which require a minyan) even if he is sleeping or davening. However, as we cited above in the name of the Mishna Berura, this leniency holds only for the tenth man.

The Tzitz Eliezer[8] relies on the opinion that holds that one person who is davening counts along with eight who have finished the amida (plus the chazan) in order to start the repetition. However, he says that it is better, when practical, to wait.

6. *Tefilla* 8:9.
7. *Berachot* 47b.
8. XII, 9.

A-11: Hosafot on Yom Tov That Falls on Shabbat

Question: On the seventh day of Pesach (which was on Shabbat, this year), the *gabbai* called up someone for a *hosafa* (additional aliya). There was some commotion as to whether it is proper to make hosafot on Yom Tov. What is the halacha/*minhag* on the matter?

Answer: On Shabbat, one is allowed to make hosafot,[1] but even then, it is preferable to avoid hosafot for two reasons. Firstly, some say that only in the time of the *gemara*, when only the first and last people called to the Torah made *berachot*, hosafot were permitted since no berachot were thereby added. Nowadays, when everyone called to the Torah makes berachot, the additional berachot due to hosafot are not sanctionable.[2] Secondly, if there are too many hosafot, it takes a toll on the congregation's patience.[3] Despite these reservations, one is allowed to make hosafot, especially if there are many people with *chiyuvim*[4] [5] or the aliyot are needed to prevent hard feelings.

On Yom *Tov*, there is an additional problem, which prompts the Rama[6] to cite an opinion that prohibits hosafot. The Ran in Megilla explains that since the number of aliyot is based on the significance of the day, adding aliyot distorts the hierarchy. For example, adding an aliya on a regular Yom Tov would make the day seem as prominent as Yom Kippur. On Shabbat, which is anyway the top of the pyramid, an increase in the number of aliyot doesn't misrepresent the hierarchy. Therefore, on Yom Tov (except

---

1. *Shulchan Aruch, Orach Chayim* 282:1.
2. See *Magen Avraham* 282:1.
3. *Mishna Berura* 282:5.
4. Occasions when one is supposed to receive an *aliya*.
5. Ibid.
6. *Orach Chayim* 282:1.

on Simchat Torah), we don't make hosafot unless there is great need. However, if Yom Tov falls on Shabbat, because of Shabbat, the maximum number of mandatory aliyot are called. Thus, adding aliyot would not make it look like a more prominent day than it is, and one may make hosafot.[7] On Yom Kippur there is an additional reason not to make hosafot. The breaks in the aliyot were carefully chosen and should not be tampered with.[8] This factor applies even if Yom Kippur falls on Shabbat.

In your case, since the 7th of Pesach fell on Shabbat, the gabbai was correct. On the other hand, many *shuls* do seem to refrain from hosafot on Yom Tov even when it falls on Shabbat. It is not clear whether this practice derives from ignorance or is based upon the desire on a Yom Tov that falls on Shabbat, with its long *davening* and with its *mitzva* of *simchat Yom Tov*,[9] not to protract the service.[10]

---

7. *Mishna Berura* 282:6.
8. *Magen Avraham* 282:2.
9. To celebrate the holiday with food, etc.
10. See *Mishna Berura* 529:1.

A-12: Covering the Torah During the Aliya's Concluding Beracha

Question: In some *shuls*, the Torah is covered after each *aliya*, before the *oleh* (one who has the aliya) makes his second *beracha*. Doesn't covering the Torah make it considered as if it is not present, as covering does to the *challot* during *Kiddush*? If so, can one make a beracha like that?

Answer: Let us explain a few concepts that we often take for granted in order to clarify this issue.

The beracha that we make before the Torah reading is primarily a *birkat haTorah*, a beracha related to Torah study. The Tur[1] cites a question raised by his brother, Rav Yechiel, concerning a case where one arrived late to shul and, as soon as he finished making his own, personal birkot haTorah, was called to the Torah. May he immediately make the same birkat haTorah again? Their father, the Rosh, said that the oleh may make the beracha because there is a set *takana* (a convention) to honor the Torah by making a blessing before and after its public reading.

The Rosh, however, does agree that the nature of the berachot of the oleh is that of birkat haTorah. Therefore, one does not need a *tangible*, open text upon which to make a birkat haTorah. Rather, it relates to the *intangible mitzva* of Torah study, whether of the Written or Oral Law.[2] Thus, even if covering the Torah were to make it as if it wasn't there, there would be no problem with reciting a birkat HaTorah. The reason that, before the oleh recites the beracha, we open the Torah and point to the place of the reading is in order for him to know what will be read.[3] This obviously is

---

1. *Orach Chayim* 139.
2. See *Berachot* 11b.
3. *Sha'arei Ephraim* 4:3; *Mishna Berura* 139:16.

unnecessary after finishing the aliya, since the oleh knows upon what he is making the beracha, namely, what has just been read.

The Torah is covered between aliyot primarily out of respect for the Torah when it is, temporarily, not in use.[4] There are two ways to cover the more important part of the Torah – its words. One way is to roll it up; the other is to cover it with something external. The implication of the Rama[5] is that rolling is a better covering than placing a cloth upon it.[6]

There is good reason to cover the Torah in some manner before reciting the concluding beracha: it should not appear that the beracha is written in the *sefer Torah*.[7] For this purpose, a single covering, accomplished by rolling, is sufficient. After the beracha, some place a cloth upon the rolled Torah, especially if there will be a long break.[8] However, the extra covering does not affect the beracha in any way.

Regarding your comparison to challot, it is interesting that there are those who specifically instruct that they be covered even during the beracha.[9] In both the case of the Torah and that of the challot, we preferably hold the object to which the beracha relates. Among other things, this connects us to them. In any event, the beracha is valid (in both cases) even if we neither see nor touch the object at the time of the beracha.

---

4. *Levush, Orach Chayim* 139:5.
5. *Orach Chayim* 139:5.
6. See *Mishna Berura* 139:21.
7. *Mishna Berura* ibid.:17.
8. *Sha'arei Ephraim* 4:21; *Mishna Berura* ibid.:21.
9. *Mishna Berura* 271:41; *Shemirat Shabbat K'Hilchata* 55:21.

A-13: Tefilla While Babysitting

Question: I am a new father, and I often take care of my infant all morning. Sometimes, after I get her to sleep and am in the middle of *davening*, she wakes and starts to cry. If this happens at a time that I am not able to stop, what am I to do?

Answer: *Mazal tov*. Of course, the best idea is to daven (if possible, with a *minyan*) before starting to watch the baby. We understand that this does not always work out; this response deals with such a situation.

Firstly, it helps to know the needs and habits of the baby (which is difficult, as they often change as fast as you learn them). Many babies will wake, cry, and fall back to sleep by themselves. Others whimper relatively calmly for a few minutes until their parents come. In such cases, it is best to reach a place in *tefilla* where one can stop before going to the baby, *if* one can concentrate. One does not have to stop davening at the first cry, nor does a parent need to interrupt another activity immediately when doing so would cause difficulty. If the baby continues to cry bitterly, the rule that the needs of a child are like those of a sick person applies.[1]

The preferred course of action depends upon the particular place in the tefilla that one finds himself. During *P'sukei D'Zimra* and *Kri'at Shema*, one can take a break to walk, motion to (which cannot be done in the first section of Kri'at Shema[2]) or make sounds to a child.[3] These are all forbidden during *Shemoneh Esrei* without an acute need.[4] It is a halachic problem during Shemoneh Esrei to hold a baby or any other item in a manner in which

---

1. *Rama, Orach Chayim* 309:1 and *Mishna Berura* ad loc.:2.
2. *Shulchan Aruch, Orach Chayim* 63:6.
3. See *B'er Moshe* III, 12.
4. *Mishna Berura* 104:1.

one may be concerned that it will fall. This problem may apply to various other parts of tefilla as well.[5]

The following are the priorities when you can't wait. If you can go to console the baby or rock her back to sleep and then continue davening, this is preferable. (If you think it is likely the baby will stir and need to be put back to sleep before you can continue davening, stand near the baby for Shemoneh Esrei in order to avoid the need to walk to the crib. At other points in the davening, it pays to not be so close, as you don't want to lose concentration at the baby's every twist and turn.) It is best to finish dealing with the baby first, provided that, by doing so, the time it takes you to recite the entire section of the tefilla you are in will not have elapsed.[6] However, if need be, you can take longer than that and continue from where you left off,[7] while being careful not to talk. It is better to hint and make signs and noises than to move from one place to another during Shemoneh Esrei.[8]

If it is likely that a very long time will pass until the baby will allow you to daven properly, then you can hold the baby while finishing to daven if that will quiet her enough to enable you to concentrate. This is because one who davened while holding something that he is afraid may fall does b'di'eved (after the fact) fulfill the mitzva.[9] The reason this is not optimal is that one's concentration is compromised. Thus, if the only way one can concentrate at all is by holding the baby, then that should be done. A better idea under these circumstances may be to put her in some type of baby carrier.[10] This is usually very soothing for the baby, especially when one sways. Logic dictates that, assuming there

---

5. Ibid. 96:1.
6. *Mishna Berura* 65:4.
7. *Tefilla K'Hilchata* 12:(198); see *Mishna Berura* 65:2 and 104:16.
8. *Mishna Berura* 104:1.
9. Ibid. 96:2.
10. Normally, carrying any load is problematic – see *Shulchan Aruch, Orach Chayim* 97:5.

is no chance the baby will fall out, this would be the best option, since one's concentration would not be adversely affected, and the restriction on holding a baby during tefilla should not apply.

A-14 When the Wrong Sefer Torah is Opened

Question: On a day that we read from two *sifrei Torah*, the *chazan* took the second *sefer* as the first. The *gabbai* discovered this only when the Torah was open on the *bima*. Should we have rolled the Torah to the right place for the first reading (it was a significant distance in the sefer) or covered up the sefer and replaced it with the correct sefer for the first reading?

Answer: Remember this rule: among the trickiest *halachot* to decide are those where there is a conflict between competing halachic preferences. While halacha requires us to act in manner *a* and in manner *b*, how do we know how to act in cases where *a* and *b* are mutually exclusive? One must either find sources that deal with a case where the two issues conflict or to independently decide (intuitively or otherwise) which issue should have precedence.

There is a rule that, out of respect for the congregation, one should not roll the sefer Torah to the right place while the congregation waits. For this reason, the *gemara*[1] relates, the *Kohen Gadol* would read part of the Torah reading on Yom Kippur by heart rather than roll the sefer from Acharei Mot to Pinchas. Nowadays, we do roll the sefer Torah when there is a need, under the assumption that the congregation is willing to compromise its honor under the circumstances.[2] Another rule found in that gemara is that one should not do anything that might imply that a sefer Torah is *pasul* when indeed it is not. For that reason, they did not have a second sefer on hand for the Kohen Gadol to switch to.[3]

---

1. *Yoma* 70a.
2. *Magen Avraham* 144:7.
3. See there why we can use multiple sifrei Torah.

While we have found no discussions among the *Rishonim* on a case where we have to choose between rolling a sefer Torah and casting aspersions on it, *Acharonim* do discuss it. The common case is where the person who has *peticha*[4] gives the chazan the wrong sefer. In the *siddur* of Rav Yaakov Emden, two opinions are mentioned: to return the sefer and take out the right one; to roll the one that was taken out. Rav Moshe Feinstein[5] says that it is hard to determine which factor takes precedence, but if the congregation is willing to forgo its honor, the sefer Torah should be kept out and rolled. He continues that if someone (not necessarily the rabbi) already gave instructions to return the sefer Torah to the *aron*, then there is a concern that overruling him will cause dispute or embarrassment. This is treated like a situation where the congregation does not withdraw its right to honor, and we return the sefer.

Our situation is different in two ways. First of all, if one does not switch sifrei Torah, it is necessary to roll both of them, which takes longer and increases the chance of disruptive discussion among congregants. More fundamentally, there should be no disgrace to or aspersions on the sefer Torah we would "pass up" by switching. After all, it would soon get its turn to be used as the second sefer. This is probably the rationale of the Sha'arei Ephrayim[6] (a 19th century work on the laws of *kri'at haTorah*) that says that if one opens the sefer for *maftir* instead of that for Bereishit on Simchat Torah, he should close it and switch sefarim rather than roll it. The Bi'ur Halacha[7] concurs with this analysis.

Another halachic factor which is all but ignored in the Acharonim's treatment of this question is the concept, "*ein ma'avirin al hamitzvot*" (we don't pass over *mitzvot* or, in this case, the sefer Torah to be used for a mitzva). One reason that it might not apply

---

4. He who opens up the aron and takes out the sefer.
5. *Igrot Moshe, Orach Chayim* II, 37.
6. 8:67.
7. On 684:3.

is that one person's error in taking the wrong sefer should not bind the whole congregation to suffer.[8] Whatever the reason, though, the consensus is that, in the case of switching two sifrei Torah that will both be used, we opt to switch the sefarim rather than roll.

---

8. See *Har Tzvi, Orach Chayim* 83.

A-15: Remembering the Exodus: Is it From the Torah? Are Women Commanded?

Question: Why is the *mitzva* of *zechirat yetzi'at Mitzrayim* (to mention twice daily the Exodus from Egypt) not counted as one of the 613 *mitzvot*? Also, even if it is a time-based mitzva, why aren't women obligated to fulfill it, as women are obligated in the performance of mitzvot that commemorate miracles they were involved in (*af hein hayu b'oto haness*)?

Answer: One of your questions is at the center of much rabbinic discussion, whereas the other is apparently not. But both are good questions and may even help answer each other. First, let us see if all of your assumptions are correct.

The *gemara*[1] treats zechirat yetzi'at Mitzrayim as a mitzva from the Torah, and the *mishna*[2] cites a *pasuk* as a source for it: "in order that you will remember the day that you left Egypt all of the days of your life."[3] We also seem to accept Ben Zoma's opinion[4] that we must fulfill this mitzva both day and night.[5] Therefore, the Magen Avraham[6] says, since zechirat yetzi'at Mitzrayim is a Torah law that applies every day, at any time of day, it is not time-based and women are obligated to fulfill it. The Sha'agat Aryeh[7] counters that there are actually two different obligations, of the day and of the night, and each one is time-based. Therefore, women are

---

1. *Berachot* 21a.
2. Ibid. 12b.
3. *Devarim* 16:3.
4. *Berachot*, ibid.
5. *Rambam, Kri'at Shema* 1:3.
6. 70:1.
7. 12.

exempt from each obligation. The Mishna Berura[8] presents both opinions, but the *minhag* seems to be that women are exempt.[9]

If zechirat yetzi'at Mitzrayim is from the Torah, why then is it not included in the list of the 613 mitzvot? (The Semak does count it,[10] but most do not.) Several explanations are given. The Ohr Samei'ach[11] suggests that zechirat yetzi'at Mitzrayim, as an independent mitzva (as opposed to a desired result of the performance of other mitzvot), may be only rabbinic. The scriptural source mentioned above that implies that this mitzva is from the Torah can be explained to mean that it is *evident from* the Torah that HaShem is interested that we remember the Exodus. Therefore, *Chazal* treated the daily practice to do so as if it were Torah law. Similarly, the Tzelach[12] says that the Torah source cited is a valid Torah source, but since it is not written in the form of a command, it is not counted.

We present one more explanation, which will help deal with your other points as well. The Beit Yitzchak[13] says that the Rambam viewed zechirat yetzi'at Mitzrayim not as an independent mitzva but as something we are to do along with the mitzva of *Kri'at Shema*. Therefore, he adds, since women are exempt from Kri'at Shema, they are also exempt from the addendum of zechirat yetzi'at Mitzrayim.

Finally, let us deal with the question of why women aren't obligated, in spite of their involvement in the miracles of the Exodus. The gemara does refer to this justification for women's obligation in a few places, including when discussing the obligation of women to drink the four cups of wine on *seder* night.[14] However, we did not find that those who discuss the obligation or

8. 70:2.
9. See *Ishei Yisrael* 7:13.
10. #110.
11. On *Rambam* ibid.
12. *Berachot* 12b.
13. *Orach Chayim* 12.
14. *Pesachim* 108.

exemption of women in zechirat yetzi'at Mitzrayim consider this factor. One can give some technical answers. For example, Tosafot[15] cites an opinion that holds that af hein hayu b'oto haness applies only to rabbinic commandments, not to Torah ones.[16] Therefore, this reasoning would not suffice to obligate women in the Torah commandment of zechirat yetzi'at Mitzrayim.

The following, fundamental approach seems to give a better understanding. The Minchat Chinuch[17] and others deal with the practical issue of why we need a mitzva to discuss yetzi'at Mitzrayim on seder night if we mention it every night anyway. Conceptually there is a major difference. On seder night, the focus of the mitzva is to praise HaShem for the miracles that saved us years ago at that time of year. During the rest of the year, it is primarily a matter of stating fundamental beliefs, that the Lord who did miracles and redeemed us is One whom we should believe in and obey.[18] For that reason, we perform the mitzva by mentioning the Exodus along with other principles of faith contained in Kri'at Shema. In that context, one's involvement in the miracles, which mandates praise, is not the critical point. Thus af hein hayu b'oto haness does not obligate women in this mitzva.

---

15. Ibid.
16. See *Maharil* 94, regarding women's exemption from the mitzva of *sukka*.
17. #21.
18. See *Shiurim L'Zecher Abba Mari* I, 1.

Section B:
Berachot (Blessings)

B-1: Teaching Berachot over Non-Kosher Food

Question: What does one do about training children in a Jewish school to make *berachot* when many of them will be eating non-kosher food?

Answer: [*We do not refer, in this response, to the educational challenges that exist in such a sensitive situation, but these challenges are taken into consideration*]. The *mishna*[1] says that people who eat non-kosher food together do not make a *zimun*.[2] The Ra'avad[3] sees this as a specific rule pertaining to zimun, an act which adds prominence to the blessings after joint eating. However, the Rambam[4] interprets the mishna more broadly, i.e., one does not make a beracha at all (before or after) on forbidden food. Thanking HaShem for enabling us to do something that He commanded us not to do is blasphemy, not a blessing.[5] The Shulchan Aruch[6] rules in accordance with the Rambam's opinion that one does not make a beracha on forbidden food, except under the rare circumstances where it is permitted to eat the forbidden food (i.e., *pikuach nefesh*[7]).[8]

The laws of forbidden foods apply to children even though they are not personally culpable for their sins. Indeed, adults violate a Torah prohibition if they feed a child a forbidden food, and those who are responsible for the children's education are also

---

1. *Berachot* 45a.
2. A joint recitation of *Birkat HaMazon* led by one of the participants.
3. *Berachot* 1:19.
4. Ad loc.
5. See *Rashi, Berachot* 47a.
6. *Orach Chayim* 196:1.
7. A situation where someone's life needs to be saved.
8. Ibid.:2.

responsible to see that they comply with the basic laws of *kashrut*.[9]
Therefore, children, as well, may not make a beracha on such food.[10]
We do not train children in the performance of *mitzvot* in such
a way that, if they were adults, their actions would not fulfill the
mitzva in question. This applies even when the action in question
is neutral,[11] and all the more so when it pertains to a forbidden
action like reciting a beracha on non-kosher food.

Even when a teacher cannot convince the children to eat only
kosher food, she is still able to train them to make berachot properly. Make sure that the children are given some kosher food upon
which they should recite the berachot. Even if the children get so
accustomed to making berachot that they will do so at home on
non-kosher food, this is not a reason for the educators to refrain
from teaching their students the important mitzva of berachot.
Furthermore, even if non-kosher food will be eaten at the same
meal, as long as the beracha is said on the kosher food, the beracha is proper. Thus, if you give the children bread and they say
HaMotzi and *Birkat HaMazon* in unison, you avoid problems and
cover almost all beracha issues. If a food other than bread is distributed, the joint beracha would be on that food. If the majority
of the children are eating kosher, then one should encourage the
group to make the berachot even if the idea we suggested cannot
be implemented. Even when a minority is eating kosher, a teacher
can still make a beracha aloud on her own food and have the children respond "Amen."

---

9. See *Shulchan Aruch, Orach Chayim* 343:1.
10. See *BeMareh HaBazak* II, p. 17.
11. See *Bi'ur Halacha* to *Orach Chayim* 657:1.

B-2: Shehecheyanu the First Time One Puts on Tefillin

Question: I recently became *bar mitzva*, and no one told me to make the *beracha* of *Shehecheyanu* the first time I put on *tefillin* as a bar mitzva. Should I have made the beracha and why?

Answer: That is a very astute question for a bar mitzva, one which shows that, already at your age, the study of Torah is not a new *mitzva* for you. There are two possible reasons to make a Shehecheyanu when beginning to put on tefillin. One is that the *performance of the mitzva* is new, as you imply. The other is that the tefillin are a new, important commodity (no less than a new suit), which brings joy even to one who has put on other tefillin for years. According to both reasons, the time to make the beracha would not be the day of the bar mitzva, but the first time one puts on the tefillin. This is usually before the bar mitzva, each young man according to his *minhag*.

The Rama[1] states that one says Shehecheyanu the first time he does *shechita* (ritual slaughtering) – not on the shechita itself, which causes damage to a living thing, but on the mitzva to subsequently cover the blood. Based on this, the Taz[2] rules that whenever one does a mitzva for the first time, he should say Shehecheyanu. However, many *poskim* take issue with the Rama and/or the Taz.[3] The main rationale of those who take issue is that, since the emphasis of the beracha is on our meriting being alive at *this time*, the mitzva must be one which is linked to a certain time of the year and, thus, be cyclical. This difference of opinion may depend on the understanding of the *baraita*, cited

---

1. *Yoreh Deah* 28:2.
2. *Orach Chayim* 22:1.
3. *Shach, Yoreh De'ah* 28:5; *Ba'er Heitev* ad loc. in the name of the Pri Chadash; see *Beit Yosef, Orach Chayim* 22.

in *Menachot*.[4] [5] The baraita relates that the *kohanim* who came to Yerushalayim to bring the *mincha* (meal offering) would recite Shehecheyanu. Rashi explains that this refers to the first time the kohen ever brought the mincha, and this would seem to support the Rama and Taz. However, Tosafot[6] says that kohanim made the beracha each time because the kohen had the privilege to do so only twice a year, making it a cyclical mitzva. As we have a rule that *safek berachot l'hakel* (when in doubt whether to make a beracha, do not possibly utter HaShem's name in vain), we do not make a Shehecheyanu on first-time mitzvot.

However, there is room to say that there is special justification for reciting Shehecheyanu on tefillin. The *tosefta*[7] says that when one makes *tzitzit* or tefillin, he makes a Shehecheyanu, and this is stated as halacha in the Rambam.[8] (There is discussion as to when the beracha is made, and we usually make berachot at a later point than the classical sources indicate.[9]) The Tur, though, cites this tosefta only in regard to tzitzit, not tefillin. The explanation appears to be that, according to the Rambam, the fact that tefillin and tzitzit are mitzvot makes their acquisition significant enough to warrant a Shehecheyanu. The Tur disagrees because only cyclical mitzvot require the beracha. He agrees that tzitzit calls for a Shehecheyanu because it is at least an article of clothing.[10] Since tefillin are not clothing,[11] their acquisition is not of *material* significance.

The Shulchan Aruch sides with the Tur, and the accepted minhag among both Ashkenazim and Sephardim is not to recite Shehecheyanu the first time one puts on tefillin or on the bar

---

4. 75b.
5. See *Yechaveh Da'at* II, 31 in the name of the Rokeach.
6. Ad loc.
7. *Berachot* 6:10.
8. *Berachot* 11:9.
9. See ibid., *Rama, Orach Chayim* 225:3, and more.
10. *Shulchan Aruch, Orach Chayim* 22:1.
11. See *Beit Yosef* ad loc. and *Har Tzvi, Orach Chayim* 21.

mitzva. However, the Mishna Berura[12] and Kaf HaChayim[13] both suggest that one put on an important new garment and say She-hecheyanu right before putting on the tefillin for the first time, having the tefillin in mind as well, to cover the doubt.

---

12. *Bi'ur Halacha* to 22:1.
13. *Orach Chayim* 22:2.

B-3: Berachot on Fruit Salad

Question: If, outside the context of a meal, I eat fruit salad containing a variety of fruit including melon, peaches, and grapes, what *beracha acharona* do I make?

Answer: You imply that you know the *beracha rishona* for the fruit salad, and this actually will affect the answer regarding the beracha acharona.

The beracha acharona on the majority of the ingredients in a standard fruit salad is *Borei Nefashot.* Assuming you eat a *k'zayit* of those fruits, you should have an obligation to say Borei Nefashot. If you have less than a k'zayit of grapes (and/or the other of the five fruits, including raisins, that require an *Al HaEtz*), then there is no possible obligation to recite Al HaEtz. The question arises when you have a k'zayit each of Borei Nefashot fruit and Al HaEtz fruit. Which of the berachot "wins out," or do you make two berachot acharonot?

The main question is how to look at a fruit salad. When one noshes from a vegetable platter, we look at the individual vegetables as separate entities. When one mashes different fruits or vegetables together until the ingredients are not distinct, then we certainly have one entity. In that case, there is a single beracha rishona that is determined by the majority (volume-wise) of the ingredients.[1] The question is: how do we categorize a food, like fruit salad, which is intended to be eaten as a combination (i.e. each spoonful contains a few varieties) but the ingredients are distinct enough to select one at a time if one desires? In this case, a significant *machloket* exists. The Mishna Berura[2] says that one makes one beracha rishona based on the majority, whereas the

---

1. *Shulchan Aruch, Orach Chayim* 208:7.
2. 212:1.

Chayei Adam[3] says that one makes separate berachot. The more accepted opinion is the Mishna Berura's, that one makes only one beracha, but there are some who follow the Chayei Adam's ruling (or try to arrange things to accommodate both opinions).[4]

The outcome of this machloket has a direct impact on the question of the beracha acharona.[5] According to the Mishna Berura, you look at the fruit salad as one unit, and, assuming the grapes (and other of the five *minim*, including raisins) do not constitute a majority, you recite only Borei Nefashot. However, if one has the practice to make two berachot on fruit salad,[6] then there is an obligation to make Al HaEtz even if the grapes are a minority, as long as he ate a k'zayit of them. Here, the situation is tricky. When one eats separately, but at the same sitting, some fruits of trees that require Borei Nefashot and others that require Al HaEtz, then the Al HaEtz exempts him from saying Borei Nefashot.[7] That is because Al HaEtz is appropriate, on a certain level, for all fruits of a tree, just that this more elaborate beracha was reserved for the five special species of fruit for which *Eretz Yisrael* was praised.[8] However, that would only exempt one from the beracha acharona on the peaches, apples, etc. But if the salad required a Borei Pri Ha'adama for melon, pineapple, etc. and one had a k'zayit of that component, then he would need to say Borei Nefashot as well. But again, the Mishna Berura's approach is the more prevalent one. Therefore, one would just make the beracha acharona that is appropriate for the majority of the fruit.

Let's end with a little mathematical/halachic riddle. If a fruit salad has 40% grapes, 35% melon, and 25% apples, what berachot (rishona and acharona) does one make, according to the Mishna

---

3. 51:13.

4. See *Piskei Teshuvot* 212:4; *V'Zot HaBeracha* 11:3.

5. See *Piskei Teshuvot* 208:14.

6. Or, according to all, in a case that the pieces of fruit are so big that they are eaten individually.

7. *Shulchan Aruch, Orach Chayim* 208:13.

8. See *Beit Yosef,* ad loc.

Berura? The answer is that, regarding each beracha, we must find the common denominator that forms a majority. For the beracha rishona, the apples and grapes join up to require a Borei Pri HaEtz. Regarding the beracha acharona, the apples and melons join up to require a Borei Nefashot. Paradoxically, the smallest component (apples) "wins" twice by teaming up to form a majority.

B-4: Birkat HaTorah for One Who Wakes Up During the Night

Question: If I get up in the middle of the night and decide to spend some time learning, what do I do about *birkat haTorah*?[1]

Answer: It is hard to avoid uncertainties in the various related scenarios of this general case, but we will try to give the general guidelines.

Rishonim struggle with the question why one doesn't make a birkat haTorah each time he learns, like he makes a *beracha* each time he eats in a *sukka*. The standard explanation is that Torah study is an ongoing *mitzva* and experience that does not lend itself naturally to interruptions.[2] Most Rishonim rule that breaks that would require a new beracha are possible, especially if one takes a significant nap during the course of the day.[3] However, there are opinions that hold that no break during the day stops the efficacy of the morning birkat haTorah, which was intended to last until the end of the person's day. The *minhag* is to employ the concept of *safek berachot l'hakel*,[4] which is the second and conclusive opinion in the *Shulchan Aruch*,[5] and not to make another beracha.

However, after going to bed at night (not merely putting one's head down on a table), almost all agree that the day's learning is over and if one wakes up and wants to learn later at night, he must make a new birkat haTorah.[6] The question arises, though, whether going back to sleep before the morning would mandate another birkat haTorah in the morning. It appears that those who

---

1. Blessing before learning Torah.
2. See variations on this idea in *Tosafot, Berachot* 11b and other *Rishonim*.
3. *Shut HaRosh* 4:1; *Beit Yosef, Orach Chayim* 47.
4. When in doubt whether to make a beracha, do not possibly utter *HaShem's* name in vain.
5. *Orach Chayim* 47:11.
6. Ibid.:13.

don't require a new birkat haTorah would halachically consider a second period of sleep like a nap. The Mishna Berura[7] explains that, according to the Shulchan Aruch's approach, one should not make a new beracha after a second sleep because we assume that a person would intend that the beracha he made during the night should be effective through the next day.

The Minchat Yitzchak[8] uses the idea of the impact of one's intention when making the beracha to come to a different recommendation in a similar case. He was asked about those who regularly take a long nap in the beginning of the night to enable them to stay up late learning. He suggests that they have in mind in the morning to have their beracha last until their *main* sleep of the night, not to have it broken by the nap. Rav Mordechai Willig not only concurs but goes as far as to say that this need not be intended cognitively but is an assumed intention. (Clearly, not all agree with this cogent position.) Certainly, in the case you discuss, where one goes to sleep *for the night* and wakes prematurely, he should make the beracha before learning at night.[9]

Be aware of the fact that it is generally legitimate (if not recommended) to make a birkat haTorah after any significant nap.[10] If one believes, but is not absolutely sure, that he should say a birkat haTorah, he should preferably make only the beracha of *"asher bachar banu..."* and not *"asher kideshanu..."*[11]

---

7. 47:29.
8. x, 7.
9. See also *Ishei Yisrael* 6: 25, 28.
10. *Mishna Berura* 47: 25, 29.
11. Ibid.:1.

B-5: Does Birkat HaMazon Cover Cake That Was Eaten Before the Meal?

Question: If I have a piece of cake and then eat bread, will *Birkat HaMazon* cover the *beracha acharona* for the cake?

Answer: If one knows that he is about to eat bread (which constitutes a meal), he should, in most circumstances, avoid eating right before the meal those foods that do not require a beracha during the meal.[1] The reason is that one should not superfluously create a situation where he makes an extra beracha. The exceptions to this rule are beyond our present scope.[2]

Your question, however, is about a case where one has already eaten food prior to the meal. Let us begin with some background information. Reciting Birkat HaMazon exempts one from reciting the beracha acharona for food that is eaten in the midst of a meal that includes bread. Does Birkat HaMazon also work *b'di'eved* (after the fact) for foods eaten without bread? *Rishonim* infer from different *gemarot* that one who recited Birkat HaMazon on wine or dates has fulfilled his obligation b'di'eved because, since these foods are satiating foods, they constitute a meal of sorts.[3] The Shulchan Aruch[4] rules, though, that if one recited Birkat HaMazon for foods made from grains, he is not exempt and must say *Al HaMichya*. However, the Mishna Berura[5] points out that many *poskim* take issue with the Shulchan Aruch, as foods made out of grain (including cake) are no less filling than dates and wine. This should also apply when one connected the eating of cake to an ensuing meal and made Birkat HaMazon with the cake in mind.

---

1. *Mishna Berura* 176:2.
2. See ibid.; *V'Zot HaBeracha*, beginning of ch. 9.
3. See *Beit Yosef, Orach Chayim* 208.
4. *Orach Chayim* 208:17.
5. Ad loc.:75.

However, the question is regarding *l'chatchila* (the proper course of action) in a case where one ate cake before the meal and became obligated in Al HaMichya. Why should the subsequent Birkat HaMazon, which is appropriate only b'di'eved, suffice? Indeed, if one eats spaghetti before his meal, he should make an Al HaMichya before partaking of the bread and, if he failed to do so, then he should recite it during the meal.[6] Only if he already made Birkat HaMazon would we say that he fulfilled his obligation and should not recite Al HaMichya. The Mishna Berura does cite a minority opinion that if one will be eating these same foods during the meal, then the eating of the food before and after the bread are combined into one eating experience subsumed under the meal, and Birkat HaMazon exempts l'chatchila. The Igrot Moshe[7] reasons that the Mishna Berura's preferred opinion is to make a beracha acharona before the meal, even in that case. However, it is best to make a reasonable break between the snack and the beginning of the meal. Then, it is clearly correct to end the snack with a beracha acharona before starting the meal.[8]

The matter is more complicated in the case of cake. There is a category of baked, grain products known as *pat haba'a b'kisnin*, for which one is required to make a beracha when he eats it as a dessert.[9] Usually, we do not make a beracha on cakes eaten at dessert because it is unclear what pat haba'a b'kisnin actually is. The Shulchan Aruch[10] cites three opinions as to the defining character of pat haba'a b'kisnin: 1) It contains a pocket of sweet filling; 2) Its dough is sweet (for Sephardim, slightly sweet; for Ashkenazim, very sweet); 3) It is thin and brittle like a cracker. Most dessert-like baked goods have one or two of these characteristics but not all. In such a case, the Bi'ur Halacha[11] says that

---

6. *Mishna Berura* 176:2.
7. *Orach Chayim* III, 33.
8. *Piskei Teshuvot* 176:1.
9. *Shulchan Aruch, Orach Chayim* 168:8.
10. Ibid.:7.
11. To *Orach Chayim* 168:8.

it as a *safek* whether it is pat haba'a b'kisnin or bread, and we do not make a beracha because of the uncertainty. If an average piece of cake might be bread, then not only could one exempt himself b'di'eved from a beracha acharona with Birkat HaMazon, but it is likely the proper thing to do. (See also opinions of Sephardic poskim on the matter in *V'Zot HaBeracha*, ch. 9 – the question was asked by an Ashkenazi).

Therefore, if one eats a standard piece of cake before the meal, the Mishna Berura[12] says not to make an Al HaMichya before the meal.[13] When reciting Birkat HaMazon, it is preferable to have in mind specifically that it refers to the pre-meal cake as well.[14]

---

12. *Orach Chayim* 176:2.
13. See *Igrot Moshe* ibid. regarding what he considers pat haba'a b'kisnin.
14. Based on *Even HaOzer* 208:17.

B-6: Does a Mistaken Beracha Exempt Other Foods?

Question: Someone made the *beracha* of *Shehakol* on a food that required a different beracha (for argument's sake, *Mezonot*). I know he is *yotzei b'di'eved* (fulfilled his obligation after the fact). However, does that mistaken beracha work to exempt other foods, either those that require Mezonot, like the food he is eating, or those that require Shehakol, like the beracha he made?

Answer: In order to answer your question, we will have to investigate some of the concepts that you correctly cite and see how they apply to your case.

One does not have to make a separate beracha on every food he eats, even if it is not part of a meal that began with bread. Rather a beracha *can* pertain to any other food that he will eat at that sitting which shares the same beracha.[1] The idea is that when one makes a beracha, he has some level of intention that it should cover other foods that he might eat later.[2]

It is also true that Shehakol works for foods that should have gotten a different beracha. This is part of a rule that more general berachot work b'di'eved for foods for which a more specific and, therefore, preferable beracha should have been said.[3]

When we put these two facts together, we have the following problem. If one makes a Shehakol on milk and then is about to eat cookies, why should he make a beracha on them? After all, doesn't the Shehakol which he said already exempt (b'di'eved) even cookies from a beracha? Rashi[4] answers that the idea of being yotzei with the more general beracha applies only when one makes it

---

1. *Shulchan Aruch, Orach Chayim* 206:5.
2. See *Rama*, ad loc. and *Mishna Berura* 206:20.
3. *Berachot* 40a.
4. *Berachot* 41a.

mistakenly on a certain food, but it does not extend to exempt other foods with the more specific beracha. Rabbeinu Yona[5] says that it actually all depends on intention. If one correctly says *Ha-Adama* on a vegetable, there is no reason to assume he intended to include a fruit that he will eat at the same sitting for which *HaEtz* is the correct beracha. The Shulchan Aruch,[6] adopting Rabbeinu Yona's approach, says that if, for some reason, one intended to use the beracha of HaAdama not only for the vegetable but also for a fruit that was there, then he would not make another beracha on the fruit.

Along similar lines, one who makes a Shehakol on something that actually requires a Mezonot usually intends to include not only that food, but all foods that require a Shehakol. Therefore, he exempts them all.[7] As we have seen, it is his inclusive intention that is crucial and overcomes the fact that the new "Shehakol foods" he desires to eat have a different beracha from the food on which he mistakenly made Shehakol. On the other hand, foods that require Mezonot are not exempted. The reason is that he did not have them in mind when making Shehakol because the Shehakol he was reciting was not the optimal beracha for them.

The more interesting question regards foods that share the beracha that he made, yet he presumably did not have them in mind. This can occur if one intended to correctly say Mezonot, and Shehakol slipped out. In this case, the Har Tzvi[8] says that since he intended the beracha for Mezonot foods, Shehakol foods are not included, and they would require a new beracha. He implies, and Piskei Teshuvot[9] states, that Mezonot foods are covered with that Shehakol because he intended to exempt Mezonot foods and made a beracha that works for them, b'di'eved.

---

5. Ad loc.
6. 206:2.
7. Based on *Mishna Berura* 209:8.
8. *Orach Chayim* 106–7.
9. 206:6.

The situation may be different for foods that were not present when the mistaken beracha was made, but that discussion is beyond our present scope.

B-7: Berachot Made by a Katan on Behalf of a Gadol

Question: Can a *katan* do *mitzvot* and make *berachot* to be *motzi* a *gadol*?

Answer: We will start with the explicit Talmudic sources concerning what a katan can and cannot do in this regard and then proceed to fill in the gaps.

The *mishna* in *Rosh Hashana*[1] says that one who is not obligated in the performance of a mitzva cannot fulfill that mitzva on behalf of one who is obligated. One example given is that a katan cannot blow shofar on behalf of adults. However, the *gemara* in *Berachot*[2] states that a katan can recite *Birkat HaMazon* on behalf of a gadol if the gadol ate an amount that obligates him in Birkat HaMazon only *mid'rabbanan*. In this case, one person who is obligated only mid'rabbanan (because of his age) can be motzi another who is obligated only mid'rabbanan (because of the amount he ate).[3]

What happens if the child also ate a relatively small amount, so that his obligation is not *mid'oraita* for two reasons (age, quantity) whereas the adult is missing only one element? A similar question is whether a katan can perform a rabbinic mitzva on behalf of a gadol. The Ran[4] cites the Ba'al HaItur, who says that a katan who is old enough to be trained in mitzvot can light the Chanuka candles on behalf of a gadol. The apparent logic is that all people who are obligated rabbinically are, essentially, on the same level of obligation, regardless of the number of reasons that

---

1. 29a.
2. 20a.
3. Ibid.
4. 10a in the *Rif*'s pages to *Shabbat*.

there is no Torah obligation. Although the Shulchan Aruch[5] states two opinions on the matter of Chanuka candles, he sides with the view that a minor cannot be motzi an adult.[6]

In the case of Birkat HaMazon, however, there is more reason to say that a katan can be motzi a gadol when both ate a small amount. One who already fulfilled his mitzva can still be motzi one who has not.[7] This is because one does not have to be presently obligated in a mitzva in order to be motzi one who is obligated now. He is a person to whom the obligation does pertain, and he has the responsibility to help fellow Jews fulfill their own obligations. These facts together place him in the category of being commanded in the mitzva. There is room to apply this logic regarding Birkat HaMazon. If a child eats a satiating meal, he becomes obligated in Birkat HaMazon on the level of a single d'rabbanan. Since that level of obligation can apply to him, it follows that he can be motzi an adult who is obligated in a single d'rabbanan even if the child did not have a satiating meal.[8][9] Despite this idea, the Mishna Berura rules that one should avoid having a katan be motzi a gadol in Birkat HaMazon if both of them ate less than a satiating meal.[10]

It is noteworthy that, when it comes to adults being motzi each other, there are distinctions between different berachot and mitzvot. We will mention a few regarding berachot on food. One *cannot* make a beracha over food on behalf of another unless the one reciting the beracha is doing so for himself at the same time.[11]

---

5. *Orach Chayim* 675:3.
6. See ibid. 689:2.
7. *Rosh Hashana* 29a.
8. *Magen Avraham* 689:4.
9. Regarding Chanuka, the katan will always have two reasons that he is obligated only rabbinically, and the gadol will always have one reason.
10. 186:7.
11. *Shulchan Aruch, Orach Chayim* 167:19, regarding *beracha rishona*; ibid. 197:4 and *Mishna Berura* ad loc.:24, regarding *beracha acharona*.

It is *proper* for one to be yotzei with another only if they are joining together to start the meal,[12] they are making a *zimun*, or one of them does not know how to *bentch* himself.[13]

---

12. *Shulchan Aruch* ibid.:11, regarding *beracha rishona*.
13. Ibid. 193:1.

Section C:
Shabbat

C-1: Rules of Lighting Shabbat Candles

Question: Is there a minimum time that Shabbat and *Yom Tov* candles must remain lit?

Answer: There are two elements included in candle lighting. The main element is a general mandate to *have enough light* to help ensure that the spirit of festivity and tranquility appropriate for the special day is maintained. The other element is to fulfill the specific rabbinic *mitzva* to create this positive atmosphere by *actively lighting candles* before Shabbat in its honor. Based upon this second element, if the house were filled with candles or other lights well before Shabbat, we would extinguish the candles and light them again soon before Shabbat for the purpose of honoring the Shabbat (or Yom Tov).[1]

We have not found an absolute minimum amount of time for which the candles must burn and assume that your question is what is the minimum duration that is appropriate. Let's start with the most preferred duration. It is appropriate to have the candles burn for as long as they serve a purpose. However, that has changed dramatically with the advent of electric lights. (We will not discuss here the pertinent question concerning the extent to which electric lights themselves can be considered "Shabbat lights.") The main element of having as much light as we need is usually achieved by means of electricity. For that reason, we no longer have the practice of lighting candles in all of the rooms and hallways of the house where light improves the "quality of life."[2]

The most important location for the candles, in order to fulfill the second element of candle lighting – to honor Shabbat, is the place where one eats the Shabbat meal.[3] It, therefore, stands

---

1. *Rama, Orach Chayim* 263:4.
2. See *Shemirat Shabbat K'Hilchata* 43:15.
3. *Mishna Berura* 263:45.

to reason that the more of the meal that is accompanied by the special Shabbat lights, the better. Preferably, they should last for the whole meal.[4] The most critical part of the meal is the beginning, when one makes *Kiddush*. In fact, there is an opinion in the *Shulchan Aruch*[5] that holds that one may not make Kiddush without the lights, although electric lights would suffice in this regard.[6] The vast majority of candles people buy do last well beyond Kiddush.

A relevant question arises when one is eating away from home but is lighting candles in her own home before leaving. (Various factors determine whether it is preferable to light at home or in the host's residence.[7]) The best option is to use candles that are long enough to still be burning when the family returns and to put them in a place where the light will then be useful. Ideally, when turning on electric lights (especially incandescent ones) around the house, one should do so right before lighting the candles with the intention that they are part of the *mitzva* to light.[8] That way, even if one doesn't benefit from the candles upon returning home, she can rely, at least partially, on the benefit she derives from the electric lights. If this is not possible, then it would be required that someone wait in the house until it begins to get dark and make use of the light of the candles. If one needs to leave before that, and certainly if one leaves the house more than an hour and a quarter before sunset, then she should light at the home of the host.[9]

---

4. *Kitzur Shulchan Aruch* 75:2; *Shemirat Shabbat K'Hilchata* 43:17.
5. *Orach Chayim* 273:7.
6. See *Perisha, Orach Chayim* 273:6.
7. See *Shemirat Shabbat K'Hilchata* 45.
8. See *Riv'vot Ephrayim* 1, 83.
9. *Shemirat Shabbat K'Hilchata* 45:8.

C-2: Swimming on Shabbat

Question: Is it permitted to swim on Shabbat? If so, is an *eiruv* required? Can one use a towel to dry off?

Answer: The *mishna* in *Beitza*[1] says that one is not allowed to swim across a body of water on Shabbat and *Yom Tov*. The *gemara* in *Shabbat*[2] explains that this prohibition even includes a pool of water that is located in an enclosed area, if the pool doesn't have a rim around it.[3] So *paskens* the Shulchan Aruch.[4] A few queries are posed by the *poskim*: whether the leniency (i.e., having a rim) applies to a pool only in a private area or even a public one, what constitutes a rim, etc. These may affect the status of an average swimming pool.

If one's body becomes wet, he is allowed to dry himself with a towel.[5] However, he should be careful not to squeeze the water out of his hair or out of the towel, as squeezing a liquid from a solid is prohibited on Shabbat. It is recommended to let the water on one's body drip off for a few moments so that there will be less chance of squeezing.

If one is in a place where he is not allowed to carry, he must dry himself before walking four *amot*[6] on the shore or shallow water, even though "carrying" the water on his body is not the regular way of carrying things.[7] This stringency does not apply while moving around in the body of water or when in the rain. Thus, in a case where swimming is permitted, one would not

---

1. 36b.
2. 40b–41a.
3. This makes it more similar to a river, where the prohibition's logic is strongest.
4. *Orach Chayim* 339:2.
5. *Shemirat Shabbat K'Hilchata* 14:20.
6. Approximately six feet.
7. *Shulchan Aruch, Orach Chayim* 326:7.

need an eiruv while in the water. However, outside the water, it's somewhat difficult to manage without an eiruv, unless one dries himself off and leaves the towel right next to the pool or waits a while to drip dry. (Regarding your reference to an eiruv, you probably realize that an eiruv is just one way to have a *reshut hayachid* [private domain], where carrying is permitted. Enclosed areas are similarly a reshut hayachid and, in many cases, are places where it is permitted to carry. If, however, the enclosed area is joint to more than one living unit, it may require a different type of eiruv. However, that matter is well beyond our scope.)

The above is the halachic background for your question. However, *halacha l'ma'aseh*, the poskim note that the accepted practice is not only to forbid swimming, but not to allow bathing either, even in cold water and even if the conditions referred to above are satisfied.[8] The Magen Avraham[9] states several reasons for our *minhag*, including the concern that one might squeeze out some water while drying off.

---

8. See *Shemirat Shabbat K'Hilchata* 14:12.
9. 326:8.

C-3: Use of Hearing Aid on Shabbat

Question: Is it permitted to use a hearing aid on Shabbat, or does the electrical mechanism make it forbidden or problematic?

Answer: While there are several issues concerning hearing aids on Shabbat from a halachic perspective, all of the major *poskim* who discussed this topic permitted their use. They were well aware that a hearing aid is used in cases of significant need and that the public understands that it is an exceptional situation. This helps explain why it wasn't forbidden or frowned upon despite the fact that its mechanism is similar to that of a microphone, which most poskim forbade. Some poskim included need as a major part of the lenient ruling's rationale.[1] Others made it an absolute condition. (For example, the Minchat Yitzchak[2] quotes Rav Yosef Henkin, who suggests that only those who cannot hear at all without the hearing aid should use it). However, as we know, people who wear hearing aids do so only when the need is substantial, and the *minhag* has developed to allow their use freely on Shabbat. We feel that this practice should be continued, certainly considering its impact on the quality of life and the enjoyment of Shabbat.

We will deal now with some of the issues that arise. [In this context, we have the liberty to deal with these issues only in a superficial manner and request our readers not to extrapolate from our discussion to other applications.] The first concerns creating circuits, which could be a problem of *boneh* (building) or *metaken mana* (fixing a utensil) or a related rabbinic prohibition. Indeed, this is a problem when one turns on a battery-operated device or shuts it off. Therefore, the hearing aid should remain on for all of Shabbat.

Another issue is the fact that speaking causes an increase in electrical current. It is far from clear that increasing the current

---

1. See *Tzitz Eliezer* VI, 6.
2. I, 37.

in an existing circuit is considered creating something new. Even if it is, there is room for leniency because the change occurs to something that has no real substance and the change is fleeting in duration.[3]

There is a general question whether devices that produce sound are included in the prohibition of using musical instruments.[4] There are several ways to deal with the issue in our context. One is based on the fact that the sound that is created is not heard by those standing around but only by the person who wears the hearing aid in his ear. Also, one who speaks does not talk directly into the instrument.[5] The fact that it is not audible to others has other halachic advantages.[6]

A further question is whether, as a battery-operated device that is usually used by turning it on and off, a hearing aid should be *muktzeh*. The Tzitz Eliezer has a variety of ways to deal with the issue. He concludes that, *at worst*, it is a *kli shemelachto l'issur* (a utensil which is generally used by doing an action that is forbidden on Shabbat). Even such an item may be moved in order to use it for a permitted purpose or because its place is needed.[7]

In summary, while this response is not an exhaustive one that deals with the subject in depth or with every pertinent question relating to the use of a hearing aid on Shabbat, we hope to have explained the general basis for its use on Shabbat. We think it also displays the interest of the poskim to find room for leniency in such a case, where the need is great, and despite the fact that one could have raised objections on several fronts.

---

3. *Tzitz Eliezer*, ibid.
4. See *Rama, Orach Chayim* 338:1.
5. See *Chelkat Yaakov, Orach Chayim* 120.
6. See *Shulchan Aruch, Orach Chayim* 252:5.
7. *Shulchan Aruch, Orach Chayim* 308:3.

C-4: Kashrut of Milk That Was Milked on Shabbat

Question: Does milk that was drawn from a cow on Shabbat by a Jew without employing any of the halachic solutions become not kosher because of the violation?

Answer: This response deals with the *kashrut* element of the issue and not with the policy of going out of one's way either to support *shomer Shabbat* dairies or to send a financial voice of disapproval to dairies that are *mechallel Shabbat*.

The *gemara*[1] cites the opinions of three *Tanna'im* regarding food that was intentionally cooked by a Jew on Shabbat (or otherwise produced in a forbidden manner[2]). The most stringent opinion, that the food becomes forbidden from the Torah for everyone forever, is not accepted as halacha. Rabbi Yehuda and Rabbi Meir agree there is only a rabbinic prohibition, but they argue about its extent. The Shulchan Aruch[3] rules like Rabbi Yehuda: the person who violated Shabbat is penalized and never allowed to eat the food, whereas others may eat the food after Shabbat. Rabbi Meir says that even the violator may eat the food after Shabbat, and a minority of *Rishonim* accepts his opinion.[4]

Either way, it would seem clear that one could drink milk that was milked by others, as it is forbidden after Shabbat only for those who violated Shabbat. The question is whether the people on whose behalf the work was done are considered like the violator himself or like others. The Magen Avraham[5] compares the result of *chillul Shabbat* to the case where one takes a forbidden

---

1. *Ketubot* 34a.
2. See *Rama, Orach Chayim* 318:1.
3. *Orach Chayim* 318:1.
4. See *Beit Yosef* and *Gra*, ad loc.
5. 318:2.

food and *purposely* combines it with permitted food in such a way that the forbidden food should become *batel* (nullified). The Shulchan Aruch[6] rules in that case that the mixture is forbidden for the person who combined the foods and for those upon whose behalf he acted. Thus, it would seem that the milk, which was produced in order to be sold to consumers, would be forbidden for them. However, the Magen Avraham continues that the Beit Yosef implies that the case where one deliberately mixed the forbidden food with other food requires a particularly strict ruling. This is because we are concerned that the perpetrator will not see the seriousness of mixing in non-kosher food with kosher. Concerning a case of *chillul Shabbat*, however, we can assume that one will take the matter seriously. Thus, almost all of the later *Acharonim* understand the conclusion of the Magen Avraham and the halacha as permitting the food to the intended recipients of the *melacha*.

However, the K'tav Sofer (son of the Chatam Sofer) complicates the matter a bit. He explains[7] that the reason a Shabbat violator may sell the food is that he is already penalized for his violation by virtue of the fact that he cannot eat the food himself. Thus, in a case where someone regularly cooks on Shabbat in order to sell the food to customers, the penalty will not be felt if he is allowed to sell the food. It, therefore, becomes forbidden for him to sell. If it is forbidden for him to sell, then it is forbidden to buy from him because of the requirement not to facilitate or even abet one who is doing a sin, in this case the sale.

It is not at all clear that we accept the K'tav Sofer's ruling, but in any event, the matter does not seem applicable to our case. After all, we do not buy the milk from the dairy farmers but from a grocer, who bought from a distributor, who bought the milk. This is too indirect for the consumer to be concerned about *lifnei iver* (facilitating a sin).

In practice, it is often a non-Jew who does the actual milk-

6. *Yoreh Deah* 99:5.
7. *Orach Chayim* 50.

ing. This situation, paradoxically, lends itself to a stricter ruling in some ways. When a non-Jew does melacha on Shabbat on behalf of a Jew, then before making use of the melacha, one must wait after Shabbat an additional amount of time equal to how long the work takes (*bichdei sheya'asu*).[8] However, in our case, this interval of time always elapses before the consumer has a chance to drink his milk.

8. *Beitza* 24b

c-5: Making Havdala on Sunday

Question: My wife did not feel well on *Motzaei Shabbat* (Saturday night) and went to sleep before I made *Havdala*. I decided to wait until she was ready, which ended up being the next morning. Should I have made a full Havdala on Sunday, including the *berachot* on *besamim* and *ner* (Havdala candle)?

Answer: There are a few questions to deal with here, starting with the question of whether you were correct to wait until the morning to make Havdala. We will assume that your wife is fully capable of making her own Havdala.

It is true that it is preferable for a woman to hear Havdala from a man because of the opinions that she is not obligated in the performance of this *mitzva*.[1] However, if necessary, she may make her own Havdala. We will now investigate the issues that might make it preferable not to have waited for your wife.

All of the classical sources, from the *gemara*[2] to the Shulchan Aruch,[3] speak about making Havdala on Motzaei Shabbat. The idea that one may make Havdala until Tuesday evening appears to apply only *b'di'eved* (after the fact). However, one can claim that these sources just describe the normal situation where, of course, one should fulfill his *mitzva* within a reasonable amount of time and do not address a situation where there is reason to delay.

There is an interesting *machloket* between the Rosh[4] and Maharam[5] about one who was exempt from Havdala on Motzaei Shabbat because he was awaiting a close relative's funeral. Is he obligated to make Havdala after the funeral on Sunday? The Taz[6]

---

1. See *Shulchan Aruch* and *Rama, Orach Chayim* 296:8.
2. *Pesachim* 106a.
3. *Orach Chayim* 299:6.
4. *Berachot* 3:2.
5. Cited by the *Rosh* ibid.
6. *Yoreh Deah* 396:2.

explains that the Rosh, who exempts such a mourner, understands that the basic obligation of Havdala is only on Motzaei Shabbat. Although one has until Tuesday to recite Havdala, that only functions as *tashlumin* (making up missed obligations) and is not part of the description of the basic obligation. In this case, as there was no obligation of Havdala on Motzaei Shabbat because of *aninut*,[7] he is exempt. The Maharam understands that the basic obligation extends beyond Motzaei Shabbat; for the mourner, it starts after the burial. According to the Rosh, it should be very problematic to delay Havdala until the morning, unless there is no choice in the matter (and, in this case, there is a choice). However, it appears that we accept the approach of the Maharam as halacha (based on Shulchan Aruch;[8] see Yabia Omer,[9] who discusses the various indications).

A further complication is that one may not eat or drink (except for water) before Havdala.[10] This is even the case upon awakening on Sunday morning, assuming one has the ability to make Havdala.[11] For Sephardim, there is yet another halachic concern. Three pillars of recent Sephardic *p'sak* (Ben Ish Chai, Kaf HaChayim,[12] Rav Ovadia Yosef[13]) rule that if one did eat before Havdala, he is able to make Havdala only if it is still Motzaei Shabbat.

Another thing to be considered by one who wants to delay Havdala is that only one who makes Havdala on Motzaei Shabbat can make the berachot on the ner and besamim.[14] Regarding ner, fire was created on Motzaei Shabbat. Regarding besamim, it

---

7. The status of a person before the funeral of a close relative, during which time one is exempt from positive commandments.

8. *Yoreh Deah* 341:2.

9. v, *Orach Chayim* 10.

10. *Shulchan Aruch, Orach Chayim* 299:1.

11. *Shemirat Shabbat K'Hilchata* 59:10.

12. *Orach Chayim* 299:26.

13. *Yabia Omer* vi, *Orach Chayim* 48.13.

14. *Shulchan Aruch* ibid.:6.

is then that one needs to compensate for spiritual letdown after Shabbat is finished. At first glance, it appears that if one waits until the next day to make Havdala, he will lose these berachot. However, one may recite them independently of the rest of Havdala on Motzaei Shabbat.[15]

We conclude that it is halachically preferable for one *not* to wait until Sunday morning to make Havdala even if he refrains from eating and even if it means that his wife will have to make Havdala herself. Since both options are neither perfect nor halachically wrong, there may be circumstances where one will want to wait until the morning (except for the ner and besamim) while not eating.

---

15. *Rama, Orach Chayim* 298:1.

C-6: Grape Juice for Kiddush

Question: I have heard that one should make *Kiddush* on wine rather than grape juice. Is this true, and, if so, does that mean that grape juice is not valid for Kiddush?

Answer: The *gemara*[1] has a rule that states that any type of wine which is valid *b'di'eved* (after the fact) for *nesachim* (libations on the altar) is valid *l'chatchila* (as a proper choice) for Kiddush. One of the examples given is *yayin migito* ("wine" that has just been pressed), which has not had the opportunity to ferment and is valid for Kiddush. This is also the ruling of the Shulchan Aruch.[2] This is what we commonly call grape juice, and, therefore, it appears clear that grape juice is totally fit for Kiddush.

That is basically the bottom line, but there are a few reservations that justify the claim you heard that wine is preferable. The Magen Avraham[3] points out that even though one may choose grape juice for Kiddush, it is more proper to use "older wine," which is at least forty days old.[4] (Be aware that before the advent of preservatives, refrigeration and vacuum packing, grape juice could not last that long without spoiling.) It follows from the way the Magen Avraham presents the halachic preference that the issue is not a need for alcoholic content. Rather, wine that has been stored for at least forty days is considered to be of higher quality, and the Shulchan Aruch[5] says that it is proper to choose good wine for Kiddush. Thus, high quality grape juice could be preferable to low quality wine, and the matter might depend on personal preference.[6]

---

1. *Bava Batra* 97a–b.
2. *Orach Chayim* 272:2.
3. Ad loc.:3.
4. *Mishna Berura* ad loc.:5, citing the Pri Megadim.
5. Ibid.:3.
6. See *Mo'adim U'Zmanim* VII, 181 in a related context.

There is some room to claim that our grape juice is halachically inferior to that which the classical sources refer to as yayin migito. In the process of making grape juice, something is done to the juice (usually including heating it to a level that is considered cooking) to prevent fermentation from taking place. This raises two issues. Firstly, there are several, important classical opinions that hold that cooked wine (*mevushal*) is unfit for use for Kiddush.[7] However, on this issue, which may also apply to pasteurized wines, the accepted ruling is to be lenient.[8]

Secondly, the Rashbam[9] implies that yayin migito is valid only because it will become alcoholic if left alone; this is not the case with our grape juice, which cannot turn into wine. However, there are several ways to deal with this issue. One is that since the grape juice is considered fit for Kiddush before pasteurization, it does not lose that status later on, since the process is not a destructive one for the juice.[10] Most poskim rule leniently on all of these issues and say that our standard types of grape juice require the *beracha* of *Borei Pri HaGefen* and are fit for Kiddush.[11]

What remains a problem is reconstituted grape juice. Here, most of its water is removed, and new water is added to it later on. Rav S.Z. Orbach[12] felt that the minority of concentrated grape juice cannot turn the majority of added water into grape juice. While we have heard that this type of grape juice is uncommon in Israel, we cannot speak for other parts of the world. (Most "organized" countries probably require producers to inform the public that the grape juice has undergone this process.) Since wine and grape juice require rabbinical supervision for reasons of *kashrut*, it is appropriate that many of the *hashgachot* have begun indicating whether they are fit for Kiddush and deserve the beracha

---

7. See opinions in the *Tur, Orach Chayim* 272.
8. *Shulchan Aruch* and *Rama* ibid.:8.
9. *Bava Batra* 97b.
10. *Minchat Shlomo* I, 4.
11. See *Yechaveh Da'at* II, 35; *Shevet HaLevi* IX, 58; *V'Zot HaBeracha*, p. 296.
12. *Minchat Shlomo* ibid.

of HaGefen. The primary importance of such a certification is to ensure that the wine is not overly diluted, which is a halachic concern, especially for Sephardim.

In short, grape juice is acceptable for Kiddush. Unless one has personal preferences (taste, health, or educational), wine is more festive and preferable, especially at night, when we are more strict.

c-7: Giving a Baby a Rattle on Shabbat

Question: May I give my baby a rattle to play with on Shabbat?

Answer: We will begin by confirming your apparent assumption that it is forbidden for an adult to use an instrument, such as a rattle, that is used to make noise. We will then see what the halacha is in regard to a baby. We also need to determine the nature of the prohibition for adults, as this may affect the answer to your question.

The Shulchan Aruch[1] forbids the use of musical instruments on Shabbat. The Rama[2] claims that this prohibition applies to all instruments that are intended for making noise, not necessarily music. The Bi'ur Halacha[3] accepts this more stringent opinion and cites sources that explain that this type of noisemaking is prohibited because it is *uvdin d'chol* (a weekday-like activity). Clearly, according to all opinions, any prohibition in this matter is at most rabbinic.

Is it permitted to let babies perform rabbinic prohibitions? Certainly, one need not try to prevent a baby, who is too young to understand the significance of his actions, from violating Shabbat or other prohibitions.[4] However, it is forbidden to "feed" prohibited things to children of any age,[5] and this is likely forbidden by the Torah.[6] This applies to all types of Torah prohibitions, whether or not related to food, and it forbids us from even *telling* children to perform prohibitions even without physically assisting them.[7]

---

1. *Orach Chayim* 338:1.
2. Ad loc.
3. Ad loc.
4. Regarding older children, see *Orach Chayim* 343.
5. *Yevamot* 114a.
6. See *Beit Yosef, Orach Chayim* 343.
7. *Mishna Berura* 343: 1, 5.

However, the Ran[8] rules that it is permitted to assist children in performing an action that is prohibited only rabbinically when it is for the child's welfare. For that reason, he explains, the *gemara*[9] permits washing a child on Yom Kippur. Thus, as many babies enjoy and consequently benefit from a rattle, the Ran would permit giving it to them on Shabbat. However, it is not altogether clear to what extent we accept the opinion of the Ran, as the Shulchan Aruch appears not to.[10] The matter may depend on how acute or *mitzva*-related the need is. Usually, rattles are not needed so acutely by babies – except those who are significantly calmed by them.

However, if we combine the two issues that we have discussed, it is logical that we can be be lenient in our case. After all, we saw above that a rattle, which is used to make noise, not music, is permitted even for adults according to the Shulchan Aruch. If it is forbidden, the probable rationale is that of uvdin d'chol, a category of prohibition that likely does not apply to a baby's toy. For this reason, the Shemirat Shabbat K'Hilchata[11] permits giving a rattle to a baby.[12] On the other hand, he does not allow the adult to shake the rattle for the infant unless the baby is very upset and the rattle calms him; in that case, he permits shaking in an unusual manner.[13] The adult should hand it to the baby gently without shaking it (faint scratching sounds inside the rattle are not considered noise).

We should note that some do prohibit giving a rattle to a baby on Shabbat.[14] Even if one is strict in this matter, the rattle is not

---

8. On the *Rif*, Yoma 1a.

9. *Yoma* 78b.

10. See *Bi'ur Halacha*, 343:1.

11. 16:3.

12. See also *Shema B'ni*, siman 34.

13. Ibid. and footnote 11.

14. See *Tiltulei Shabbat*, p. 26, who forbids doing this and implies, in footnote 29, that Rav Moshe Feinstein was of that opinion.

muktzeh, as it serves the baby who certainly may independently use the rattle.[15] All should also agree that it is permitted to put the rattle in a place where he expects the child to find and use it.[16]

---

15. Ibid., footnote 28 in the name of Rav Feinstein.
16. Based on the story of Rav Pedat, *Yevamot* 114a.

C-8: Killing Mosquitoes on Shabbat

Question: Is it permitted to kill mosquitoes on Shabbat? There are a lot of mosquitoes in my area. They cause my family much grief and, perhaps, even danger.

Answer: Ridding oneself of living creatures could involve the *melachot*[1] of *tzad* (trapping) and/or *shochet* (killing). If one does either of these in order to prevent personal harm, not to get benefit from the animal, then it is a *melacha she'eina tzericha legufa*, a melacha not done for a classic positive outcome. We *pasken* that melacha she'eina tzericha legufa is prohibited only rabbinically. Regarding the trapping of some creatures, including mosquitoes, there is an additional point of leniency. Trapping creatures belonging to a species that, as a rule, is not hunted for use is also only rabbinically prohibited.[2] If one has reason to fear that the animal is about to bite him, he may remove it by hand, which includes trapping, to avoid pain.[3] However, since it is halachically worse to kill these creatures than to trap them, killing is not permitted unless there is a strong danger of more significant pain.[4] Thus mosquitoes, which usually cause discomfort but not significant pain, should in most circumstances not be killed on Shabbat.

A few significant exceptions exist. One who has a specific allergy or sensitivity to mosquito bites may kill them to prevent being bitten. It would seem, in our unprofessional estimation, that applying a repellent (application by stick must be done before Shabbat) and/or spraying the immediate area are more effective and halachically preferable types of prevention.[5] Another

---

1. Activities that are forbidden on a Torah level on Shabbat.
2. *Shabbat* 106b–107b.
3. *Tosafot*, ad loc.; *Shulchan Aruch, Orach Chayim* 316:9.
4. *Shulchan Aruch* ibid.: 9–10; *Mishna Berura* ad loc.:46.
5. See *Shemirat Shabbat K'Hilchata* 25: (28).

exception exists when an infestation is likely to bring about multiple bites, which, cumulatively, can cause significant pain. However, in many cases, it is questionable whether killing a few mosquitoes before going to bed would make a substantial difference.

In areas affected by malaria or West Nile Disease, a determination may be made that there is a *safek pikuach nefesh* (possibility of mortal danger). If so, anyone would be allowed to take various necessary steps, including killing mosquitoes. This determination should be made by a competent *posek*, in consultation with health authorities.

C-9: Clearing a Table That Will Not Be Used Again on Shabbat

Question: How does one deal with dishes and food that remain at the end of a Shabbat meal when he will not need them again on Shabbat. How does one avoid problems of *hachana* (preparations for after Shabbat)?

Answer: The idea of hachana is simple, but its practical parameters are difficult to define. One must not do actions in order to enhance his situation after Shabbat. However, if the action enhances Shabbat itself, it is permitted even if it enhances the weekday even more, provided that one does not do more of the action because of the weekday.[1]

When one finishes a meal, he usually has a few reasons to clear the table. In addition to preparing it for the next meal (which might be after Shabbat), most people are interested in a tidy dining room. Thus, one may clear the table. However, it is problematic to scrub the table or to do a thorough sweeping job if the room looks fully presentable for Shabbat. Similarly, if the dining area will neither be used nor seen until Shabbat's conclusion, or if Shabbat is about to end, one needs other grounds for leniency.[2]

The Magen Avraham[3] and Mishna Berura[4] say that one may perform an action on Shabbat that in and of itself is permitted, in order to prevent damage to an object that is needed after Shabbat. Indeed, one is allowed to move a non-*muktzeh* item "from the sun to the shade" in order to protect it,[5] and halacha mentions no qualification that this is only when the owner might use the item

---

1. *Shemirat Shabbat K'Hilchata* 28:70.
2. See ibid.:79.
3. 321:7.
4. 321:21.
5. *Shulchan Aruch, Orach Chayim* 308:4.

on Shabbat. This is the main *heter*[6] for refrigerating leftover foods on Shabbat and even freezing them for later use.[7] In many cases, there is probably another reason for leniency. When one clears off the food, he has to find some place to put it. Since the refrigerator and freezer are as legitimate storage places as anywhere else, one has the right to store the food there, even if he also benefits from its use on a weekday. The heter of preventing loss is necessary only if the food is already removed from sight and one decides to put it in the freezer for longer-term storage. Shemirat Shabbat K'Hilchata[8] extends the leniency of preventing loss to instances where there is a legitimate concern that leaving food to spoil or crumbs on the floor will attract ants and other bugs.

There are two further innovative points of leniency at which Rav S.Z. Orbach[9] arrived, one of which dramatically expands the idea of preventing loss. Not only may one take steps to prevent a permanent loss, but he may also preserve a status quo from deteriorating even though the deterioration is easily rectified. Rav Orbach's case in point is allowing one to *soak* dishes in water so that the residue will not harden, making washing dishes after Shabbat harder than it would be had they been washed right away. (This would not permit *rinsing* the dishes to remove residue, which is an additional action done to save time after Shabbat, not to preserve the status quo.) It appears that many previous *poskim*, including the aforementioned Magen Avraham and Mishna Berura, did not assume that this was the correct understanding of "preventing loss."

A second idea, which is more compelling but for which it is hard to set parameters, is that actions that one does naturally under normal circumstances, without giving a second thought,

---

6. Grounds for a lenient ruling.
7. *Minchat Yitzchak* viii, 24 – see his discussion concerning whether one is allowed to freeze liquids.
8. 12:2.
9. Cited in *Shemirat Shabbat K'Hilchata* 28:81; see *Minchat Shlomo*, ed. ii, 36.

do not constitute hachana. Let us offer some examples. One who returns *sefarim* to a bookcase as a matter of course after having finished using them may do so even if, in this case, that action has value only after Shabbat (e.g., a *siddur* after Mincha, a *birkon* after *se'uda shlishit*). Accordingly, one who regularly removes his utensils and leftover food right after eating may do so even after se'uda shlishit. One mustn't say he is doing so to prepare for after Shabbat.[10]

---

10. *Shemirat Shabbat K'Hilchata* ibid.

C-10: Doing Work on Motzaei Shabbat Before Havdala

Question: On *Motzaei Shabbat*, I have a lot of laundry to do so I can send my children off to school for the week. It would be helpful if I could start the first load before my husband has returned from *shul*. However, I heard that it is a problem to do serious work before *Havdala*, even after saying *HaMavdil* (a shortened Havdala). Is that true, and does it apply in this case?

Answer: Our small survey of knowledgeable people had the following results. Most (including *talmidei chachamim*) have never heard of the practice you mentioned. A few follow it. Others are "wishy-washy" about what they heard or do. We hope that some more knowledge will help clarify matters and put them in perspective. There are two *possible* reasons to refrain from serious work before Havdala. One is a weak (or mistaken) halachic concern. The other is a *minhag* of classical origin, but one that was apparently not widely accepted.

The *mishna*[1] says that, as the end of Shabbat draws near, one may walk to his field for the purpose of guarding it and may return after Shabbat carrying fruit. The *gemara*[2] is troubled how he could do such work (picking fruit) before Havdala, and it arrives at the conclusion that work is permitted after saying HaMavdil. Rashi[3] says that reciting HaMavdil, which is a partial fulfillment of the requirement of Havdala, is sufficient mention of the departing Shabbat to allow work to be done before full Havdala over wine. The same, he says, is true after saying *Ata Chonantanu* in *Maariv*.

---

1. *Shabbat* 150a.
2. Ibid. 150b.
3. Ad loc.

Although both the Rosh[4] and Rambam[5] have a somewhat more stringent approach, the Shulchan Aruch[6] and the accepted practice follow Rashi's opinion.

Is there a distinction between different types of work? Rabbeinu Yerucham,[7] when discussing these *halachot*, says that the need for HaMavdil applies only to "work like weaving and writing, not to lighting a candle or carrying." The Rama[8] cites Rabbeinu Yerucham as a minority opinion, yet the Taz[9] defends him. The Taz hints[10] that the prohibition on work before Havdala is not a continuation of Shabbat's prohibitions but an independent problem of starting the week's work before "saluting" Shabbat as it leaves. This idea helps to explain Rabbeinu Yerucham's distinction. According to him, simple work, even that which is forbidden on Shabbat, is not a problem even *before* saying HaMavdil. We do not accept this opinion and forbid any type of Shabbat violation before saying HaMavdil.[11] On the other hand, the Sha'ar HaTziyun[12] mentions one opinion that uses Rabbeinu Yerucham's distinction to derive a stringency: strenuous work is forbidden even *after* HaMavdil. The practice you cited may be based on this opinion, making it a very stringent halachic opinion, or it could be a mistaken application of Rabbeinu Yerucham.[13]

Now, let us explore minhag. The *gemara*[14] says that he who does work on Motzaei Shabbat will not see good fortune. It is clear from both context and language that this is a minhag, not a

---

4. See *Tur, Orach Chayim* 299.
5. See *Beit Yosef, Orach Chayim* 299.
6. *Orach Chayim* 299:10.
7. 12:20.
8. *Orach Chayim* 299:10.
9. *Orach Chayim* 299:9.
10. See *Acharonim* on *Rambam* (*Shabbat* 29:5).
11. *Mishna Berura* 299:39.
12. 299:51.
13. See *Machatzit HaShekel* 299:17.
14. *Pesachim* 50b.

halacha, and it is not cited in the Shulchan Aruch. Tosafot[15] and the Tur[16] limit the minhag to waiting until the end of Ma'ariv or Havdala. If the work the gemara refers to is serious "weekday-like work" (as is logical), this minhag could be the source of your mysterious practice.

Given that refraining from exerting work before Havdala is a mistake, an extreme position, or a sparsely kept minhag, you can decide whether you want to follow the practice, especially in your circumstance. (If yes, state that it is *b'li neder*.) We do not recommend to one who never followed the practice to feel a need to start now. You can opt for the Kaf HaChayim's[17] approach as a compromise. He says that HaMavdil was intended to allow a woman "to do temporary (*ara'i*) work, but she is obligated to hear a proper Havdala." In other words, she should not get overly involved to the point that she forgets about Havdala, but she can act to make productive use of her time *until* her husband returns for Havdala. (Regarding your specific question about laundry, one can also distinguish between sorting and scrubbing and simply dumping clothes in and turning on the machine.)

---

15. Ad loc.
16. *Orach Chayim* 299.
17. *Orach Chayim* 299:61.

C-11: Eating on Shabbat by Midday

Question: I thought that one must make *Kiddush* on Shabbat morning by *chatzot* (astronomical midday). However, I cannot find a source for such a *halacha*. Does one exist?

Answer: Your impression has a basis but is not precise. Let us explain.

We fulfill the main *mitzva* of Kiddush (verbally sanctifying Shabbat) on the evening of Shabbat by making a special *beracha* ("*mekadesh haShabbat*") both in *tefilla* and before eating. When it comes to the daytime Kiddush (called *Kiddusha Rabba*[1]), the main purpose is simply to add prominence to the meal by beginning it with wine[2] [or possibly a substitute – beyond our present scope]. If, for whatever reason, one did not make Kiddush at the morning meal (i.e., after *davening*), then he begins *se'uda shlishit* with Kiddush.[3] The time element of Kiddush (i.e., having to make Kiddush by chatzot) is not an inherent issue. Rather, whenever the first Shabbat day meal is, Kiddush should precede it. The question, then, is whether the meal must be started by chatzot.

There are classical sources that refer to the three meals of Shabbat as taking place at night, in the morning and in the afternoon, respectively.[4] However, it is not clear whether the stated times are halachic requirements, assumptions or suggestions.[5] There is extensive discussion among *poskim* concerning the questions of whether the first meal must be at night and whether the third must be in the afternoon. In contrast, there is little discussion

---

1. *Pesachim* 106a.
2. *Shemirat Shabbat K'Hilchata* 50:4.
3. *Sha'ar HaTziyun* 291:9.
4. *Shabbat* 117b; Rambam, *Shabbat* 30:9.
5. The *Aruch HaShulchan, Orach Chayim* 288:2 is of the opinion that it is a halachic requirement, although he admits that this does not appear to be the accepted opinion.

about whether the second meal must begin in the morning, and the common practice is to not be careful that it is. See an interesting discussion of possible reasons for this phenomenon in Yisrael V'Haz'manim.[6]

The more serious problem is that of fasting on Shabbat. All agree that, under normal circumstances, it is forbidden to fast on Shabbat, the day the Torah[7] and *Nevi'im*[8] refer to as a day of eating and indulging. The Shulchan Aruch[9] says that one may not fast on Shabbat beyond the end of six hours (a standard term for chatzot) even if he does not intend to fast.[10] The Rama[11] rejects the minority opinion[12] that holds that one who is preoccupied with tefilla or Torah study need not be concerned about chatzot. Thus since one must eat by the end of six hours and he may not eat or drink before Kiddush,[13] he *ostensibly* has no choice but to make Kiddush by chatzot. Of course, one can satisfy the requirement of not fasting by having Kiddush and cake before chatzot. He does not need to eat *challa* by that time.

However, there are grounds and means for leniency (if you call not eating leniency). Most commentators[14] say that the significance of six hours into the day is that after that time the stomach is so empty that it is not receptive to food, a situation one really should avoid all week long. The Magen Avraham[15] and Mishna Berura[16] say that, in this regard, the period of six hours[17] is cal-

---

6. Vol. I, pp. 432–438.
7. *Shemot* 16:25.
8. *Yeshaya* 58:13.
9. *Orach Chayim* 288:1.
10. *Magen Avraham* and *Mishna Berura* 288: 1.
11. *Orach Chayim* 288:1.
12. See *Beit Yosef, Orach Chayim* 288.
13. *Shulchan Aruch, Orach Chayim* 289:1.
14. Including *Taz, Orach Chayim* 288:1.
15. 157:1.
16. 157:2.
17. *Z'maniyot,* or half of daytime.

culated from the time a person awakens. This solves the problem for those who start eating late because *shul* starts late.

However, on Shabbat, there may be an independent problem of fasting until midday, even if one has not been up for six hours.[18] One can remedy this by drinking a cup of water before the beginning of tefilla (before there is a need for Kiddush). After that, not eating is not considered fasting. It is unclear whether this also remedies the issue of an empty stomach.[19]

In summary, Kiddush, per se, need not be made by chatzot, but one may not fast until that time. Since most people eat within six hours of awakening, it is possible that there is no problem, and, if there is, it can be remedied by drinking water before tefilla.

---

18. See *K'tzot HaShulchan* 90:1 & *Badei HaShulchan* ad. loc.: 1.
19. See ibid.

C-12: Making Tea on Shabbat

Question: What is the proper way to make tea on Shabbat?

Answer: There are many opinions, including widely varied ones, on this matter. We will have to be satisfied with referencing the main issues and suggesting two of the mainstream approaches. There are other approaches, some more lenient (especially among Sephardic *poskim*) and some stricter. Our omission of these opinions is not meant to discount them.

If one pours from a *kli rishon* (the utensil in which the cooking took place) onto a food, it likely cooks at least part of the food, which is forbidden.[1] However, in general, we say that water in a *kli sheini* (a utensil into which hot food is transferred directly from a kli rishon) does not cook foods.[2] Thus, to prepare tea on Shabbat, it would seem to suffice to pour the water into the cup (a kli sheini) before putting in the tea bag.

However, in order to reconcile an apparently contradictory *mishna*, Tosafot[3] makes the following limitation on the leniency of kli sheini. Placing most uncooked foods into a kli sheini looks like cooking (*michzi k'mevashel*), and this is rabbinically forbidden. According to many authorities, tea leaves belong to the majority of foods to which this prohibition applies.[4]

There is another potential limitation on the leniency of kli sheini, which is likely to apply to our case. The *gemara* mentions two foods, salted fish and salt, that are or may be[5] considered cooked even when exposed to heat sources that usually are not sufficiently intense to use for cooking. The heat of a kli sheini is

---

1. See *Shulchan Aruch, Orach Chayim* 318:10.
2. *Shabbat* 40b.
3. *Shabbat* 39a.
4. *Mishna Berura* 318:39.
5. Depending on the opinion in the *gemara*.

probably considered such a source. The question arises in the discussions of the *Rishonim* and *Acharonim* whether salted fish and salt are a closed list (and a limited problem) or two examples of a broad concern. The exact opinion of the Shulchan Aruch and Rama is somewhat unclear,[6] but the Mishna Berura[7] is stringent on the matter. Others note that tea leaves, which are very thin, are likely easily cooked.[8] So, most poskim looked for a different system to prepare tea.

One simple method, which enjoys the blessing of many poskim (including Rav Moshe Feinstein[9]), is to pour the hot water from the first cup to another. Certainly, they reason, neither of the aforementioned stringencies should apply to a kli shlishi (a utensil where food was transferred from a kli sheini). However, others reason that if the water is hot enough to cook with, as it appears to get the job done with the tea, it doesn't matter that it passed through one more utensil.[10]

Another issue is *borer* (selecting). A tea bag is made in a way that allows the tea flavor to seep out while the leaves stay put. As long as this takes place underwater there is no problem. However, when one lifts up the bag and waits for the last drops to fall into the cup (instead of on the table), he has used a specialized device to select the drops from the leaves (hence, borer).[11] Thus, we normally instruct those who use this method to remove the tea bag with a spoon and discard any tea droplets that materialize.

The "safest" mainstream approach (you don't want to know what the Chazon Ish reportedly did!) is to prepare an essence before Shabbat by pouring boiling water from a kli rishon onto tea bags. Out of concern that not all the leaves are totally cooked, we do not reuse the leaves on Shabbat. One may pour the essence into

---

6. See *Shulchan Aruch*, ibid.: 5.
7. 318:39.
8. *Shemirat Shabbat K'Hilchata* 1:53 and ibid., footnote 152.
9. *Igrot Moshe, Orach Chayim* IV, 74.15.
10. *Aruch HaShulchan, Orach Chayim* 318:28.
11. See *Shulchan Aruch, Orach Chayim* 319:1.

hot water on Shabbat, as it has already been cooked, at least to the level of cooking it undergoes on Shabbat. Although many assume that cooked liquids may not be re-heated on Shabbat after cooling off,[12] they may be re-heated in a kli sheini.[13] Therefore, we put the water into the cup first and then pour in the essence.[14]

---

12. *Shulchan Aruch* ibid.:4.
13. *Mishna Berura* ibid.:23.
14. Ibid.:39.

C-13: Taking Lactase Pills on Shabbat

Question: In order to digest milk properly, I need to take lactase pills. Is it permitted to take such pills on Shabbat, in light of the prohibition of *refuah* (medical treatment)?

Answer: Before we try to solve your specific problem, let us "digest" the topic a little more broadly.

There is a rabbinic prohibition to undergo medical treatment on Shabbat.[1] This prohibition was instituted out of concern that one might violate Shabbat in the course of the treatment or, in the classical situation, in preparing medicines (by grinding). However, the breadth of this prohibition is reduced at two opposite ends. When one is truly sick, he is permitted to take medicine to improve his condition. Also, some health-related actions are too minor to be considered medicinal.

Food, in addition to being tasty and to providing energy for the day's activities, may also have medicinal value in a variety of ways. Yet, even specifically healthful foods are not included in the prohibition of refuah.[2] Those things, including some herbs and tablets, that are arguably food-like but are normally eaten only when one is ill are prohibited.[3] Does this prohibition pertain also to a person who is well? The Shulchan Aruch[4] says that healthy people are permitted to consume these items because they do not need refuah. Some explain the reason for this halachic distinction as follows. Although one who is ill may be distressed enough to inadvertently violate Shabbat when seeking a remedy, this concern does not apply to a healthy person.[5] On the other hand, the

---

1. *Shulchan Aruch, Orach Chayim* 328:1, from *mishna, Shabbat* 111a.
2. *Mishna, Shabbat* 109b.
3. Ibid.
4. Ibid.:37
5. See *Tzitz Eliezer* XI, 37.

Magen Avraham, one of the Shulchan Aruch's primary commentators, tries to prove that medications are prohibited even for those who are not suffering at all.[6] The Tzitz Eliezer[7] and Rav Ovadya Yosef[8] accept the Shulchan Aruch's opinion, but Rav Moshe Feinstein[9] says that it is difficult to dismiss the Magen Avraham under normal circumstances.[10]

An apparent, common application of this *machloket* concerns whether a healthy person can take vitamins, which are not really food (we don't make a *beracha* on them). However, Rav Feinstein rules that it is permitted to take vitamins on Shabbat, even according to the Magen Avraham. He reasons that a medicine must make some type of improvement to the body. If a compound just helps prevent disease by providing the body with substances that keep it working smoothly, then it cannot be considered medicine.

What about lactase pills? There are different ways to look at the matter. On one hand, the person feels fine when he takes it. On the other hand, he has an existing deficiency which will, given that he ingests milk, cause him discomfort in the relatively short term without the pills.[11]

Fortunately, when it comes to lactase pills, there are additional grounds for leniency, based on how they work. Most medicines strengthen the body or fix problems that have arisen in it. Interestingly, *lactase replacement pills* act differently from most pills. They provide the enzyme without which the consequences of lactose intolerance follow. They simply break down milk's lactose into sugars that the body can absorb. In fact, the active enzyme can be added directly to the milk, and the desired breakdown will occur outside the body. Thus, the pill just causes that the problematic condition never arises. The body's deficiency is

---

6. 328:43.
7. Ibid.
8. *Yabia Omer* IV, *Orach Chayim* 29.
9. *Igrot Moshe, Orach Chayim* III, 54.
10. This is the implication of the *Mishna Berura* 328:121 as well.
11. *Shemirat Shabbat K'Hilchata* 34:18 is stringent in such cases.

not addressed, as it is not healed into producing its own lactase enzyme. Therefore, the situation is more lenient than even that of vitamins, which help give the body strength and resources to deal with future problems.

C-14: Benefiting on Shabbat From Work Done by a Child

Question: My three-year-old son mischievously turned the dining room lights off and back on again on Shabbat. Were we allowed to continue eating in the room?

Answer: Your question raises standard Shabbat questions, which we will address briefly, along with the question about *melacha* (forbidden work) done by a child on Shabbat. We will not discuss the contentious question of when, if ever, it is permitted to have a child do something on Shabbat that is forbidden for an adult.[1]

The prohibition of receiving benefit from melacha done on Shabbat arises in the Talmud in two contexts. One is as a *k'nas* (penalty) on a Jew who violates Shabbat, in order to curtail possible benefit that results from desecrating it.[2] The second is not to benefit from melacha done by a non-Jew on Shabbat on behalf of a Jew, even though the non-Jew did nothing wrong. Regarding the latter instance, Rashi[3] says that benefiting from the melacha of a non-Jew on Shabbat is an intrinsic (rabbinic) problem of inappropriateness. Tosafot,[4] in contrast, explains it as a concern that if a Jew gets used to benefiting in such a way, he may come to ask a non-Jew in a forbidden manner to do the work for him. What about a child's melacha?

No penalty is appropriate regarding a child, who is halachically no worse (and is likely better) than one who violates Shabbat accidentally, even if the child has reached the age of *chinuch* (education).[5] The question we must investigate is whether

---

1. See *Orach Chayim* 343.
2. See *Ketubot* 34a and *Shulchan Aruch, Orach Chayim* 318:1.
3. *Beitza* 24b.
4. Ad loc.
5. We will not dwell on that issue since a three-year-old, even one who "knows" about Shabbat, is below the age of chinuch.

there exists a prohibition of having benefit, lest one come to ask the child to do melacha.

The *gemara*,[6] in discussing whether one has to prevent a minor from doing what is prohibited for an adult, relates the following story. Someone lost keys in the public domain and needed to retrieve them from that area on Shabbat. Rabbi Pedat suggested that small children be taken to the area to play so that they might find the keys and return them. Tosafot[7] wonders why, regardless of whether one can let a child take the keys, it wasn't forbidden to benefit from the keys, as would be the case had a non-Jew retrieved them. Tosafot answers that it was permitted because the children brought the keys without having the needs of others in mind. (When a non-Jew does melacha for himself, Jews may benefit from it). The Magen Avraham[8] infers from here that if a child does melacha for someone, that person may not benefit from it on Shabbat. The Pri Megadim[9] explains that this is because of a fear that an adult will ask the minor to do melacha and he will comply.[10] One leniency that can be implied from Tosafot is that if the child acts on his own behalf but does more than his needs require, we are not concerned that he had others in mind as well, as we are when a non-Jew does the melacha.[11]

Let's get back to your case. If your son turned the lights off and on in one act of mischief, then it was all done for his own purposes and there is no problem of receiving benefit. However, maybe he shut them and, after regretting the situation that everyone was sitting in the dark, decided later to put them back on to improve the situation for his family. In that case, there should be a problem because we look at the turning on as acting to benefit others, even if he also hoped it would save him from punishment.

---

6. *Yevamot* 114a.
7. *Shabbat* 122a.
8. 325:22.
9. Ad loc.
10. See *Yevamot* ibid.
11. See *Magen Avraham* ibid. and commentaries.

Without reviewing all the laws of benefit from melacha on Shabbat, let us recall one rule. If a room can be used without the melacha, even with difficulty, then the extra benefit that results from the melacha is not considered forbidden.[12] Most homes have enough light that, even if the dining room lights go off, it would still be possible to dine there. Thus, the only question was probably about reading, and that, as explained, depends on the circumstances.

---

12. *Shemirat Shabbat K'Hilchata* 30:58.

C-15: Is a Rock Collection Muktzeh on Shabbat?

Question: I have a very extensive rock collection. Is it *muktzeh* on Shabbat?

Answer: Often, regarding issues of muktzeh, only the person who asks the question can answer it, as we will explain.

Rocks are, in general, one of the classic examples of muktzeh[1] because, in their simple form, they do not have a defined use that would make them considered a *kli* (utensil). However, if one does something to prepare them to be used for a given purpose or if their owner decides, even without an act of preparation, to use them *permanently* for a purpose, then they are not muktzeh.[2] Thus, rocks that were collected for and, even more so, incorporated in a rock collection are not necessarily muktzeh.

The only question is whether one's high regard for the collection causes problems, as we will explain. Things that are purposeless are muktzeh, as there is not expected, when Shabbat begins, to be a good reason to move them. The fact that later, on Shabbat, a use does arise does not change their status. There is a factor, however, that makes something more muktzeh specifically because of its value. This category is called *muktzeh machmat chisaron kis*.

The classical cases of muktzeh machmat chisaron kis that are discussed in the *gemara* and early *poskim* deal with utensils that are designed to perform functions that are forbidden on Shabbat (*keilim she'melachtam l'issur*). Such a utensil can be moved only under limited circumstances (details of which are beyond our present scope). If, additionally, the kli is so important to its owner that he is careful not to use it for anything other than its

---

1. *Shulchan Aruch, Orach Chayim* 308:21.
2. Ibid.:21–22.

main purposes, then it is muktzeh machmat chisaron kis. As such, it is further off limits and cannot be moved at all.[3]

What happens if the second level of a "muktzeh factor" exists without the first? In other words, what is the status of a kli that was made for permitted use (*kli shemelachto l'heter*), but because of different reasons, including its value, its owner is careful that it not be moved around? Two things are quite clear. Firstly, the Rambam[4] states that, sometimes, one's absolute decision to set an item aside can cause it to be muktzeh machmat chisaron kis even if its ultimate use is for permitted activities.[5] An example of this is an item that one has set aside with the intent of selling it. Secondly, a kli shemelachto l'issur can more easily be muktzeh machmat chisaron kis because its range of possible uses is limited even before the issue of its value comes into play.[6] A kli shemelachto l'heter needs a higher level of concern about its damage to be muktzeh machmat chisaron kis. The question is where to draw the line.

Cases which are disputed by recent poskim include pictures and clocks that are hung on a wall. Rav Moshe Feinstein[7] says that these are not muktzeh. His implied rationale seems to be that hanging them up on the wall is the way to use them, not the way to remove them from use. However, Shemirat Shabbat K'Hilchata[8] says that since one is careful not to move them from their places out of concern they may get damaged, they are set aside as immovable objects.[9] (The Chazon Ish[10] implies that even if something is not moved because there is no reason to move it,

---

3. Ibid.:1.

4. *Shabbat* 25:9.

5. See *Aruch HaShulchan, Orach Chayim* 308:11.

6. See *Mishna Berura* 308:8 and *Shulchan Aruch HaRav, Orach Chayim* 308:4.

7. Responsum #13 in "Tiltulei Shabbat."

8. 20:22.

9. Along the lines of the *Mishna Berura* ibid.

10. *Orach Chayim* 43:17.

it is muktzeh). Presumably, if one often removes or rearranges the clock or picture, then it would not be muktzeh, but most people do not do so.

Your case depends on you. If you move around rocks in the collection or take out individual rocks on a semi-regular basis, then they are not muktzeh. If you are consciously careful to keep them untouched for extended periods, then the matter depends on the opinions of the poskim mentioned; Rav Feinstein would permit it, and the Shemirat Shabbat K'Hilchata would forbid it.

C-16: Guest Who Does Not Find Pre-Cut Toilet Paper for Shabbat

Question: I was at a friend's house on Shabbat and found only a roll of toilet paper in the bathroom, with no cut paper. What does one do in such a situation?

Answer: To properly address this question one must deal with two distinct issues. The first is simply what to do when there is no prepared toilet paper for Shabbat. The other involves dealing with the concern of possibly insulting friends who have different halachic standards on certain issues.

The overwhelming majority (at least) opinion is that one may not rip toilet paper from a roll on Shabbat. One who rips it on the perforation, which creates a measured piece of paper, violates the *melacha*[1] of *mechatech* (cutting). If one rips off a piece in an unmeasured manner (e.g., not on the perforation), it is a matter of considerable discussion whether he violates the Torah prohibition of *korei'a* (ripping for a constructive purpose) or just a rabbinic violation of *metaken kli* (fashioning a utensil).[2] The crux of the issue is whether korei'a applies to a case where one cuts a part of an object from the rest of the object in order to use only one of the two parts.[3]

Several *poskim* rule that where there is no viable alternative, one may rip the toilet paper in a way that only a rabbinic law, not a Torah one, would be violated.[4] This is based on the principle that in cases of significant need of *k'vod haberiyot* (preserving human

---

1. One of the 39 categories of forbidden work on Shabbat.
2. See *Shulchan Aruch, Orach Chayim* 340:13; *Bi'ur Halacha*, ad loc.; *Tzitz Eliezer* XI, 30.
3. *Bi'ur Halacha*, ibid.
4. *Shemirat Shabbat K'Hilchata* 23:16; *Tzitz Eliezer*, ibid.; *Piskei Teshuvot* 340:28.

dignity), rabbinic laws may be pushed off.[5] Although we need to apply this rule with care,[6] we do have precedent for using something *muktzeh* as toilet paper.[7] One can make the issue a rabbinic violation by tearing the toilet paper in a significantly unusual way. (Using elbows and legs are among the poskim's suggestions, as is wetting the paper away from the perforation so that it will rip easily in a halachically less severe manner.)

This, of course, assumes that there is no other way to deal with the k'vod haberiyot issue without ripping the toilet paper. Other solutions may be available. The most direct solution, if the problem is discovered in time, is to ask the hosts for tissues or precut toilet paper (one may open a package by destroying it), which they may have forgotten to put out. One need not be ashamed to ask – it probably has happened to all of us. On the contrary, one who says nothing can cause embarrassment if the hosts discover later that they put their guest in an uncomfortable situation. A more difficult question arises in situations where one is convinced that the hosts are unaware or have purposely been lenient (with an unusual rabbinic ruling or without one) on the matter.

What would happen if one would raise the need for pre-cut paper, either explicitly or with a statement like "I didn't find the Shabbat toilet paper"? This may not be pleasant for the guest or the host. However, the alternative could be that the hosts will find out years and many guests later that they were unaware of or not careful about something that their peers were and they had put their guests in uncomfortable positions. If the hosts will not listen or you are in a community where you are one of the few who is careful on the matter, then one can, in many cases, apply the rule of *mutav sheyihiyu shogegin* (it is better that people violate

---

5. *Berachot* 19b.
6. See *Tosafot, Shevuot* 30b.
7. *Shulchan Aruch* and *Rama, Orach Chayim* 312:1; see also *Shemirat Shabbat K'Hilchata*, ibid.

something unknowingly, or partially so, than knowingly).[8] It is trickier when a person might listen, but he is in a fragile religious state where he could also react negatively to what he sees as religious meddling. We cannot address the guidelines in a paragraph, as a book would be needed. The basic advice is to be smart (including bringing your own provisions to a home where you expect such a problem).

---

8. *Beitza* 30a.

C-17: Removing Excess Milk From Cereal on Shabbat

Question: When I give cereal to my baby, I usually pour enough milk in to make it wet and soft, but then strain most of the milk out into the sink so that he should not make too big a mess. On Shabbat, I simply hold back the cereal with my fingers, as using a utensil is a problem of *borer* (sorting). Is that sufficient to solve the problem?

Answer: There are three major requirements to avoid borer. The three are (1) taking the desired element (*ochel*) from the undesired (*pesolet*), (2) not using a utensil that enhances the sorting process, (3) using the ochel in the short term.[1] Although using your fingers satisfies requirement (2), you still fail requirement (1) because you remove the undesired milk. You may choose any of the following ways to rectify the situation:

1. Remove the cereal from the bowl, leaving the milk. This simply eliminates the problem that we mentioned by taking the ochel from the pesolet. You could even use a spoon to do so, as the spoon is not specifically designed for sorting/straining, and, in theory, your fingers could be just as efficient as a spoon.[2] You must be careful, though, if you happen to take a spoonful that has too much milk in it, that you don't rectify the situation by purposely tilting the spoon to make the excess milk fall out. You are allowed, however, to take the spoon out of the bowl at an angle from the start. Depending upon how much your baby eats, this system might be tedious.

2. Have someone drink the milk you pour off. The problem you have stems from the fact that you are treating the milk as pesolet, something not to be used, at least in the short term.

---

1. See *Mishna Berura*'s introduction to *siman* 319.
2. See *Shemirat Shabbat K'Hilchata* 3:45.

However, if the baby or someone else drinks the milk in the short term, then the milk is considered another type of ochel, and it is permitted to remove one ochel from another to eat immediately. Even if someone removes an element that he does not desire and does not eat, if he takes it out to give to someone nearby who does want it, no violation has been done.[3]

3. Remove some cereal along with the milk. The Taz[4] says that if one wants to remove a fly from soup, where the fly is obviously the pesolet, he may do so by taking out some soup along with the fly. The reasoning is as follows. The prohibition of borer exists when a person takes one element from another, not when he takes a certain percentage of the two elements that make up a mixture from the rest of the mixture in a manner that changes the relative concentration. The *chidush*[5] of the Taz is that even if by removing a particular percentage of the two elements only one element (fly-less soup) is left, it is still permitted. That is because halacha is concerned with that which one *removes*, in relation to the original mixture, not with that which *remains*.[6] Since there was a mixture of soup and a fly and one is removing a mixture of soup and a fly, there is no problem. Although some disagree with the Taz, the Mishna Berura[7] and a broad consensus of *poskim* accept his view. Your situation is even better, as you will be leaving some milk in the bowl, just at a lower concentration. You must be careful to consistently remove the milk and cereal together. If you spoon out some milk by itself, then the fact that you subsequently throw in some cereal will not retroactively fix the previous act of borer. If you use this system correctly, it is not considered a process of borer at all, and it would therefore not make a difference whether the baby eats the food shortly thereafter or significantly later.[8]

---

3. Ibid.:23.
4. *Orach Chayim* 319:13.
5. New insight.
6. *Eglei Tal, Borer*, note 6.
7. 319:61.
8. See *The 39 Melachos*, vol. II, p. 433.

C-18: Encouraging a Non-Jew to Buy Tickets on Shabbat

Question: I want to attend a sporting event. Ticket sales begin on Shabbat and are expected to be finished by the day's end. May I ask a non-Jew to buy tickets for himself, hinting that I will buy them from him after Shabbat for a higher price?

Answer: The general rule about arranging before Shabbat for a non-Jew to do work for you on Shabbat is as follows. If the non-Jew is considered to be acting independently for his own benefit, it is permitted, even though the Jew gains from the action. If halacha views him as serving as some type of *shaliach* (agent) of the Jew, it is forbidden. Based on this rule, the classical *poskim* arrived at a variety of practical distinctions.

One may not pay a non-Jew to be his employee (*po'el*) on Shabbat. However he may give a non-Jew a job to do if he is paid for the specific job (*kablan*), not for his commitment to do work on the Jew's behalf.[1] There are many details and distinctions in these halachot, such as how we treat extended work relationships and *marit ayin* issues that arise when it looks like he is the Jew's daily employee. However, these are beyond this response's scope. What is most pertinent to us is the rule that the Jew may not demand even of a kablan that he do the work on Shabbat.[2] Even if the Jew does not specify that he work on Shabbat, if, in order to accomplish the job as specified, the non-Jew must work on Shabbat, the prohibition still applies.[3] This seems to apply in your case, as paying him for the task of buying the tickets requires that he do so on Shabbat.

However, the non-Jew is considered working for you only if

---

1. *Shulchan Aruch, Orach Chayim* 247:1.
2. Ibid.
3. *Mishna Berura* 307:15.

the work relates to you directly. Therefore, although you may not give money to a non-Jew to purchase a commodity for you on Shabbat, you may *suggest* that he buy it with his own money and hint that you will likely buy it from him after Shabbat.[4] Hagahot Maimoniot[5] and Hagahot Mordechai[6] derive this from the fact that one can sell *chametz* to a non-Jew with the understanding that he will buy it back.[7] Since several *Acharonim* allow a Jew to give an oral assurance to buy back the chametz if the sale is unconditional,[8] one can likewise promise the non-Jew to buy the tickets from him after Shabbat.[9] There are those who even allow the Jew to lend the non-Jew money to buy the chametz because, at the time of the purchase, the money belongs to the non-Jew.[10]

In summary, you may suggest a deal; just don't tell him to buy them *for you*.

---

4. *Shulchan Aruch, Orach Chayim* 307:3.
5. *Shabbat* 6:2.
6. *Shabbat* 452.
7. See *Shulchan Aruch, Orach Chayim* 448:4.
8. *Mishna Berura* 448:23.
9. Ibid. 307:13.
10. *Shulchan Aruch HaRav, Orach Chayim* 307:10.

C-19: Sorting Silverware on Shabbat

Question: After washing silverware on Friday night, I need to arrange each type in its proper place. How do I do this without violating the prohibition of *borer* (selecting)?

Answer: The basic rule of borer[1] requires that three conditions be fulfilled in order to permissibly separate an object that is in a pile from others: 1) One takes the *desired* object (*ochel*) from the *undesired* objects (*pesolet*). 2) One plans to use the desired object soon. 3) One does not use a utensil made especially for selecting in the process. Your case seems to fail #2. However, it is possible that there is no problem, as we will explain, and there are also relatively simple ways to obviate the possible problem.

Rav Ovadya Yosef[2] justifies the practice of those who, in order to expedite the setting of the table on Shabbat morning, remove forks, knives, and spoons from a pile of silverware and arrange them in groups. In classic form, he does so by offering several possible reasons why the procedure may be permitted, even though each reason is not sufficiently convincing in its own right.

The Aruch HaShulchan[3] wonders how it is permitted to pick out one type of silverware from a bunch of assorted ones. His first suggestion is that because of their large size, each utensil is distinct in the eyes of the one who selects. Thus, the process of removing what he wants is not considered borer but simply taking. In fact, the Terumat HaDeshen[4] already posited this idea but was reluctant to rely upon it without further indications of leniency.

---

1. See *Orach Chayim* 319.
2. In *Yabia Omer* v, *Orach Chayim* 31.
3. *Orach Chayim* 319: 8,9.
4. #57.

However, several *Acharonim* question this proposition.[5] The matter may depend on how tightly packed the silverware is.

The Pri Megadim[6] raises the following important point. The Rambam[7] rules that if one has two useful types of items before him, he may take out the one he wants to use *soon*. The time factor can be understood in two ways. Perhaps the fact that one will be used before the other turns the former into ochel and the latter into relative pesolet. As mentioned above, the rule is that we may take ochel from pesolet, but not vice versa. If that is the issue, reasons the Pri Megadim, then in a case where one will use both groups of items at the *same time* in the future, there would be no problem because there is no distinction between ochel and pesolet. The Bi'ur Halacha[8] is convinced that this is not the explanation of the time factor. Rather, there is a special dispensation for one who takes an object to use in the short term, as this is considered "in the manner of consumption," and it is, therefore, permitted. In contrast, selection for later use is more like classical borer.

There are additional, weaker grounds for leniency. One is the possibility that the Torah prohibition of borer applies only to things which grow from the ground. Another is the claim that preparations for the next meal are considered short-term even if the meal is significantly later.

We note that, based on the aforementioned reasons and others, many are of the custom to allow separating the silverware unconditionally. However, we will share suggestions to conform to the majority opinion among *poskim,* who are not lenient.[9] One is to keep the silverware in a pile and set the table soon before the meal begins, as indicated by the Rambam. Please note that it is not sufficient to do the separation soon before setting the table, if that

---

5. *Shemirat Shabbat K'Hilchata* 3:78; *Piskei Teshuvot* 319:6.

6. Cited in *Bi'ur Halacha* 319:3.

7. *Shabbat* 8:12.

8. Ibid.

9. See *Shemirat Shabbat K'Hilchata* 3:78–79; *Hilchot Shabbat (Eider)* x,G,4.

is long before the meal commences.[10] Another possibility is to not select utensils from the pile but to use the opportunity when the utensils are in your hand to create separate piles for each category, as follows. After taking them one by one indiscriminately in order to wash or dry, put each one in a separate pile by type. With a little organization, this system need not waste too much time. Others suggest artificially undoing the mixture by throwing it across a surface (like pick-up sticks) and then selecting as desired.[11]

---

10. *Mishna Berura* 321:45.
11. Rav Moshe Feinstein, response #11 to Rav Eider.

C-20: Insulating Hot Food Taken From an Oven on Shabbat

Question: Is it permitted on Shabbat to take hot food in a pan from an oven and transfer it to an insulated or thermal container to keep it warm?

Answer: This response does not relate to use of an oven on Shabbat, which has potential pitfalls and solutions beyond our present scope. We are also assuming that the food is fully cooked.

Hatmana (insulating hot food) is rabbinically forbidden in two basic circumstances: 1) when it takes place on Shabbat; 2) if the hatmana is done in a medium where heat is being added, even before Shabbat.[1] You refer to hatmana on Shabbat, so we will have to look for situations where the prohibition of hatmana does not apply.

In order to be considered hatmana, the food or its utensil must not only be covered but must be surrounded relatively tightly by the insulating material[2] on all sides (at least for Ashkenazim[3]). Only then is it similar to hatmana in *remetz* (a mixture of sand and coals), the prototype of the prohibition. In some cases, an insulating container gives a relatively snug fit; in others, the food's container and the insulation do not come in such close contact. In the latter case, there is no problem. Let us continue to look for solutions for cases that meet the general description of hatmana or are borderline in this regard.

The *gemara*[4] cites Rashbag, who says that if one has moved food from the utensil in which it was heated into *another* utensil,

---

1. *Shulchan Aruch, Orach Chayim* 257:1.
2. Ibid.:8.
3. *Shemirat Shabbat K'Hilchata* 1:66. The *Shulchan Aruch*, ibid. is stringent in a case that is no longer common. Rav Shlomo Zalman Orbach's opinion on this matter is unclear. See question C-21, footnote 10.
4. *Shabbat* 51a.

he can do hatmana (that does not add heat) to the second utensil even on Shabbat. The gemara explains that, normally, hatmana is prohibited because there is a concern that it might lead a person to violate Shabbat in his desire to make sure it is hot. Here, however, since the person cooled down the food by moving it into another utensil, we do not have to be concerned that he will now reheat it. Thus, the following system should solve all problems. Before putting the hot food into the insulation, first transfer the food into another pan or container, using Rashbag's leniency, which is accepted as halacha.[5]

Is our case, though, a legitimate application of Rashbag's leniency? An important *machloket* exists between the Rambam and Rashi whether Rashbag's logic applies in a case where the food was moved to a second utensil without intention to cool it off. The Rambam[6] writes that the prohibition exists only in the *"kli rishon shenitbashel bo"* (the utensil that the food was cooked in) without further distinction, as Rashbag's statement implies. Rashi[7] implies that there must be intention to cool off the food for the leniency's logic to apply. The major *poskim* accept the Rambam's view.[8] A possibly more stringent application is heated water that is poured into a thermos, where the transfer was done specifically to maintain the heat for as long as possible. Still, most poskim permit the matter based on the Rambam, as the hatmana occurs in a *kli sheini* (a utensil that was not heated up). Additional factors are raised that might allow even Rashi to be lenient regarding a thermos.[9]

We must consider whether our case is more problematic than that of a thermos. Liquids that are poured into a new utensil cool

---

5. *Shulchan Aruch*, ibid.:5.
6. *Shabbat* 4:5.
7. *Shabbat* 51a.
8. *Beit Yosef, Orach Chayim* 257; *Magen Avraham* 257:14; *Mishna Berura* 257:29.
9. See *Chazon Ish, Orach Chayim* 37:32; *Igrot Moshe, Orach Chayim* I, 95; *Minchat Shlomo* II, 8.

off significantly and are said to be in a kli sheini, where several halachic leniencies exist. However, many rule that a solid (*davar gush*) is not very affected by a kli sheini's cold walls, maintains its heat, and retains the status of kli rishon.[10] Thus, one could claim that Rashbag's leniency does not apply to solids, as in our case. However, the Rambam's wording[11] implies and the Pri Megadim[12] states clearly that hatmana is forbidden only in the actual utensil where the food was heated. It does not apply in another utensil, even when the food has a halachic status of being in a kli rishon.[13]

In summary, if one wants to put food heated in an oven pan into a tight-fitting insulating container, it is necessary and sufficient to transfer it into another utensil before insulating.

---

10. *Shach, Yoreh Deah* 94:30, arguing on *Rama, Yoreh Deah* 94:7.
11. Ibid.
12. *Mishbetzot Zahav* 257:5.
13. See *Minchat Shlomo*, ibid.

C-21: Insulating a Warm Challa Before Shabbat

Question: After baking a *challa* soon before Shabbat, I like to wrap it in aluminum foil so that it stays warm. Is this permitted? May I also leave the wrapped challa in an oven that is turned off but is still warm?

Answer: The problem of wrapping, to which you refer, is the rabbinic prohibition of *hatmana* (insulation). We cannot get into all of the details,[1] but we will touch on some of the major points, especially those that are relevant to your cases.

The *gemara*[2] forbids two basic types of hatmana. One type is wrapping food on Shabbat in order to maintain its heat. This rabbinic prohibition arose out of the fear that one who is so concerned about keeping the food hot might actually come to heat the food before he wraps it. The second type of hatmana is wrapping food, even before Shabbat, in a manner where heat is being added to the insulated food (*mosif hevel*). The reason to prohibit this type of hatmana even before Shabbat is that there is a concern that the heat-adding insulation might be done with *remetz*, a mixture of sand and coal, in which case one might come to stoke the coals at some later point. However, in the case of your first question, you have "the best of both worlds." You do the hatmana *before* Shabbat in a simple insulation of aluminum foil, *which does not add heat*. Thus, it is permitted.

The answer to your subsequent question, whether you may put the wrapped challa in a warm oven, is much more complicated. The gemara, in reference to the type of hatmana that is mosif hevel, discusses insulating materials which are thermodynamic.[3]

---

1. Most of which are found in *Orach Chayim* 257; see also question C-20.
2. Shabbat 34a–b.
3. Heat emanates from them through chemical processes.

Aluminum foil does not add heat itself, but it does serve as a conduit for heat, in this case, the heat of the oven. There is a *machloket* among the *Rishonim* whether such a situation is considered mosif hevel and is forbidden even before Shabbat. The Shulchan Aruch[4] is stringent on the matter. The Magen Avraham[5] discusses the practice of putting an insulated pot on top of a hot oven and cites some of the *Rishonim*'s justifications for it. The Mishna Berura[6] feels that the leniency is legitimate (but not unanimous[7]) but only in a case where the heat source is no longer present and the heat is residual. Furthermore, if there is little heat left in the oven and it will dissipate before the time that you plan to take the challa out, there is even more room for leniency.[8] However, if you leave your oven on, even on a very low setting, then you should not put the wrapped challa in it for the purpose of insulation.

Rav Ovadya Yosef[9] is generally more accepting of leniency even when the heat source remains and says that it is fine to put the insulated food on a non-adjustable heat source, such as a Shabbat hotplate. Another option that will work according to most opinions is to leave a noticeable section of the challa uncovered, so that it is not considered hatmana at all.[10]

---

4. *Orach Chayim* 257:5.
5. Ad loc.:8.
6. Ad loc.:43.
7. *Sha'ar HaTziyun* ad loc.:41.
8. See *Shulchan Aruch, Orach Chayim* 258:1, *Taz* ad loc.:1 and *Mishna Berura* ad loc.:2.
9. *Yabia Omer* VI, *Orach Chayim* 34.
10. Rav Mordechai Willig pointed out that, apparently, according to Rav S.Z. Orbach, hatmana applies when even a simple majority of the food/pot is insulated. Rav Willig agrees with this view.

Section D:
Mo'adim (Festivals)

D-1: Tashlich on Shabbat

Question: When is one supposed to do *Tashlich* when Rosh Hashana falls on Shabbat?

Answer: First a little background on the origin of Tashlich, which will also have pertinence to the answer to your question.

The first known mention of the *minhag* is by the Maharil,[1] towards the beginning of his discussion of Rosh Hashana. The rationale for the timing of the practice is based on a *midrash*.[2] Avraham and Yitzchak were walking on the way to *Akeidat Yitzchak* and were impeded by the Satan, who formed a river. They continued into the water up to their mouths and turned to HaShem to allow them to complete their *mitzva*. Since that day was Rosh Hashana, we use a body of water, which conjures up the memory of the merit of the forefathers, as an appropriate place to ask that HaShem "throw (*tashlich*) all our sins into the depths of the sea."[3] Others see a river as a sign of blessing because of how it flows or as the historic place for the coronation of kings.[4] In any case, this minhag, which apparently has its origin in Ashkenaz, has spread throughout the Jewish world (in part, due to the Arizal), and a minhag of Israel is considered like Torah.

There is nothing innate in the process of Tashlich that makes it *halachically* inappropriate to do it on Shabbat. There is a difference of opinion as to whether it is proper from the perspective of *Kabbala*, and we do not have what to add on that point. In fact, it can be clearly inferred from the Maharil that the practice was to do Tashlich on Shabbat as well. Yet, over the last few hundred

---

1. Early 15th century *l'minyanam*, Ashkenaz (Germany).
2. *Yalkut Shimoni, Vayeira* 99.
3. *Micha* 7:19, recited at Tashlich. This is not only the source of the name Tashlich, but also captures its content, at least according to some explanations.
4. See *Yechaveh Da'at* I, 56.

years, minhagim have arisen to restrict its performance on Shabbat.

The main issue appears to be the possibility of being *mechallel Shabbat* by carrying something to the riverside.[5] The question already arose in the discussion of the Maharil. He objected to the minhag of some to throw bread to the fish during Tashlich. Whereas his main concern regarded the laws of feeding animals on *Yom Tov* (beyond our present scope), he also objected to carrying the bread without an *eiruv*. This can be a problem on Yom Tov[6] but is an even bigger problem on Shabbat. Of course, when the river is outside the eiruv, one cannot carry anything there on Shabbat, but it is still possible that one can go the riverside without carrying.

Tracing the sources historically,[7] the following theory seems likely. In the time of the Maharil, only the few *p'sukim* of "*Mi kel kamocha …*" were said, and it was probably not necessary for people to carry *siddurim* with them. So Tashlich went on unimpeded on Shabbat. However, as additional *tefillot* were added to Tashlich, people started bringing siddurim with them. Thus, *chillul Shabbat* in places without an eiruv (or an eiruv that did not extend to the river) became a real problem, and minhagim developed to stop Tashlich on Shabbat. Accordingly, when Rosh Hashana falls on Shabbat, we do Tashlich on the second day of Rosh Hashana. Carrying a siddur then is permitted, as it is done for the needs of Yom Tov. Rav Ovadya Yosef[8] rules as practical considerations seem to dictate. That is, communities that use an eiruv that reaches the body of water should do Tashlich on the first day, even on Shabbat; places without such an eiruv should wait. The more common minhag is to always delay.

When we were teenagers, some of our *rabbeim* reacted to the

---

5. *Pri Megadim, Eshel Avraham* 583:5; *Mishna Berura* 583:8.
6. See *Maharil* and *Pri Megadim*, ibid.
7. See *Yabia Omer* IV, *Orach Chayim* 47.
8. *Yabia Omer*, ibid.

questionable atmosphere in some places at Tashlich by claiming that we picked up more *aveirot* than we got rid of there. We can apply similar reasoning to this matter. It is legitimate for a *rav* to decide to go either way on this issue. However, whether the community minhag is to postpone Tashlich or it is to go as a group on Shabbat, an individual should conform to the minhag and avoid *machloket* over a public matter on this holy day.

D-2: Blowing Shofar on Behalf of Women

Question: After *davening* on Rosh Hashana, I often blow the sho-far for women who couldn't make it to *shul* for health or family reasons. Are there any special guidelines for such a situation or issues of which I should be aware?

Answer: Women are exempt from hearing shofar blowing.[1] Al-though it is forbidden to blow a shofar on *Yom Tov* not in the context of the *mitzva*, the optional mitzva for women provides sufficient justification to blow.[2] In fact, the Maharil points out that for centuries, women have treated the mitzva as if it were obliga-tory. Although women may blow for themselves or for each other, a man also may blow for them, as is customary.[3] Therefore, your practice is very praiseworthy.

The *minhag* is to blow thirty *kolot* (sounds), three of each set (*tashrat, tashat, tarat*). In general, there is much debate whether *shevarim-teru'ah* should be done in one breath or two. Therefore, in order to fulfill both opinions, one alternates between the two methods when blowing 100 kolot. Here, when blowing thirty kolot, one should do them in one breath.

There is a specific problem regarding the *berachot*. As you know, one of the berachot includes the phrase "and *commanded us* to hear the sound of the shofar." The *Rishonim* disagree whether women may recite such berachot on mitzvot about which they, personally, are not commanded (Rabbeinu Tam) or not (Ram-bam). While Sephardic women do not make the berachot, the Rama reluctantly confirms the minhag of Ashkenazic women to make the berachot.[4] Thus, an Ashkenazic woman may her-

---

1. *Shulchan Aruch, Orach Chayim* 589:3.
2. *Tur, Orach Chayim* 589 in the name of the *Ra'avya* and *Rosh*.
3. *Shulchan Aruch* ibid.:6.
4. See *Beit Yosef* and *Darchei Moshe, Orach Chayim* 17 and 589.

self make the berachot. However, a man who already fulfilled his mitzva should not say the berachot for them.[5] The reason for this is that one can make a beracha for someone else only when one of them is obligated.[6] Since the man fulfilled his mitzva and the women are exempt, he may not say the berachot. Rather, one of the women should make the berachot for herself and have in mind to include the others.

---

5. *Rama, Orach Chayim* 589:6.
6. *Rashi, Rosh Hashana* 29a.

D-3: Outlook of One Who Must Eat on Yom Kippur

Question: I have multiple sclerosis, and I take many pills to deal with a variety of related conditions. Even so, I am relatively happy with my lot in life. I had fasted all of my life on Yom Kippur, but I am getting older and cannot fast anymore. My wife has told me, "You are not allowed to fast! The Talmud says that it is a sin for you to fast!" Where is this written, or is she just trying to make me feel better?

Answer: Someone who, by fasting, would be putting his life in danger is permitted *and* commanded to eat and/or drink, even on Yom Kippur. This should be determined in consultation with one's doctor and rabbi. This law can be found in the Talmud in the final chapter of tractate *Yoma*[1] in both the *mishna* and corresponding *gemara*. The Rambam[2] equates one who loses his life in order to keep a commandment for which he is not required to do so to someone who commits suicide. Since halacha treats real danger the same as certain death, it would also be a sin to endanger oneself because of Yom Kippur.[3] It is important to understand that following halacha requires discipline. Heroism is not defined by the degree of daring but in the resolve to follow the rules accurately, even against one's inclination. In cases like this, avoiding risks is true heroism.

When possible, it is proper to eat very slowly (approximately one fluid ounce of food and of liquid in nine minutes[4]). This reduces the severity of what, for other people, would be a violation

---

1. 82a–84b.
2. *Yesodei HaTorah* 5:1.
3. See *Mishna Berura* 618:5.
4. See *Shemirat Shabbat K'Hilchata* 39:18–20, who permits a little more liquid.

of Yom Kippur. On all other fast days, anyone who is sick, even without any danger, may eat according to his needs.

Keep up the noble approach to your illness. Accepting hardship with love of HaShem is one of the highest spiritual levels a person can reach. It is indeed an honor to answer your question. May a full cure be found for your condition, and may you continue to serve HaShem with love and with the addition of good health.

D-4: Children Fasting on Yom Kippur

Question: I have children aged ten and below. What should my policy be about their fasting on Yom Kippur?

Answer: *Children below age nine:* There are no limitations on these children's eating on Yom Kippur.[1] There is discussion regarding whether this halacha is in order not to jeopardize their health or simply because the mitzva to fast does not apply to them.[2] If it is due to health concerns, one could say that the child's eating should be limited to her actual needs. However, the practical halacha is to let such a child eat as much as she wants whenever she wants.[3] Even if the child wants to fast, we do not allow it.[4] This does not mean that the child must be forced to eat at the outset. Rather, on Yom Kippur, parents should not allow their children to refrain from eating to a degree that they would normally consider unhealthy for them.

Children age nine and above. The *gemara*[5] says that healthy children aged nine (or weak children aged ten) should fast "for hours" for the purpose of *chinuch*.[6] The gemara explains that a child should eat the morning meal an hour after the time she usually does. The Shulchan Aruch[7] adds that the amount of delay depends upon the strength of the child.

The aforementioned gemara discusses delaying the morning meal. Some *Acharonim* understand this as an indication that the child had not eaten until this point, including Yom Kippur night. Therefore, a child of this age should fast at night and, at

---

1. *Shulchan Aruch, Orach Chayim* 616:2.
2. See *Mikra'ei Kodesh* (Frank), *Yamim Nora'im* 43.
3. *Yalkut Yosef* v, p. 92.
4. *Rama, Orach Chayim* 616:2.
5. *Yoma* 82a.
6. Literally, education.
7. Ibid.

that time, should be given a drink only if she complains of great thirst.[8] Others understand the gemara as meaning that all meals should be delayed during the course of the day.[9] However, once she has broken her fast, if she is still hungry, she may eat regardless of how it fits into her meal schedule.

In a case where a child is permitted to eat, adults are allowed to feed her. If she wants to eat earlier than she should, there is a halachic debate regarding whether an adult may feed her.[10]

---

8. *Yalkut Yosef* ibid.
9. *Shemirat Shabbat K'Hilchata*, ed. 1, 32:41.
10. See *Magen Avraham* 616:2; *Sha'ar HaTziyun* 616:9.

D-5: Why is Simchat Torah Celebrated Sukkot Time?

Question: Why is Simchat Torah celebrated after Sukkot and not on Shavuot, the anniversary of the giving of the Torah?

Answer: Simchat Torah, celebrating the completion of the public reading of the Torah, occurs at the end of Sukkot, apparently for one or more of the following reasons.

1. We celebrate the most happy occasion of finishing the reading of the Torah during the holiday on which happiness is most stressed by the Torah, namely, Sukkot.[1]

2. The reading of V'Zot HaBeracha, Moshe's blessing to Bnei Yisrael, at the conclusion of the Torah, is appropriate at this time, as it corresponds to *Shlomo HaMelech*'s blessings to the nation at the end of Sukkot after the inauguration of the *Beit HaMikdash*.[2]

3. Another parallel is that Simchat Torah is the last day of the *shalosh regalim* of the year.[3] Rav S.R. Hirsch explains in Horeb that the specific significance of Shemini Atzeret / Simchat Torah is to "gather in" the spiritual lessons of the holidays and to concentrate on having them last through the long winter. This idea could also apply to the completion of the Torah cycle.

Regarding your suggestion that we finish and restart the Torah reading on Shavuot, consider the following. The Torah was given on Shavuot, but not specifically the text of the Torah that we complete on Simchat Torah. There are two opinions in the Talmud[4] concerning when the Torah was written down. One opinion holds that Moshe wrote it in sections, as matters transpired, and

---

1. *Machzor Vitri, siman* 385.
2. Ibid.
3. The cycle of holidays, which begins with Pesach and finishes with Sukkot. There are *halachot* based on this order.
4. Gittin 60a.

completed it directly prior to his death. The other opinion holds that the entire Torah was written down at the time soon before Moshe's death. Certainly, it was not presented in its current written form at *Har Sinai*. At Har Sinai, on or around the time of Shavuot, HaShem gave most of the laws of the Torah with their explanations and halachic implications along with the principles of the Torah – not the exact text of the *Chumash*. Therefore, Shavuot need not be the right time to finish the Torah cycle.

D-6: Taking a Lulav and Etrog to the Kotel

Question: I understand that, after the first day of Sukkot, the main *mitzva* of *netilat lulav* is performed only in Yerushalayim. Should I go to Yerushalayim on *Chol HaMo'ed* in order to fulfill the mitzva properly?

Answer: It is true that the Torah-level *mitzva* of netilat lulav applies only on the first day of Sukkot; afterward, the obligation is only rabbinic, instituted as a *zecher laMikdash* (remembrance of [the time of] the *Beit HaMikdash*).[1] In the *Beit HaMikdash*, the mitzva was in effect for seven days, as it says, "… and you shall rejoice *before HaShem, your God*, seven days."[2] Regarding a possible requirement of netilat lulav in modern Yerushalayim on Chol HaMo'ed, there are several issues:

1. Location – According to Rashi,[3] the mitzva of seven days pertains only in the area of the Beit HaMikdash itself, not the *Kotel* plaza, which is right outside of the Temple Mount. Even if all of Yerushalayim is included, as the Rambam[4] implies, that would refer only to the boundaries of the Second Temple period, which include the Kotel and significant parts of the Old City.

2. Kedusha – The Rambam and Ra'avad[5] disagree whether the *kedusha* and special halachic status of Yerushalayim apply after the destruction of the *Beit HaMikdash*.

---

1. See *Sukka* 41a.
2. *Vayikra* 23:40.
3. *Sukka* 41a.
4. Commentary on the *Mishna*, Sukka 3:10.
5. *Beit HaBechirah* 6:14.

3. Requirement to fulfill a second time – One who is outside the described area of Yerushalayim is obligated in the mitzva of netilat lulav during Chol HaMo'ed only rabbinically. Therefore, his fulfillment of the mitzva would only seem to be of a rabbinic nature. There is a wide-ranging discussion whether one who fulfills a mitzva when obligated rabbinically must fulfill the mitzva a second time when the obligation becomes from the Torah.[6]

4. Requirement to obligate oneself – Most *poskim* rule that the seven-day mitzva of lulav applies only to those who are at the place of obligation. One is not required to travel to the Beit HaMikdash or to Yerushalayim (when there is no requirement of *aliya laregel*) to create an obligation.[7]

The Tzitz Eliezer[8] points out that there was no custom among *Yerushalmim* to do a second netilat lulav at the Kotel, apparently because of the multiple doubts concerning its necessity. If one specifically wants to be stringent, he should not make a *beracha* and probably can use a borrowed set.[9]

---

6. See *Mikraei Kodesh, Sukkot* 11, 13.
7. See *Mikraei Kodesh*, ibid.
8. x, 2.
9. *Aruch LaNeir, Sukka* 36b.

D-7: Buying a Separate Lulav for Boys Under Bar Mitzva

Question: Does one have to buy a set of *arba'at haminim* (= lulav) for sons before *bar mitzva,* or can they share the father's?

Answer: The *gemara*[1] says that one should not transfer ownership of his lulav to a minor on the first day of Sukkot because a minor can accept ownership of an object but cannot transfer it to others. On the first day, one must fully own the lulav when performing the *mitzva.*[2] If a father gives his lulav to his son, no adult will subsequently be able to use it to fulfill the mitzva. Therefore, the simplest advice for a parent is to buy a kosher lulav for his child from the time the child should be trained in the performance of this mitzva (when he can shake the lulav appropriately[3]).

The Shulchan Aruch[4] does cite a dissenting, lenient opinion (Ran) that holds that a child who has reached the stage of *pe'utot* (who understands buying and selling, usually at age six) is able to halachically give the lulav back.[5] Many *poskim* counter that the minor can acquire the lulav on the Torah level (when it is given to him by an adult) but can return it only rabbinically. Therefore, adults who subsequently use this lulav will not have the Torah-level ownership they require. The Ran might argue that a minor can acquire an object only rabbinically, and he can return it on the same level.[6] Others explain that the *machloket* depends on the classic question whether *kinyanim*[7] of rabbinic origin are effective

---

1. *Sukka* 46b.
2. *Shulchan Aruch, Orach Chayim* 649:2.
3. Ibid. 657:1; *Bi'ur Halacha*, ad loc.
4. Ibid. 658:6.
5. See *Shulchan Aruch, Choshen Mishpat* 235:1.
6. See *Bi'ur Halacha*, ad loc.
7. Acts of acquisition.

in regard to *halachot* from the Torah.[8] The Shulchan Aruch's first, stringent opinion is considered the more authoritative one.

The Shulchan Aruch[9] presents another (partial?) solution – that the adult should hold on to the lulav[10] or otherwise maintain *ownership* as the child shakes it.[11] This certainly solves the halachic issue for adults who subsequently use this lulav. However, it may create a problem for the child. The Mishna Berura[12] cites two opinions concerning whether one fulfills the mitzva of *chinuch*[13] of a child with a borrowed lulav. Rav Feinstein[14] explains that the basis for the two approaches is whether practical training suffices to fulfill the mitzva of chinuch or if he must perform the mitzva in a manner that is fully valid for an adult. Rav Feinstein sides with the stringent opinion. Although he acknowledges that the practice in Europe was not to buy a lulav for children, Rav Feinstein says that this was so because sets were few and very expensive, but in our days a father should buy a set for his son(s). Minchat Yitzchak,[15] addressing a much poorer community with larger families, reconfirms the legitimacy of leniency for financial reasons.

When Sukkot starts on Shabbat, we start taking the lulav on the second day. In *Eretz Yisrael*, we do not need ownership of the lulav on the second day.[16] Therefore, a father can *lend* his lulav to his children. Even in a year when Sukkot starts on a weekday, he can give it to his child after all adults who are to use this lulav have done so. (The child will, regrettably, not be fulfilling the mitzva during *Hallel* with this system). In *chutz la'aretz*, ownership is needed on the second day because the second day is treated like

---

8. *Melamed L'Ho'il* I, 120.
9. Ibid.
10. Ibid.
11. *Mishna Berura* 658:28.
12. Ibid.
13. Educating a child to perform mitzvot
14. *Igrot Moshe, Orach Chayim* III, 95.
15. IX, 163.
16. *Shulchan Aruch, Orach Chayim* 658:3.

the first.[17] Thus, the only safe way to share in chutz la'aretz is to give the lulav to the child after the adults are done on the second day and only lend it to him on the first, which, according to Rav Feinstein, deprives the child on the first day.

---

17. *Mishna Berura* 658:23.

D-8: Categories of Forbidden Work on Chol Hamo'ed

Question: I know that a lot of things that are forbidden on *Yom Tov* are permitted on *Chol HaMo'ed.* Are all rabbinic prohibitions, such as *muktzeh* and *amira l'nochri* (requesting a non-Jew to do the work), permitted on Chol Hamo'ed?

Answer: There isn't a blanket distinction, with regard to Chol HaMo'ed, between Torah and rabbinic prohibitions. In general, there are three approaches among the *Rishonim* as to the basis for the restriction on working on Chol HaMo'ed. Some say that it is derived from the Torah but has more areas of leniency than does the restriction on working on Yom Tov. Some hold that its source is entirely rabbinic. There is also a third, fascinating approach, as follows. The Torah decreed that some areas of *melacha* would be forbidden, yet it empowered *Chazal* to determine under which circumstances work would be forbidden and under which it would be permitted.[1]

There are significant differences between the laws of melacha on Yom Tov and those of Chol HaMo'ed. These differences depend primarily upon the category of melacha of a given act of work, the nature of the act, and its purpose, not necessarily upon whether the prohibition in question is from the Torah or rabbinic. Chazal's general approach was to distinguish between activity that is related to enhancing the festive spirit of the *mo'ed* and that which occupies a person with other, tiresome activity.[2] Chazal determined how to apply that general rule, and we are bound to follow their guidelines, which we can be found in the classical sources.

If one studies *sugyot* of Chol HaMo'ed, he will not find explicit references to the classic laws of muktzeh. (The concept of

---

1. See a summary in the *Beit Yosef* in the beginning of *Orach Chayim* 530.
2. See *Mo'ed Katan* 2b.

muktzeh l'mitzvato does, however, arise.) The *poskim*[3] conclude that, indeed, muktzeh was never included in the prohibitions of Chol HaMo'ed.

In contrast, the rabbinic prohibition of amira l'nochri, which appears primarily in regard to Shabbat, may apply throughout the Torah[4] and certainly extends to Chol HaMo'ed.[5] The logic of forbidding amira l'nochri is that there is a concern that the Jew might come to do the work himself[6] or that involvement in work through a proxy is often not conducive to the spirit of the day.[7] This prohibition applies whether one holds that melacha on Chol HaMo'ed is forbidden by the Torah or is rabbinic.

There are, however, some points of leniency regarding amira l'nochri on Chol HaMo'ed. The most pertinent is: the Magen Avraham[8] says that one may ask a non-Jew to do work in order to facilitate a *mitzva* that will be needed on Chol HaMo'ed.[9] He explains that since there is an opinion that permits a non-Jew to do melacha on a Jew's behalf in the case of a mitzva even on Shabbat, one can certainly be lenient on Chol HaMo'ed. The Levushei S'rad[10] understands that the leniency is based on the assumption that the entire prohibition of work on Chol HaMo'ed is rabbinic. Nevertheless, it is generally assumed that one can rely on the Magen Avraham's conclusion even if one is of the opinion that the melacha prohibition is from the Torah.[11]

---

3. See *Tosafot, Shabbat* 22a; *Darchei Moshe, Orach Chayim* 544:2; *Shemirat Shabbat K'Hilchata* 68:26.

4. See *Bava Metzia* 90a.

5. *Mo'ed Katan* 12a; *Shulchan Aruch, Orach Chayim* 543:1.

6. See *Chol HaMo'ed K'Hilchato* 2:(245).

7. *Aruch HaShulchan, Orach Chayim* 543:1.

8. 543:1.

9. When there is a mitzva need, it is *often* permitted for a Jew to do the work himself (*Shulchan Aruch, Orach Chayim* 545:3). However, it is important to know that there is a specific leniency of using a non-Jew for those situations when it is forbidden for a Jew.

10. On Magen Avraham 543:1.

11. *Shemirat Shabbat K'Hilchata* 68:(144).

D-9: Going to Work on Chol Hamo'ed

Question: I am a social worker in a (Jewish) old-age home. I have a certain number of vacation days during the year, and I prefer to take them in the summer. May I work on *Chol HaMo'ed* in order to leave my vacation privileges for a different time?

Answer: Two *halachot*, one permissive and one restrictive, are at the heart of this question, and we must see how they interact in this case. The first halacha is that one may do unskilled *melacha* on Chol HaMo'ed in order to provide for festival needs (*tzorchei mo'ed*).[1] The second is that melacha done for tzorchei mo'ed should either be done by the one who has the festival need or by another person on his behalf for free, but not for pay.[2] Now let's analyze and apply these principles to your case.

Our assumption is that your presence at the old-age home on Chol HaMo'ed enhances the atmosphere for the residents (individually and/or collectively). Thus, any melacha that you need to do in your workplace or in order to get there is permitted, as tzorchei mo'ed, assuming that you can avoid skilled work (*ma'aseh uman*), which would be permitted only for communal needs.[3] The classification of skilled work is determined by the technical aspect of the work. For example, writing in a sloppy manner is considered unskilled work even if one writes complex poetry.

The problem is that one should not be paid for such work (as above) unless it is occurs while performing community needs[4] which, we imagine, your job includes but is not limited to. You may be able to apply the Noda B'Yehuda's leniency. He writes[5] that

---

1. *Shulchan Aruch, Orach Chayim* 533:1, 544:1.
2. *Shulchan Aruch, Orach Chayim* 542:1.
3. *Shemirat Shabbat K'Hilchata* 68:6.
4. Ibid.
5. Ed. II, *Orach Chayim* 104.

the prohibition of taking money for work on Chol HaMo'ed is only for melacha but one can be paid for simple, non-melacha activity for tzorchei mo'ed. Thus, for example, it is permitted to take money for regular babysitting on Chol HaMo'ed.[6] If your job is, or can be arranged for Chol HaMo'ed to be, not based on melacha, then your pay would relate to permitted activity. Incidental melacha, which is not an integral part of the job, is considered unrelated to your salary and, thus, could be done for tzorchei moed. You are not paid to drive to work, and it is permitted to do so for the tzorchei mo'ed elements of the job.

Even if you have to do significant amounts of melacha (such as writing – refer to the laws of writing on Chol HaMo'ed, which are beyond our present scope), it should still be permissible for you to attend your job. The *gemara*[7] relates that the people who regularly set the table at the Exilarch's home could fix the table on Chol HaMo'ed if it broke, since they received only the privilege of eating there and did not get paid separately. We see from here that there is a distinction regarding the form of payment. "To receive money on Chol HaMo'ed is in the manner of the weekday (*uvdin d'chol*)," but to receive the privilege to eat "does not look like renting oneself out."[8] Your case is somewhere in the middle. On one hand, you are paid on a yearly basis, not for the job that you do specifically on Chol HaMo'ed. On the other hand, it is part of your regular job, for which you are paid in a normal, monetary fashion. Here we can say that the payment is permissible for the following reason. In several halachic contexts, it is permitted to receive payment *b'havla'ah* (the problematic payment is included in an undifferentiated lump sum that also includes allowable payments). Several *poskim* apply this rule in similar cases to yours and

---

6. *Chol HaMo'ed K'Hilchato* 9:39.
7. *Moed Katan* 12a.
8. *Beit Yosef, Orach Chayim* 542.

even in more tenuous cases.[9] Thus, one who is paid on a monthly or yearly basis can certainly rely upon these opinions.

We would usually suggest that a worker make an effort to show respect for the *mo'ed* by taking off on Chol HaMo'ed, if possible. However, in your case, the residents' quality of life balances out that factor.

We did not discuss the issue of loss of income, which applies to some cases of work on Chol HaMo'ed, but does not appear to apply in this case.

---

9. See *Shemirat Shabbat K'Hilchata* 66:(163); *Moadim U'Zemanim* VII, 155; *Piskei Teshuvot* 542:3.

D-10: The Validity of Artistic Chanukiyot

Question: We, in the community of Judaica artists, are confused about the "*kashrut*" of *chanukiyot*. Do the lights really have to be in a straight line in and be the same height?

Answer: Many people subscribe to an "absolute fact" that the lights of a *chanukiya* (Chanuka *menora*) must be in a straight line. However, there is no fundamental description of the required formation of a chanukiya that mandates this. Rather, its purpose is to prevent problems.

The *gemara*[1] says that one may put two wicks into one oil bowl (*ner*), and, thus, it may be used for two people. However, if one puts several wicks around the circumference of a bowl and leaves it uncovered, no one fulfills the *mitzva* because it looks like a *medura* (bonfire) rather than a flame. It follows from the gemara that if one would solve the problem of looking like a medura, it would not be a problem that the candles are in a circular position.[2]

How does one obviate the problem of medura? Several *Rishonim* say that it is sufficient that there be a finger's breadth between the wicks, but others require that the wicks should be separated by a partition.[3] The Rama's[4] opinion is even more stringent. He says that even if the wicks are in different cups, they should not be in a circular configuration because it could still look like a medura. The Magen Avraham[5] extends this stringency to a zigzag pattern. This is the source of the common practice that the candles

---

1. *Shabbat* 23b.
2. See *Shulchan Aruch, Orach Chayim* 671: 3, 4, from which it is clear that the same halachot that apply to single candles of different people also apply to multiple candles of one person.
3. See *Tur, Orach Chayim* 671.
4. *Orach Chayim* 671:4.
5. Ad loc.:3.

should be in a straight line. However, the Rama himself continues that it is acceptable to use candles in a candelabrum because, not only are they separate *nerot*, but they also are far away from each other.[6] Thus, there shouldn't be a problem, even according to the Rama, if the candles are far enough from each other that they do not resemble a medura by any stretch of the imagination. If this is so, zigzags of different types, which are just an extension of the stringency of a circle, should not be worse than a circle and should be acceptable as long as the lights are not too close together.

The other "fact" – that wax candles must be of the same height and, similarly, that the candles' bases must be on the same level, is also perplexing. Apparently, the first source for this requirement is the Chayei Adam,[7] who lived in the early 19th century. He mentions it in a matter-of-fact manner when discussing the requirement of a straight line. It is unclear if this too is somehow related to the medura issue or if there is a different reason.[8] Several later *poskim*[9] cite this stringency without disagreeing. However, the Mishna Berura does not mention it.

If an individual were to ask whether to light a standard shaped chanukiya or an innovative one, we would suggest that he conform to the standard practice. You, however, are coming from the point of view of an artist. Most observant people who buy an artistic chanukiya use it for decoration, not for lighting. A God-fearing artist, though, would not want a potential user of his chanukiya to forfeit the proper performance of the mitzva. Nevertheless, one who follows the letter of the law in designing the chanukiya (presumably, even if he does not conform to the

---

6. See *Terumat HaDeshen* 105 and *Pri Megadim, Mishbetzot Zahav* 671:2.

7. 154:10.

8. The issue might be that it is hard to see that they belong to the same lighting. However, we should remember that, according to the basic law, one candle per household is sufficient.

9. *Kaf HaChayim, Orach Chayim* 671:29; *Kitzur Shulchan Aruch* 139:9.

Chayei Adam's description) need not be concerned that some purchasers may not want to be as conservative on the matter as most of us like to be.

D-11: Lighting Chanuka Candles Away From Home

Question: My wife and I will be spending part of Chanuka in a guesthouse as part of a group. The group will be the only ones on the premises. Part of my family will be at home. Do I light Chanuka candles where I am and, if so, where?

Answer: The *gemara*[1] says that a guest is obligated to light Chanuka candles at his host's home, but it is sufficient to give money for some of the oil that is used to be included in their lighting. (Some say that more oil must be added in order for the contribution to be significant.[2]) The gemara adds that Rav Zeira, who used to pay toward the oil, stopped doing so once he got married (but was sometimes away from home by himself) because his wife would light for him in his home.[3]

Thus, it would seem that as long as there are *bar/bat mitzva* age children at home lighting, you are exempt from lighting away from home. The Taz[4] posits that a wife is automatically assumed to light with her husband in mind. However, others in the household (e.g., bar mitzva age children) should have their relative(s) specifically in mind. Yet, there are additional factors that complicate matters, and these factors are different for Ashkenazim and Sephardim.

The Maharil, one of the pillars of Ashkenazic *p'sak* and, especially, *minhag*, says that nowadays a person who is staying at an inn should light his own candles (even if his wife is lighting at home). This is because two realities have changed. One is that the place of lighting with the related *pirsumei nisa* (publicizing

---

1. *Shabbat* 23a.
2. *Mishna Berura* 677:3.
3. The understanding of most *poskim*.
4. *Orach Chayim* 677:1.

the miracle) has been moved indoors. Secondly, now it is customary that all the members of the household light. Therefore, if one of the guests does not light, others may think that he has chosen not to take part in the *mitzva*; they may not realize that he has a household that is lighting for him. The Terumat HaDeshen[5] rules that, even though one is exempted by his family, since there is a concept of *mehadrin*,[6] a guest who is interested in lighting may do so with a *beracha*. Moreover, in general, there is a preference that a person light his own candles rather than add on to the host's oil.[7] This is all the more so in a case like yours where you are part of a group where everybody is a guest at a commercial institution. This is different from joining an *existing* household, which more naturally incorporates others.[8]

As far as where to light, the Rama[9] says that the location where people eat is the proper place to light. One could argue whether it is preferable to light also in or outside the room where one sleeps [beyond our scope], but given that most guesthouses are understandably reluctant to permit fire hazards, the lighting in the joint dining hall should suffice.

For Sephardim, there are two major differences. Firstly, the Shulchan Aruch[10] does not accept the Terumat HaDeshen's permission to make a *beracha* when his household will exempt him. Secondly, the Shulchan Aruch states that when the guests have sleeping quarters with a different entrance than that of the *baʾal habayit* (homeowner), they should light there; otherwise, it might be suspected that the occupier of the dwelling is not lighting. It is unclear whether that situation requires lighting with or without a beracha (when there is a candle-lighting at home). The Kaf

---

5. #101.
6. To have more Chanuka lighting than is minimally necessary.
7. *Mishna Berura* ibid.
8. See *Chovat HaDar, Chanuka* 2:9.
9. *Orach Chayim* 677:1. One can distinguish between the cases, but this seems to be the better solution here for a combination of reasons.
10. See *Beit Yosef, Orach Chayim* 677.

HaChayim,[11] therefore, suggests hearing the beracha recited by someone who is certainly obligated. Where there is a problem getting permission to light in the room, it may be reasonable for Sephardim to light without their own beracha in the joint dining area and to try to ensure that someone lights in front of the building or wing where they sleep on behalf of all of them. Another rationale of leniency is that in a campus that is occupied by one group whose members light uniformly, the issue of suspecting one another is weaker than usual.

---

11. *Orach Chayim* 667:9.

D-12: Does One Need a Minyan for Megillat Esther?

Question: If one cannot make it to *shul* for the reading of *Megillat Esther*, does he or she need a *minyan* at home for this purpose?

Answer: Both men and women should make all reasonable efforts to fulfill the *mitzva* of hearing the reading of *Megillat Esther*, both at night and during the day.[1] Regarding whether this requires a minyan or not, Rav and Rav Asi dispute the point.[2] Rav Asi says that a minyan is required, and Rashi[3] explains that the minyan is needed for *pirsumei nisa* (publicizing the miracle of Purim), which is part and parcel of the mitzva. Rav holds that, as long as the reading takes place on Purim itself,[4] a minyan is not required. Rashi explains that on Purim, since everyone is obligated and will be reading in one venue or another on the same day, the individual is part of the framework of pirsumei nisa.

There is extensive discussion among the *Rishonim* concerning whether the *machloket* between Rav and Rav Asi is only *l'chatchila* (proper course of action) or even *b'di'eved* (after the fact) and concerning how we should *pasken*.[5] The Shulchan Aruch[6] rules that one should try to have a minyan, but, if it is not possible, an individual or a small group may read the *megilla*. The Rama[7] adds that one makes the *berachot* before such a reading (the Shulchan Aruch

---

1. *Shulchan Aruch, Orach Chayim* 689:1; see also *Mishna Berura* 689:1.
2. *Megilla* 5a.
3. Ad loc.
4. In Talmudic times, there was a practice that villagers could read the *megilla* on the previous Monday or Thursday – see *Megilla* 2a.
5. See *Beit Yosef, Orach Chayim* 690.
6. *Orach Chayim* 690:18.
7. Ad loc.

apparently agrees) but not the *beracha* after the reading.[8] (On *Purim Meshulash* the situation is somewhat more stringent.[9])

The Rama adds that if there was already a minyan in town that read the megilla and, thus, there was pirsumei nisa, an individual has no problem in reading without a minyan. The Mishna Berura[10] notes that this opinion is not universally accepted. Thus, it is still *preferable* (not mandatory) for an individual to try to find ten people for his/her reading.

What happens if people are asked to form a small minyan at someone's home rather than go to shul? Generally, it is better to hear the megilla reading in shul than in a small minyan because of *b'rov am hadrat melech*.[11] [12] Therefore, they need not give up their optimal fulfillment of the mitzva to enable another individual to fulfill his mitzva optimally. If they agree to go or to hear the megilla a second time in order to form a minyan for the person (male or female) who could not come to shul, they are doing a *chesed*. The importance of the chesed is greater regarding a sick person who would feel disappointed in not taking part in a "proper reading."

---

8. *Rama*, ibid.: 692:1.

9. See *Mishna Berura* 690:61 and *Purim Meshulash* 2:6.

10. 690:64.

11. It is more glorifying to the King when there is a multitude of people.

12. *Bi'ur Halacha*, ad loc.

D-13: Giving Matanot La'Evyonim Before Purim

Question: Can I give *matanot la'evyonim* before Purim if it will be given to the poor on Purim? I'm not even sure whether it will be Purim day for us when the *matanot* are actually distributed in Israel.

Answer: Firstly, it is good to give matanot la'evyonim both locally and from *chutz la'aretz* to Israel. Besides avoiding possible halachic quandaries like this one, it encourages increased *tzedaka*, which is very much in the spirit of Purim.[1]

There is much discussion concerning whether the main factor in *mishlo'ach manot* and matanot la'evyonim is the giving or the receiving. This discussion has several halachic ramifications. The consensus seems to be that the more important element is the receiving. In fact, the Magen Avraham[2] understands the Ba'al HaMa'or as saying that the reason not to give matanot la'evyonim before Purim is for fear they will finish the food received before Purim. This implies that if we were confident that the recipient would still have the donation when Purim came, it would not bother us that it was given before Purim. Even if it must be given on Purim, it appears to be sufficient that it be Purim for the recipient.

Many, indeed, have the practice to give matanot la'evyonim before Purim to be distributed on Purim.[3] However, this practice can be justified in various ways, with significant differences between them. One justification is, as above, that it may be sufficient that the needy receive or possess the presents on Purim

---

1. See *Mishna Berura* 694:3.
2. 694:1.
3. See *BeMareh HaBazak* II, p. 59.

(implication of Magen Avraham[4]). However, it is also possible that the distributor of the matanot la'evyonim on Purim is acting as an agent for the senders. It is, thus, as if they themselves are giving the presents on Purim.[5] One difference between the above two approaches is whether matanot la'evyonim can be sent before Purim with a non-Jewish courier. According to the second approach, even if they arrive on Purim, in the absence of a halachic agent, they were given too early.[6]

Another difference could be the matter of time zones. If one needs to *give* (either himself or by an agent) on Purim, then the agent would need to make the delivery when it is the right time at the place of the senders. Regarding this point it is not clear whether *b'di'eved* one can fulfill the mitzva of matanot la'evyonim on the night of Purim in the U.S., when it would be morning in Israel.[7] When Purim day begins in California, it is near its end in Tel Aviv, making the system logistically challenging. (Many distributors give most of the matanot la'evyonim early, to help the recipients, and some late in the day, to remove halachic doubt for givers in the U.S.)

Another interesting issue involves money that is collected outside Yerushalayim to be given the next day, on the Holy City's Purim. Logic dictates that if it was given on the donor's Purim and distributed on the recipient's Purim, one would fulfill the *mitzva* whether the emphasis is on giving or receiving.[8]

---

4. Ibid.; see *Pri Megadim*, ad loc.
5. *Aruch HaShulchan, Orach Chayim* 694:2.
6. See *Mikraei Kodesh (Frank), Purim* 45.2.
7. See ibid. 45.3.
8. See letters of Rabbis Weiss and Halberstam in *Y'mei HaPurim* p. 197. Rabbi Mordechai Willig does not feel that this system would remove all halachic doubt.

D-14: Rushing to Eat Afikoman

Question: It seems that every year we have a conflict between those who want to rush to eat the *afikoman* by *chatzot* (astronomical midnight) and those who want to allow the *seder* to advance at its own pace. What should we do?

Answer: It is generally difficult for one to decide whether someone else should be stringent. In this case, the intention to be stringent in terms of the time of afikoman often causes reduced observance of other elements of the seder. In addition to the feelings of a wife/(grand)mother who slaved to prepare a meal fit for those celebrating liberation, there is also the issue of curtailing the *mitzva d'orayta* (from the Torah) of *sipur y'tzi'at Mitzrayim* (telling the story of the Exodus) or rushing the children, whom *Chazal* saw as central figures in the seder experience. Therefore, one cannot compare the situation of those who can easily reach the target of chatzot with a little planning with those who have understandable difficulty. Study of the sources is needed to put the matter into perspective.

There are two main elements of the *mitzva* of eating the afikoman. Firstly, it is part of the mitzva to eat matza on the seder night, and, according to a minority of *Rishonim*,[1] is the main fulfillment of this mitzva. Secondly, as the Rosh[2] stresses, the afikoman is a reminder of the *Korban Pesach*, which we no longer have. Therefore, like the Korban Pesach, it is eaten on a relatively full stomach and is not to be followed by other food.

By when do these elements need to be fulfilled? Rabbi Elazar ben Azaria and Rabbi Akiva dispute whether the Korban Pesach

---

1. *Rashi, Rashbam* on *Pesachim* 119b.
2. *Pesachim* 10:34.

must be eaten by chatzot or by the morning.[3] Rava[4] says that the time for eating the Korban Pesach is also the time for eating matza. Thus, both aforementioned elements of the afikoman depend on this *machloket*. The Rambam[5] and, apparently, the Rif *pasken* like Rabbi Akiva, that we have until the morning. Yet, the Shulchan Aruch[6] writes: "One should be careful to eat [the afikoman] before chatzot." This statement must either have been made out of deference to those who pasken like Rabbi Elazar or because Rabbi Akiva agrees that one should distance himself from possible sin and eat the Korban Pesach and the matza by chatzot.[7]

Usually, the terminology of "one should be careful," when used in the Shulchan Aruch, is somewhat more than a suggestion but somewhat less than an outright, binding halachic decision. This is logical based on the sources we have seen. We must remember also that we are not talking about eating either the Korban Pesach itself or our first matza of the night after chatzot, only the additional *matza* for the purpose of the afikoman.[8]

Therefore, the following guidelines should provide a good balance. Try to start the seder promptly. Proceed through it without looking at the face of the clock, but at the faces of the children and others who should be learning, sharing, and enjoying the full experience of the seder. It is during the meal that one should start trying to "make it by chatzot." It is best for all concerned to get used to the idea that there is usually too much food at the seder. If less is prepared, and we remember that there are seven or eight days to partake in the bounty, there will be less chance of insult should it be decided to skip dessert. Also, although the afikoman should be eaten on a full stomach, it is best that some appetite be

---

3. *Pesachim* 120b.
4. Ibid.
5. *Chametz U'Matza* 6:1.
6. *Orach Chayim* 477:1.
7. *Bi'ur HaGra*, ad loc.
8. The *Mishna Berura* (477:6) makes this distinction.

left for its consumption.[9] However, habits are hard to break, and feelings should not be ignored.

(Some are aware of a sharp halachic trick to obviate the problem. It has both merit and potential problems and is beyond the scope of our discussion.[10])

---

9. *Rama* 476:1; *Mishna Berura* ad loc.:6.
10. See *Teshuvot V'Hanhagot (Shternbach)* II, 239.

D-15: An Ashkenazi Eating From Pots Used for Kitniyot

Question: On Pesach, may I (an Ashkenazi) eat *kitniyot*-free food at the house of a Sephardi friend if the food is cooked in pots that my friend uses to cook kitniyot, which Sephardic custom permits?[1] If so, why?

Answer: The various questions regarding kitniyot on Pesach seem to have become so divisive recently that one can barely open his mouth on the topic without fear of attack or of offending someone. However, the answer to this question *should* be acceptable to all "combatants" on the topic.

The Terumat HaDeshen[2] (one of the pillars of early Ashkenazic *p'sak*) says that although we are strict not to eat kitniyot, if a grain of kitniyot falls into a pot of food on Pesach, we are not so strict as to forbid the food. This is because the prohibition of eating a mixture containing a *mashehu* (tiny amount) of *chametz* on Pesach does not apply to kitniyot. The Rama[3] concurs with this ruling. (If identifiable, the kitniyot must be removed.[4]) The Terumat HaDeshen apparently permits the food in the pot only when there is a tiny amount (less than one-sixtieth of the volume of the entire mixture), which, in the case of standard food prohibitions, would be *batel* (nullified). Relative to actual chametz on Pesach, which cannot be nullified, this is a leniency. However, most *poskim* understand that the Rama includes in his leniency

---

1. Kitniyot are legumes and other foods that are not *chametz* but have some similarity to grains that can become chametz. Ashkenazic custom forbids eating these foods on Pesach out of concern that they will be confused with or contain chametz.
2. #113.
3. *Orach Chayim* 453:1.
4. *Mishna Berura* ad loc.:8.

any case where the kitniyot is a minority.[5] Based on these poskim, the Ashkenazi would surely be allowed to eat food cooked in pots used to cook kitniyot. We never know exactly how much flavor comes out of the walls of a pot that has absorbed non-kosher food. However, we know that there will not be a majority of kitniyot in the "kosher for Ashkenazim" food that is cooked in the pots in question.

One might suggest that our case is more severe than the case that the Rama discussed, because here one is purposely setting up a situation where he will rely on the fact that the minority of kitniyot will be batel. (There, the grain fell in accidentally.) There is much to say about this distinction, but we will concentrate on the halachic question at hand.[6] In our case, the kitniyot is not *be'ein* (actual pieces or juices directly in the food), but it is only flavor that is expelled from the walls of the pot. Therefore, in spite of the fact that one is setting up the situation where the kitniyot will be batel, the halachic conclusion is that it is permitted.

There is yet another halachic rationale to be lenient in our case. There are other foods that are permitted by certain communities and forbidden by others. (Regarding kitniyot, it is quite clear that the stringency, while binding on Ashkenazic communities, is more based on custom than on its own merits.[7]) The Rama[8] discusses the custom of the Jews of the Rhine region to eat a certain type of animal fat that most other Jewish communities felt was forbidden. He rules that although members of other communities should not eat this fat or a food of which it constitutes at least one-sixtieth, they may use the utensils this fat was cooked in. Therefore, we can draw the following conclusion about food that some, but not all, consider unacceptable. There is more halachic

---

5. *Pri Chadash, Orach Chayim* 453:1; *Chok Yaakov* 453:5; *Mishna Berura* 453:9.
6. See *BeMareh HaBazak* IV, 51.
7. See *Beit Yosef, Orach Chayim* 453.
8. *Yoreh Deah* 64:9.

latitude to use a pot in which this food was cooked than there is to eat something that contains a significant minority of the same food. As we have already seen, most poskim permit eating a food that has in it a significant minority of kitniyot. It is also quite clear that the likelihood of a serious prohibition is greater in the case above involving the fat than for kitniyot. Thus, it follows that it is permitted according to the Rama (who is the posek who presents the Ashkenazi tradition of kitniyot) to eat from "kitniyot pots." See also *Yechaveh Da'at*,[9] which presents this conclusion after citing several other precedents.

Stringency on Pesach has positive elements and, at times, one has reason to consider where he should be eating. However, it is neither beneficial nor halachically warranted in our case to preclude such a large group of Jews from hosting another large group.[10]

---

9. V, 32.
10. See *Rashi, Yevamot* 88a.

D-16: Chametz Found on or After Pesach

Question: In the past, after weeks of Pesach cleaning, I have found *chametz* on or after Pesach. Does this mean that I have sinned accidentally? What should I do when this happens?

Answer: Although there is a prohibition of possessing chametz on Pesach, you probably have no need to feel guilty about not finding all the chametz. If you are referring to insignificant crumbs, you need not worry, since they are not included in this prohibition.[1] Regarding significant pieces, you still don't need to worry, as long as you followed the prescribed pre-Pesach procedure of cleaning, culminating in *bedikat chametz*, and *bitul* (nullification of) *chametz*. This is so for the following reasons: 1. One who checked properly (as can be expected of a human) has fulfilled his *mitzva* and does not violate the prohibition of possessing chametz, even if some chametz remained unnoticed. This is either because it is an *oness* (beyond control) or because, according to some, one violates the prohibition only with chametz that he knows about.[2] 2. The Rabbis were concerned, even after a person has performed bedikat chametz, that he may discover chametz in his possession and, *at that point*, will violate the prohibition of owning chametz. Therefore, they instituted bitul chametz, whose text can be found in *siddurim* and in bedikat chametz kits. Once bitul has been done, one no longer violates the prohibition of owning chametz, even if he finds chametz in his possession on Pesach.

Still, if one finds chametz on Pesach, he may not rely on the bitul but should destroy it at the first opportunity.[3] If one finds

---

1. *Pesachim* 6b.
2. See *Ran* and *P'nei Yehoshua* on *Pesachim* 2a; *Pesachim* 6a, 6b, 21a with commentaries.
3. *Shulchan Aruch, Orach Chayim* 446:1; see *Mishna Berura* ad loc.: 1, 2.

chametz on *Yom Tov*, it is *muktzeh* and it should be covered with a utensil to avoid the possibility that it will be eaten accidentally.[4]

The prohibition, after Pesach, of benefiting from chametz that was in Jewish possession on Pesach (*chametz she'avar alav haPesach*) is a rabbinic injunction as a penalty to those who violated the prohibition of possession.[5] To strengthen the injunction, it was applied even to cases where the owner of the chametz is not to be blamed for the mishap or even when he did bitul.[6] Thus, if one finds (unsold) chametz in his house after Pesach, he should throw it out. If this will cause great loss, he should consult his local rabbi.[7]

---

4. *Shulchan Aruch* ibid. and *Mishna Berura* ad loc.:3.
5. *Pesachim* 30a.
6. *Shulchan Aruch* ibid. 448: 3, 5.
7. See *Mishna Berura* ad loc.: 25.

D-17: Time of Selling Chametz for a Traveler

Question: Where does one who is traveling for Pesach sell his *chametz*?

Answer: All things being equal, it is better to sell chametz in the place where the chametz is found because it makes it easier for the non-Jew who buys it to claim the chametz. Despite the fact (or possibly because of the fact) that the sale is somewhat unrealistic from a commercial perspective, it is proper to make it as practical as we can.

However, other factors are involved. If one is traveling significantly eastward, for example, from New York to Israel, then selling one's N.Y. chametz in N.Y. presents complications. The laws of Pesach and other time-based *mitzvot* are determined by the halachic time in the place where one is located, regardless of his place of origin. When one is in Israel at the time that his chametz becomes prohibited and he is obligated to destroy it, the law applies to all chametz that one owns, including the chametz that is in his N.Y. home. Furthermore, once the sixth hour of *Erev Pesach* arrives, one may not derive benefit from the chametz, and it becomes halachically impossible to sell.[1] When that takes place in Israel, it is still the previous night in N.Y. and usually chametz has not yet been sold. Therefore, the sale has to be done in Israel at the appropriate time for the person, even though his chametz is in a place where it would not yet seem to be problematic.

One can solve the problem by approaching a N.Y. rabbi who carries out two sales, the earlier one being called a *mechirat yud gimmel*. This early sale, done before the time of *bedikat chametz* (searching for chametz), is primarily intended to exempt those who will be away for all of Pesach from checking their homes.[2] By

---

1. See *Pesachim* 6b.
2. See *Mishna Berura* 436:32.

selling their chametz and renting out their house at that time, the obligation to check the house never starts. This sale also solves the timing issue for our Israel-bound traveler, as it precedes Erev Pesach morning in Israel.

Someone traveling west who leaves chametz in Israel has fewer problems getting rid of his chametz before Pesach. If he sells in Israel, he is "covered" time-wise.[3] Regarding the possibility of selling "Israeli chametz" in N.Y., the matter may be problematic. Assume, as is reasonable, that the sale takes place after it is already too late in Israel (the sixth hour of the morning). We must decide how to regard chametz that is located in an area (Israel) where the prohibitions already apply but the time has not yet arrived for the owner (in N.Y.). It is true that a person violates the prohibition of possessing chametz only if he himself is in a place where the prohibition applies.[4] However, Rav Moshe Feinstein[5] says that we should not allow chametz to be in Jewish hands when the chametz in *its* place is forbidden. This, he says, is true even if, for the owner, the time of the prohibition has not yet begun.[6] Although Rav Moshe presented his position tentatively and the majority opinion that disagrees with him seems logical, it is hard to discount his view.[7] (An early sale in N.Y. solves this problem.)

The problem for a westbound traveler who sells in Israel is the re-purchase after Pesach. When the rabbi buys back the chametz after Pesach in Israel, it is still Pesach for the owner in N.Y. (According to Rav Moshe, this problem exists also for one selling his N.Y. chametz in Israel.) Therefore, the seller should inform the rabbi that he will be abroad and that the re-purchase should not

---

3. It is preferable but probably not absolutely necessary to let the rabbi know who will have access to his apartment to enable the non-Jew to claim his chametz on Pesach.

4. See following source.

5. *Igrot Moshe, Orach Chayim* IV, 94.

6. He bases this view on a precedent that the laws of *issur hana'a* and *chametz she'avar alav haPesach* apply even in cases where there is no personal liability.

7. See *Mechirat Chametz K'Hilchato* 3: 14–17.

apply to his chametz until after Pesach is over for him. If the seller forgets to tell the rabbi and cannot reach him, he should declare before two witnesses that he cancels the rabbi's authority to buy back his chametz until later.

D-18: Can a Chazan Who Missed a Day of Sefirat Ha'Omer Recite the Beracha?

Question: If one missed a day of *sefirat ha'omer* and is now serving as the *chazan* for *Ma'ariv* in a place where it is customary that the chazan recites the *sefira* with a *beracha* aloud, may he do so?

Answer: This matter has been debated by the *Acharonim*, and it is worthwhile to understand the various logical arguments and their relative strengths to help decide how to act.

We will start with the assumption that after missing a day of sefirat ha'omer, one may not continue counting with a beracha because the forty-nine days constitute one *mitzva* of counting.[1] The Pri Chadash[2] offers the following, tentative suggestion. Although the beracha is inappropriate personally for one who has missed, it is proper for him to recite it as the congregation's representative for the public recital of sefirat ha'omer. The public mitzva, even if everyone present is capable of performing the mitzva himself, creates an obligation on the public level, as it does regarding *chazarat hashatz*. Alternatively, the Beit HaLevi reportedly[3] suggested that someone in the *minyan* can be asked to refrain from making his own beracha and be *yotzei* with the person who forgot a day. That way, the beracha becomes appropriate based on the rule that one can make a beracha on someone else's behalf even if the person making the beracha is not doing the mitzva himself at that time.[4]

The Pri Chadash[5] goes on to reject these possibilities because the person who forgot a day, assuming, as above, that he is unable to fulfill the mitzva of sefirat ha'omer, is akin to one who is not

---

1. *Shulchan Aruch, Orach Chayim* 489:8.
2. Ad loc.:8.
3. See *Mikraei Kodesh* (Frank) *Pesach* ii, 66.
4. *Rosh Hashana* 29a.
5. Ibid.

obligated in the mitzva. Such a person is incapable of making the beracha to be *motzi* someone else.[6] He reasons that although the person in question is generally obligated in sefirat ha'omer, the fact that he has no practical obligation at this time makes him equivalent to the person in the following case of the Yerushalmi. The Yerushalmi says that one whose obligation to read *Megillat Esther* is on the fourteenth of Adar cannot read on behalf of those who are obligated on the fifteenth of Adar.

The Birkei Yosef[7] cites (but rejects) those who take issue with the Pri Chadash's comparison, as follows. In the case of *megilla*, the person in question has no obligation to read on that day. In contrast, our *chazan* is obligated today and just a technical (halachic) impediment prevents him from fulfilling the mitzva. Rav Frank[8] points out that the Talmud Bavli posits that the responsibility to help another Jew fulfill his mitzva (*arvut*) makes it considered as if he has a personal obligation. Thus, he reasons, the Bavli must reject the aforementioned Yerushalmi. Although there is not a clear conclusion on the matter, the majority opinion seems to follow the Pri Chadash, that the person who missed a day of sefirat ha'omer should not use the Beit HaLevi's trick to enable him to make the beracha.[9] On the contrary, he should have in mind to be yotzei with one who has not missed a day.

One very subjective, pertinent factor is the element of embarrassment. *K'vod haberiyot* (avoiding embarrassing people, including oneself) has great, halachic weight. Thus, there are those who allow a *rav* who customarily does the sefira aloud and for whom it would be a disgrace to publicize that he missed a day of sefirat ha'omer to rely on the very significant opinions among *Rishonim* that missing one day of sefirat ha'omer does not disqualify the

6. *Rosh Hashana*, ibid.
7. *Orach Chayim* 489:19.
8. *Mikraei Kodesh* ibid.
9. See *Sha'arei Teshuva* 489:20; *Yabia Omer* VIII, *Orach Chayim* 46.

mitzva thereafter.[10] Someone other than the rav should probably not be so embarrassed in such a situation, and the rav can *pasken* for himself. Therefore, our suggestion is that a regular *chazan* should preferably offer to someone else the honor of saying the sefira aloud or perhaps avoid being the *chazan* during that period if he will be embarrassed. (Regarding mourners, they usually do not miss days anyway.)

10. *Shevet HaLevi* III, 96.

D-19: Counting Sefirat Ha'Omer in a Non-Standard Base System

Question: This sounds like a crazy question, but what is the halachic ruling on counting *sefirat ha'omer* in a base other than the standard decimal system? In other words, could a person say, "Today is one, one, zero, one in base two," on day thirteen (1101 in base two equals thirteen in the decimal system)?

Answer: From a practical perspective, this does seem like a crazy question, but trying to answer it gives us the opportunity to define more clearly how one performs the *mitzva* of counting. Let us give one practical scenario. If one is asked the day of the *omer* before he has counted with a *beracha*, he is not supposed to answer in a way that can be used to fulfill the mitzva.[1] Can he respond in base two in order to give the information without fulfilling the mitzva?

The Shulchan Aruch's[2] suggestion to avoid fulfilling the mitzva prematurely is to say what the count was the previous day. We see, then, that hinting at the correct count in a clear manner does not fulfill the mitzva. Otherwise, saying yesterday's date would be like giving today's date. Thus, one has to say something relatively direct about the number that corresponds to the day in the omer. But how formal does it have to be?

Firstly, the *poskim* understand as a simple matter that one can say sefirat ha'omer in any language that he understands.[3] Some say that one does not fulfill the mitzva if he does not understand the language, even if it is Hebrew.[4] So one can say that the important thing is getting the point across in reference to the day's count, and it makes no difference if it is expressed in a different language

---

1. *Shulchan Aruch, Orach Chayim* 489:4.
2. Ibid.
3. *Magen Avraham* 489:2.
4. Ibid.

or by using the binary number system. Actually, though, many *Acharonim*[5] dispute or have doubt about whether one fulfills the mitzva by saying the number in *gematria* form (e.g. "*yud gimmel*" for thirteen). One might claim that the answer to your question depends on this dispute, as all numerical systems are probably the same. Furthermore, the Ba'er Heitev[6] says that one fulfills the mitzva by saying "*arbaim chaser echad* (forty minus one)" for the thirty-ninth day, which is even a further use of arithmetic computations.

However, there is a logical distinction between your case and the aforementioned. It is true that our definition of what a number is may be broad enough to include gematria. However, gematria is at least a normal way for many people to express numbers. In Talmudic Hebrew, "forty minus one" is also a catch phrase for thirty-nine.[7] (One can, therefore, take issue with the B'er Moshe[8] who simply equates "five minus one" with "forty minus one.") In contrast, "talking in binary" is not normal in any language (if one, properly, excludes computer languages).

The matter may depend on the careful reading of earlier sources. The Tur[9] cites the Ra'avya's opinion that when one is in between multiples of seven days, he doesn't declare the total number of days. Rather, he states only the number of weeks and the remainder of days. For example, one would recite only "a week and six days" for thirteen. Apparently, "a week" is an accepted way of saying seven days and it seems to be equivalent to the gematria case. Yet, the Tur feels compelled to explain that this way of counting is valid only because on day number seven, he said, "seven days, which is a week." The Chok Yaakov[10] says, in fact, that if on

---

5. See *Sha'arei Teshuva* 489:6; *Bi'ur Halacha* on 489:1; *Kaf HaChayim, Orach Chayim* 489:24.
6. *Orach Chayim* 489:6.
7. See *Shabbat* 73a.
8. III, 82.
9. *Orach Chayim* 489.
10. 489:8.

day number seven one simply says "a week," the Ra'avya agrees that he does not fulfill the mitzva. Only after formally stating in our counting that seven days is equivalent to a week are they then interchangeable on subsequent days.[11]

In the final analysis, if counting in gematria is invalid, then doing so in number bases other than decimal is certainly invalid. If one accepts gematria, there is a possibility to consider binary numbers. However, logic still dictates that one must express the count in a numerical system that is an accepted means of speaking in the language one is using.

---

11. Some argue with the Chok Yaakov, and one can suggest that the Tur's explanation is needed only to clarify why the Ra'avyah's system is legitimate l'chatchila, whereas you are likely interested in the ruling b'di'eved.

D-20: Getting Married on Yom HaAtzma'ut or Yom Yerushalayim

Question: Is it permitted to get married on *Yom HaAtzma'ut*[1] and *Yom Yerushalayim*?[2]

Answer: As you know, there is an ancient custom not to marry during the period of *sefira*, when we commemorate the death of the students of Rabbi Akiva.[3] There are opinions that are lenient in a variety of cases of need and *mitzva*,[4] but the *minhag*, in general, is kept strictly.

Chief Rabbi Nissim[5] felt that celebrating the miracles and Divine blessings associated with Yom HaAtzma'ut is reason enough to allow a full suspension of the minhagim of sefira on that day. Thus, it would be permissible even to celebrate a wedding. Other distinguished contemporaries of Rav Nissim, although they appreciated the importance of the crucial, historic events of Yom HaAtzma'ut, believed that allowing marriages on that day despite sefira was a leniency too revolutionary to adopt in our generation. See the responsa of Rav Ovadya Hadaya[6] and Chief Rabbi Unterman,[7] who expressed the latter view. After confirming with religious councils in Israel that the practice is to not allow marriages on Yom HaAtzma'ut, we feel that this custom should be followed. However, those who decide to have the wedding then have upon whom to rely.

The situation on Yom Yerushalayim is different because it falls after *Lag BaOmer*. Since, according to the minhag of many,

---

1. Israel Independence Day (5 Iyar).
2. Jerusalem Liberation Day (28 Iyar).
3. *Shulchan Aruch, Orach Chayim* 493:1.
4. See a survey of opinions in *Yein HaTov* II, 11.
5. Ibid.
6. *Yaskil Avdi* VI, 10.
7. *Shevet MiYehuda* 60

the restrictions of the sefira period are over then,[8] there is significantly more room for leniency. Consequently, the Chief Rabbinate Council, under the presidency of Chief Rabbis Unterman and Nissim, issued a directive to allow marriages on Yom Yerushalayim. In *BeMareh HaBazak*,[9] we cited this ruling and stressed its particular relevance for those who have not yet fulfilled the mitzva of *pru u'revu*.[10]

---

8. See *Shulchan Aruch* ibid.:2 and *Mishna Berura*, ad loc.
9. III, p. 100.
10. Procreating by having at least a boy and a girl.

D-21: Why Are There Two Days of Shavuot?

Question: I understand the reason for celebrating two days of *Yom Tov* in *chutz la'aretz* for all *chagim*, except for Shavuot. Since we count forty-nine days of *sefira* and the fiftieth day is Shavuot, how could there be uncertainty?

Answer: You make an excellent point. Let's start with the background necessary to fully appreciate your question.

The length of each Jewish month must be either twenty-nine or thirty days. Until about 1,600 years ago, the *beit din* would declare the new month based on the sighting of the moon, but the rest of the Jewish world needed to be notified so that they would know when the upcoming chagim would fall. Originally, they used a system of quickly informing most Jewish communities (even in Babylonia) by means of lighting torches on mountaintops.[1] At that time, the few communities who weren't notified kept two days of Yom Tov. When the *Kutim*[2] disrupted the reliability of the system, a slower system of couriers was adopted. Word did not arrive in many communities even in time for the mid-month *Yamim Tovim* of Pesach and Sukkot, forcing them to keep two days.[3] We continue the *minhag* of keeping two days in those places even though the calendar is now predetermined.[4]

By Shavuot time, everyone must have known when Nisan had begun and could count fifty days from Pesach. Indeed, Shavuot does not depend on the date of the month and can technically fall on the fifth, sixth or seventh day of Sivan[5] (although our set calendar always puts it on the sixth). Therefore, Shavuot did not

---

1. *Rosh Hashana* 22b.
2. A sect that did not accept Rabbinic authority.
3. *Rambam, Kiddush HaChodesh* 5:3–12.
4. *Beitza* 4b.
5. *Rosh Hashana* 6b.

depend on when the *Rosh Chodesh* of Sivan would be declared, and the extra day seems superfluous, as you suggest.

The *gemara* addresses a similar question in the following scenario. The emissaries of the beit din could not violate Shabbat or Yom Tov in carrying out their charge. Thus, in Tishrei, because of Rosh Hashana and Yom Kippur, these emissaries were not able to get as far by Sukkot, the fifteenth of Tishrei, as they could in Nisan by Pesach, the fifteenth of that month. Therefore, there should have been some communities where they kept two days of Yom Tov for Sukkot out of uncertainty but only one day for Pesach. Yet, the gemara[6] says that any place where the emissaries of Tishrei did not reach in time for Sukkot would keep two days of Yom Tov on Pesach even if the emissaries reached them. This was because of a *g'zeira* (rabbinic injunction), lest there be confusion between the two sets of holidays. The Rambam,[7] in discussing this concept of not distinguishing between holidays, states explicitly that the same idea applies to Shavuot, thus answering your question.

---

6. *Rosh Hashana* 21a.
7. Ibid. 3:12.

D-22: Eating New Fruit During the Three Weeks

Question: Why is eating new fruit considered such a pleasure that it is forbidden during the Three Weeks (between 17 Tammuz and 9 Av)? Also, is it permitted on Shabbat during that time?

Answer: As far as the actual practices of the Three Weeks and the Nine Days are concerned, we prefer not to rule definitively, as the practices depend very much on family and/or community *minhag*. These are best handled on the local level. However, it is worthwhile to address some of the confusion about the source, rationale, and parameters of this halacha/minhag.

The issue is actually not the eating of the new fruit, per se, but the fact that when eating new fruit, one is required to make the *beracha* of *Shehecheyanu*. The wording of that beracha implies that we are happy to have reached a particular period of the year. However, the sadness associated with the Three Weeks makes such a statement inappropriate then. The source is actually post-Talmudic (as is not uncommon regarding these *halachot*). The Sefer Chasidim[1] says:

> There were pious ones … who would not eat any new fruit between 17 Tammuz and 9 Av, for they said: "How can we make the blessing that 'He gave us life, sustained us, and allowed us to reach this time'?" There are those who make the beracha on new fruit when they came across them on the *Shabbatot* between 17 Tammuz and 9 Av.

The Shulchan Aruch[2] phrases it as follows: "It is good to be careful not to say Shehecheyanu on fruit and clothes during the

---

1. #840.
2. *Orach Chayim* 551:17.

Three Weeks, but on a *pidyon haben* you say it and do not lose out on the *mitzva*."

The weak language of these sources implies that the practice of avoiding the recitation of *Shehecheyanu* is in a lower category than halacha or even a standard minhag. The Gra[3] calls this practice an extreme stringency. He proves that even a mourner on the day of a parent's death may recite *Shehecheyanu* if the need arises, and, therefore, there is no way that the Three Weeks could be more severe. However, the Magen Avraham[4] makes a fundamental distinction between the Three Weeks and mourning, which many accept (but the Gra does not). He says that it is not that a person should be too sad to recite Shehecheyanu but that the period is a tragic one. That is, the Three Weeks is an objectively sad time for all, as opposed to the occasion of mourning, where the individual is sad, not the period in time.

The aforementioned sources do not say that to make a Shehecheyanu during this time is out of the question, but that the situation should be avoided by not eating new fruit or wearing new clothes. (For clothes, there are additional problems during the Nine Days, beyond the issue of Shehecheyanu.[5]) Not only do we say Shehecheyanu at a pidyon haben, but the Rama[6] says that if the only time the fruit will be available for one to make a Shehecheyanu is during the Three Weeks, then one should not lose the opportunity.

One common question about which there is major discussion among *poskim* is, as you asked, whether one may recite Shehecheyanu on Shabbat. On one hand, even though the laws of *aveilut* almost disappear on Shabbat, our issue here is whether one may praise the time of year. Even on Shabbat it would, apparently, be inappropriate to praise the Three Weeks. On the

---

3. Ad loc.
4. 551:42.
5. See *Shulchan Aruch*, ibid.:6.
6. *Orach Chayim* 551:17.

other hand, because of the mitzva of *oneg Shabbat*,[7] we do not want to refrain from adding to our enjoyment. Although there is no clear consensus on the matter, different factors can help a person decide whether it is preferable to eat the foods and make a Shehecheyanu or not.[8] One factor is how close it is to Tisha B'av. Another factor is how important eating the new fruit is for the enjoyment of Shabbat.

In general, with regard to the laws and customs of the Three Weeks, it is important to keep things in perspective. Many of the specific customs are relatively recent, and sometimes the extent to which they are binding on a given community is questionable. On one hand, the existence of customs, many of which are halachically binding, are crucial in creating a pervasive atmosphere of dampened joy. On the other hand, the heart of the mitzva is the atmosphere itself.

---

7. Physical enjoyment of Shabbat.
8. See *Piskei Teshuvot* 551:53.

D-23: How to Spend Tisha B'Av

Question: Besides refraining from forbidden activities, how should one spend Tisha B'Av?

Answer: For a few reasons, the answer depends on the individual. As usual, some matters depend on the local *minhag*. In this case, it is even more individualistic, as different people arrive at the proper frame of mind in different ways. Furthermore, we have to be realistic. Not everyone who will refrain from a given practice will be sitting all day crying about the *Beit HaMikdash*. I remember a group of people who were careful not to learn Torah on Tisha B'Av, but they used the afternoon for an annual softball game. A little "leniency" regarding something more suitable might have been better. In any case, we will use *halachot* to arrive at a general approach to what is appropriate.

There are two major elements to the various halachot that govern activities on Tisha B'Av (other than those that are directly fast-related). One element is to concentrate on the *aveilut* (mourning) over the national destruction that the day commemorates. The other is to refrain from things that we categorize as joyful.

The *mishna*[1] presents two minhagim regarding whether work is permitted on Tisha B'Av. The main reason not to work is, apparently, in order to keep one's mind on aveilut.[2] The mishna instructs each person to follow the local minhag, as does the Shulchan Aruch.[3] (In the Beit Yosef, he reports a widespread practice of stringency, which some Sephardic *poskim* accept as a final ruling.[4]) The Rama[5] states that the Ashkenazic minhag is to ab-

---

1. *Pesachim* 54b.
2. *Mishna Berura* 554:43.
3. *Orach Chayim* 554:22.
4. See *Torat HaMo'adim* 8:24.
5. *Orach Chayim* 554:22.

stain from work of even a moderately serious nature until *chatzot* (midday). (The halachot are similar to those of *Chol Hamo'ed* and are beyond our present scope.) This leads us to the conclusion that until chatzot one should act in a way that keeps his mind on aveilut. This is supported by the minhag to postpone preparing the night meal until chatzot,[6] to sit on or near the floor, and to recite *kinot* (mournful liturgy) until close to chatzot.[7]

After chatzot, the main focus is on not doing things that are joyous. Of course, there are different levels of happiness, and there is some distinction between activities that are formally forbidden and those that fall within the realm of the spirit of the law. Torah study is formally classified as something that makes one happy and is forbidden even for those who do not derive from it a strong, conscious joy. Only Torah topics that are objectively sad or aveilut-related are permitted.[8] There are sources and logic that support both sides of the question of whether works of *mussar* (literally, rebuke) are permitted to be studied on Tisha B'Av. The matter may depend on the nature of the work (e.g., the extent to which *p'sukim*, *midrashim*, and interesting philosophical insights are incorporated[9]).

The spirit of the law is also expressed in the law. The Shulchan Aruch[10] says that one should not stroll in the marketplace, lest he come to frivolity. The Mishna Berura[11] urges those with the minhag to visit the cemetery to do so in small groups to avoid it turning into "a happening." These are just a couple of halachot that help set a tone and give a direction to follow.

A practice has developed to have daylong programs of talks on topics of soul-searching. While Tisha B'Av is intended to be more a day of sadness than of self-improvement, most people are

---

6. *Shulchan Aruch, Orach Chayim* 559:10.
7. *Shulchan Aruch* and *Rama* ibid.:3.
8. See a (partial?) list in *Shulchan Aruch, Orach Chayim* 554:1–2.
9. See *Riv'vot Ephrayim* I, 386.
10. Ibid.:21.
11. 559:41.

better served by taking part in such forums than staying at home, attempting the difficult task of maintaining the proper frame of mind on their own. Whereas in the morning the focus should be on the kinot (recitation or explanation), the afternoon may be spent on forums of contemplation and soul-searching. Lecturers and participants should do their part to ensure that the content and atmosphere are somber and do not foster socializing, which is against the spirit and halachot of the day.[12]

---

12. *Shulchan Aruch* ibid. 554:20.

D-24: Caffeine Pills on Fast Days

Question: On fast days other than Yom Kippur, is it permitted to swallow a caffeine pill without water in order to prevent caffeine withdrawal headaches?

Answer: Someone who is sick is permitted to swallow medicine (without water or washed down by an inedible, bitter liquid) on fasts other than Yom Kippur if the medicine is not normally edible.[1] According to several opinions, this is permissible even on Yom Kippur.[2] There are two complicating factors regarding a caffeine pill:

1. Caffeine is not a medicine that heals. Rather it is an ingredient in regular foods that is missing during a fast.

2. One usually takes this pill when perfectly healthy to prevent a future decline in his condition.

(The following guidelines do not apply to Yom Kippur.) However, the above considerations don't preclude the use of caffeine pills, just limit it. Caffeine withdrawal is not a lack of nutrition but a disease-like situation caused by an acquired dependency upon caffeine. When, based on experience, one expects to feel ill to the extent that it will affect his ability to function, as is the case with a severe headache, he can take the pill in advance to prevent deterioration.[3] If he is affected enough to be confined to bed, then he could take the pill with water if needed.[4] If only a mild headache is expected, then he should not take the pill. After all, healthy people don't always feel great on a fast day. If one is likely to get a bad headache but can prevent it by taking the pill when the symptoms begin, he should delay taking it until it becomes

---

1. See *Tzitz Eliezer* x, 25.22.
2. See *Tzitz Eliezer*, ibid; *Shemirat Shabbat K'Hilchata* 39:8.
3. See *Shemirat Shabbat K'Hilchata* 33:1.
4. See *Shulchan Aruch, Orach Chayim* 554:6.

evident that a serious headache is coming on. In general, in borderline cases, there is more reason to be stringent on Tisha B'Av
than on the other fasts.[5]

Some people solve the problem by avoiding caffeine all year
long or by slowly weaning themselves during the weeks before the
fast. If these solutions are practical, they are also preferable.

5. See ibid.:5, 6.

Section E:
Kashrut

E-1: Milk and Poultry – Why Is It Forbidden?

Question: If the prohibition of eating meat with milk is based on the Biblical passage: "You shall not cook a kid in its mother's milk," why does it apply to chicken? After all, chickens do not have milk.

Answer: The prohibition of meat and milk is a *chok*, a commandment whose reason is not readily apparent. *Chazal*[1] taught that "kid" and "mother's milk" are just examples of meat and milk. However, there are laws derived from the choice of these words that show that your question has much merit.

Rabbi Akiva derives from the three-fold repetition in the Torah of "a kid" that fowl and certain other animals are excluded from the prohibition. Rabbi Yossi HaGelili says that the law applies to any mammal that requires *shechita*.[2] He agrees that species that have no mother's milk (like chicken) are excluded.[3] Rabbi Akiva and Rabbi Yossi HaGelili also argue whether there is a rabbinic prohibition on fowl and milk.[4] The halacha follows the opinion of Rabbi Akiva that there is a rabbinic prohibition to eat fowl and milk.[5] The reason for the a rabbinic prohibition is that if people become accustomed to eating the meat of chicken in milk, they may forget the aforementioned distinction and eat beef cooked in milk.

Some of the regular restrictions that apply to meat and milk apply to fowl as well. One may not eat fowl and milk together even if they were not cooked together, may not have milk on the table

---

1. The rabbis of Talmudic times.
2. Ritual slaughter.
3. *Chulin* 113a.
4. Ibid. 116a.
5. *Shulchan Aruch, Yoreh Deah* 87:3.

when he is eating fowl (unless he uses a halachic reminder),[6] and must wait up to six hours between eating fowl and dairy.[7]

There are, however, some differences. From the three-fold repetition in the Torah of the above passage we learn that the prohibition includes not only eating meat and milk that were cooked together but also the act of cooking itself and deriving benefit from the cooked mixture. When, however, eating is prohibited only rabbinically, cooking and deriving benefit are permitted.[8] Thus, one could, for example, cook fowl and milk together in order to sell to a non-Jew. (Of course, the pot would then be unfit for cooking food for a Jew.)

---

6. Ibid. 88:1.
7. Ibid. 89:1.
8. Ibid. 87:3.

E-2: Kashering China

Question: Can you *kasher* a set of *treif* china and, if so, under what conditions and how?

Answer: In general, one cannot kasher china, as it is assumed to belong to the category of *kli cheres* (earthenware). The *gemara*[1] states that the Torah testifies that one cannot remove from a kli cheres all that it has absorbed.

However, when there is a confluence of 1) a variety of mitigating circumstances and 2) a significant need, one can permit a special system of kashering of such utensils. Regarding a full set of china, we can assume that not being able to use part of the set would be considered a *hefsed merubeh* (a great loss) for most people. We are also assuming that most use of the utensils was as a *kli sheini* (i.e., the hot food was removed from the pot that was on a flame before it made contact with the dishes.)

The following system can be used in such a case. The dishes must not be used for twelve months so that the absorbed matter can dry out.[2] One fills a large pot with water so that it preferably contains sixty times the volume of the dishes that will be in the pot at one time. The water should be brought to a boil and kept boiling. The dishes must be cleaned of all residues before the kashering process can begin. Each dish from the set should be placed in the pot for a few seconds so that the water covers it and then is removed and rinsed. The process should be repeated three times, a system which works, according to a minority view, even under normal circumstances for a kli cheres. Some say that the water should be switched before each repetition of the process.

This discussion is a synopsis taken from BeMareh HaBazak.[3]

---

1. *Pesachim* 30b.
2. See *Shulchan Aruch, Yoreh Deah* 135:16.
3. II, p. 68.

One can find there additional sources and reasoning for our specific issue and should study the laws of kashering in greater depth.

E-3: Kashering Utensils From Meat to Dairy

Question: When can one *kasher* utensils from *fleishig* to *milchig* or vice versa?

Answer: Let's start with a basic understanding of the problem. From the perspective of the *gemara*, and even of the *Rishonim*, one may kasher between fleishig and milchig. (We will refer to milchig and fleishig interchangeably, as the direction of the switch makes no difference.) However, the Magen Avraham[1] reports a *minhag* not to do so. The rationale is that if one were allowed to kasher freely, he might decide to use a given utensil for both milchig and fleishig on an ongoing basis. *Chazal* were opposed to this situation, as the gemara[2] states that one should have three different knives to use for different functions and not rely upon himself to clean them well between uses. This minhag has been widely accepted and is considered binding in the Ashkenazic community. Rav Ovadya Yosef[3] points out some weaknesses in the minhag and says that Sephardic *poskim* did not accept it.

Some important poskim understand that the prohibition does not really pertain to the *use* of a formerly milchig utensil for fleishig, but rather to *kashering* a utensil for that purpose. Consequently, if one kashered a utensil in order to prepare it for Pesach, he can change it from milchig to fleishig.[4] Similarly, if the utensil became *treif* and was subsequently kashered, it can be changed, as well.[5]

Rav Moshe Feinstein suggests that if no recognizable taste remains in the utensil (e.g., after kashering was already performed

---

1. 509:11.
2. *Chulin* 8b.
3. *Yabia Omer* iii, *Yoreh Deah* 4.
4. *Shut Chatam Sofer, Yoreh Deah* 110.
5. *Pri Megadim* on *Magen Avraham*, ibid.

or after twelve months of nonuse), it *might* be permissible to change.[6] [7] Others permit kashering by a new owner, as he never used the utensil in a different manner and, thus, will not come to mistakenly use it for what it was originally (milchig or fleishig).[8] An interesting *machloket* exists regarding whether one can switch from milchig to *pareve*, given that even if he forgot to kasher the utensil before using it, the halachic stakes are much lower.[9] It is easier to be lenient when a pareve utensil accidentally becomes milchig because, without kashering, it can no longer be used for its original intended purpose.[10]

[*The above is a brief survey of the topic and not a p'sak on any particular case.*]

---

6. *Igrot Moshe, Yoreh Deah* I, 43.
7. In the latter case, with kashering.
8. See *Darchei Teshuva* 121:59.
9. See *Tzitz Eliezer* IX, 38.
10. *Darchei Teshuva*, ibid.

E-4: Children Checking Food for Insects

Question: If a child under the age of *bar/bat mitzva* inspects grains or vegetables for insect infestation, is that inspection halachically sufficient?

Answer: Your question is a very important one, and it has broad application. In fact, since the applications are too numerous and complex to exhaust, we will, for the most part, only address the general principles.

The *gemara*[1] says that minors are believed when they attest that a house was checked for *chametz*. The gemara explains that this is so because, assuming *bitul* (nullification of) *chametz* was done, the problem of having chametz in his home is only rabbinic. Thus, we have our first guiding principle for deciding when one may trust a child: we may trust a child regarding a rabbinic law, but not regarding a Torah law.

However, the gemara's case may be lenient for two additional reasons: 1. There is no known, pre-existing prohibition that needs to be rectified (*lo itchazek issura*).[2] 2. The child who is attesting has the ability to rectify the situation himself (*beyado*), since he can check the house for chametz.[3] The Rama[4] rules that a minor is believed only when these three lenient factors coincide, i.e., the law is rabbinic, the prohibition is not known to have pre-existed, and the child can rectify the situation himself. Many[5] take issue with the Rama and claim that when it is *beyado*, a minor is believed even regarding itchazek issura. Tosafot[6] requires that the child himself will be relying upon his own testimony (e.g., eating

---

1. *Pesachim* 4a.
2. *Rama, Yoreh Deah* 127:3.
3. *Tosafot ad loc.*
4. *Yoreh Deah* 127:3
5. Including the *Shach* ad loc.:31.
6. *Eruvin* 31b.

the food), and some *poskim* prefer that we rely on their checking only in such a case.[7]

A specific case where poskim "hammer out" the issues is the question whether a minor is trusted that he performed *tevillat keilim* (immersing utensils). The Shulchan Aruch[8] rules that a minor is not believed. The Taz[9] explains that this is because tevillat keilim is a Torah law. A major *machloket Acharonim* exists regarding tevillat keilim of a glass utensil, for which there is only a rabbinic obligation.[10]

The situation regarding checking food for infestation really depends on several factors. Since there is no knowledge that a problem did exist, there is no issue of itchazek issura. On the other hand, to check many foods properly requires concentration and toil, which may challenge the child's capabilities and credibility. We suggest the following. If the likelihood of a problem is not very high, a child can be believed since there is only a rabbinic requirement to check. It is best if the child will also be eating from the food. In certain cases, where the likelihood of infestation causes a Torah requirement to check, a child is not believed.

Of course, any leniency must assume that the specific child is fully capable of doing a proper job.

---

7. See *Shaar HaTziyun* 437:19; *Bedikat HaMazon KaHalacha* 6:2.
8. *Yoreh Deah* 120:14.
9. Ad loc.:16.
10. See *Rav Akiva Eiger* and *Pitchei Teshuva*, ad loc. and a summary in *Tevilat Keilim* (Cohen) 8: (2*).

E-5: Exchanging Non-Kosher Wine

Question: I received a bottle of non-kosher wine worth about $140 as a gift from a non-Jewish coworker. Our liquor store will exchange it for kosher wine of similar value if they can sell mine. May we make the exchange?

Answer: What you suggest is the equivalent of selling the non-kosher wine. If it is *asur behanaʾa*,[1] what you describe is forbidden.

However, the status of regular, non-kosher wine is the source of a major dispute. There are two parts to the *rabbinic* prohibition of *stam yeinam* (wine which has been exposed to non-Jewish contact). One part is a prohibition to *drink* the wine, out of fear that such behavior might lead to intermarriage.[2] There is, at times, a *Torah-level* prohibition to *benefit* from wine when it is involved in idol worship. Because these two prohibitions could be confused one with the other, *Chazal* added a second rabbinic prohibition of benefit on stam yeinam.[3]

Regarding stam yeinam's rabbinic prohibition of *benefit*, the classic sources indicate that there is significant room for leniency in various cases. The Shulchan Aruch[4] states that non-Jews who are not involved in idol worship do not create a prohibition of benefit, only a prohibition of drinking. The Rambam[5] applies this rule to Moslems. Regarding religions with less perfect forms of monotheism, the situation is less clear.

The Rama[6] provides the "bottom line" for Ashkenazi Jews: "Nowadays, when it is uncommon for non-Jews to perform libations for purposes of idolatry, some say that a non-Jew's touching

---

1. Forbidden to receive benefit from it.
2. *Avoda Zara* 36b.
3. *Avoda Zara* 29b; see *Beit Yosef, Yoreh Deah*, beginning of *siman* 123.
4. *Yoreh Deah* 124:6.
5. *Maʾachalot Asurot* 11:7.
6. *Yoreh Deah* 123:1.

of our wine does not prohibit benefit, [it] only [prohibits] drinking. Similarly, benefiting from their unsupervised wine (stam yeinam) is permitted. Therefore, one may take wine from a non-Jew as payment to prevent losing a debt or to prevent other losses (i.e., relating to transactions that he already performed). However, he should not initiate such sales in order to profit. There are those who are lenient even in such cases [to initiate], but it is proper to be strict." The Chochmat Adam[7] concurs.

If your situation is that the present was received as a bonus from an employer or you are expected to reciprocate with a present of your own, etc., one could consider the sale of the wine a way to prevent loss. Additionally, nowadays, when there is little true idol worship, one can be more lenient regarding what kind of contact creates a full prohibition.[8]

---

7. 75:14.
8. See *Rama, Yoreh Deah* 124:24.

E-6: Commerce With Non-Kosher Food

Question: May a Jew deal commercially with prohibited foods if he has no direct contact with the food and he has a non-Jewish partner?

Answer: The *gemara* derives from the *pasuk*, "*Vesheketz yiheyu lachem*," that one may sell non-kosher species (and some other forbidden foods) that have come into his possession, but he may not make efforts to acquire the foods in order to sell them. Be aware that this prohibition of purposely acquiring the non-kosher food applies only to food that is forbidden from the Torah (as opposed to rabbinically).[1] Primarily, meat and fish products are likely to fit into this category, although the matter is more complicated than we can address in our context.

According to most *Rishonim*, the prohibition of trading in forbidden foods is on a Torah level.[2] The Rashba[3] says that the reason is to minimize the possibility of eating forbidden foods; others say it is a *gezeirat hakatuv* (heavenly decree without a known reason).

The consensus of *poskim* is that this prohibition applies as long as a Jew owns the food, even if he is not expected to come in direct contact with the food.[4] It is debatable whether holding a small amount of stocks is considered partial ownership of a company and would be forbidden in this regard.[5]

As mentioned, it is prohibited only to purposely obtain these foods. If one "chances upon them," he is allowed to sell them. There are many complicated questions regarding the distinction

---

1. *Shulchan Aruch, Yoreh Deah* 117:1.
2. See *Shut Chatam Sofer, Yoreh Deah* 104–106, 108; *Yabia Omer* VIII, *Yoreh Deah* 13.
3. *Responsa* III, 223.
4. *Chatam Sofer* ibid. 108, cited in *Pitchei Teshuva, Yoreh Deah* 117:6.
5. See *Mishneh Halachot* V, 102.

between purposely and unintentionally obtaining. For example, what is the halacha concerning buying mutual funds, when it is known that some percentage of the stocks that will be acquired on his behalf are of companies that deal with prohibited foods? In the case of mutual funds, we can be lenient for a combination of reasons.[6] However, it is more problematic to directly buy stocks of, for example, McDonald's. One is not allowed to be a merchant of prohibited foods if he actually owns the food. In a case where most of the food is permitted and business circumstances require the owner to include some non-kosher food, there is some room for leniency.[7] This is not the case, though, when buying stock in McDonald's, which conducts most of its business with non-kosher food. A partnership with a non-Jew does not help.

If you have a specific question, please let us know. Often, small details can make a big difference, and this summary is not meant as a *p'sak* for a specific case.

---

6. *Mishneh Halachot*, ibid.

7. See *Taz, Yoreh Deah* 117:4; *Aruch HaShulchan, Yoreh Deah* 117:26.

E-7: Use of Fleishig Oven for Pareve Food

Question: I use my oven for baking *fleishig* foods. If I haven't used the oven for twenty-four hours and then bake a *pareve* cake, may I eat it with milk?

Answer: Please be aware that there are diverse *minhagim* in different communities regarding the use of ovens for various types of foods. What we write here is not intended to delegitimize any ruling you may have received from a competent rabbinic authority.

We start with the case where you use pareve ingredients for a cake baked in a fleishig pan. Does the fleishig taste, which the pan absorbed, get transferred yet again to the pareve food and turn it into fleishig? This double-removed potential taste, known as *nat bar nat*, is the subject of a far-reaching *machloket* between the Shulchan Aruch and the Rama.[1] The Rama's ruling, accepted by Ashkenazic Jewry, is that it is proper to treat the formerly pareve food as fleishig in regard to not eating it with milchig food.

However, if the pan has not been used for twenty-four hours, then the taste remaining in its walls is considered "spoiled" and is not halachically significant. It is true that *Chazal* did not allow us to use non-kosher utensils even after they have remained unused for twenty-four hours. However, since, in this case, even within twenty-four hours, the fleishig status of the food is the subject of the aforementioned machloket, the cake baked in such a pan (after twenty-four hours) is considered pareve. For this reason, the Gra[2] permitted the use of such a pan for the purpose of eating it with milk. On the other hand, many *Acharonim* subscribe to the opinion of the Chochmat Adam,[3] with which the Rama[4] mildly

---

1. *Yoreh Deah* 95:2.
2. Ad loc.:10.
3. 48:2.
4. Ibid.

implies that he agrees, that one should not set up such a situation *l'chatchila*.[5] In other words, if one planned to eat the cake with fleishig or pareve, and then a situation arose where he decided to eat it with milchig, he may do so. However, he should not bake with the intention to eat the cake with milk. Thus, the proper thing, based upon the above, is to use a pareve or disposable pan.

Using a fleishig oven, however, still presents halachic challenges. The Rama[6] rules that, when two foods were baked or roasted in an oven at different times, taste is transferred from one food to the other only if there was condensation (*zei'ah*) from both foods on the walls of the oven. A "fleishig oven," presumably, had fleishig condensation at some time during its use. However, it is unclear how liquid a food and how insulated an oven have to be in order that there be zei'ah to transfer the fleishig taste from the walls to the food.[7] Bread and relatively dry cake batter probably do not create zei'ah in a normal oven and will remain pareve. (One must make sure that the pan does not touch a surface with fleishig residue on it.) However, a liquid batter may create zei'ah. Practical rulings on the matter depend not only on the case's details but also on the approach of one's rabbi. If zei'ah is present, it compromises the pareve status of both the cake and the pan. (If the oven was well-cleaned and had not been used within twenty-four hours, the pan would not need to be *kashered* and the cake remains pareve).

There are at least two good solutions to the problem of zei'ah in an oven. One solution is to cover the cake batter (where feasible) so that escaping moisture is insufficient to transfer taste.[8] The other solution is to do *libun kal*[9] on the oven before baking the cake to remove the fleishig taste from the walls and to burn

---

5. Of his own choice.
6. *Yoreh Deah* 108:1.
7. See *Igrot Moshe, Yoreh Deah* I, 40.
8. *Rama* ibid.
9. A form of kashering.

any surface residue. A half-hour of heating at the oven's highest temperature is usually sufficient to accomplish libun kal. (More time is needed if there was significant spillage that one did not remove prior to heating.) Even one who relies upon the afore-mentioned Gra must ensure that there is no edible residue on the walls of the oven that zei'ah could transfer to the food. If there are tiny quantities of edible residue on the wall, they will not make the food fleishig *b'di'eved*,[10] [11] but, with direct contact, they may affect the status of the pan.

---

10. After the fact.
11. See *Igrot Moshe* ibid.

E-8: Milk That Fell on Hot Meat

Question: I was making a roast, and a drop of milk spilled on it. Is the meat still kosher?

Answer: When milk falls into a pot that contains meat, it can create the forbidden substance known as *basar b'chalav*[1] if there is enough milk to give a taste to the meaty food. The halachic assumption is that if the volume of milk is at least one-sixtieth of the volume of the meaty food, the milk's taste will be noticeable in the mixture and make it forbidden.[2] This method of measuring works well when the milk spreads uniformly throughout the contents of the pot, which happens when the food is soupy. However, if the milk fell onto a solid piece of meat, then we have to ascertain how far into the food the milk penetrated, as we shall see. (If the milk fell into a pot containing solid pieces of meat protruding from gravy, the situation is much more complicated and beyond our present scope.[3])

Several factors affect if and how far the taste of one food is absorbed by the solid food on which it falls. The most basic factor is the heat of the food. In a case where the bottom food is cooking, there is significant absorption even if that which falls upon it is cold (Shulchan Aruch,[4] based on the rule, *tata'ah gavar*[5]). However, even if the drop of milk is absorbed, will it spread throughout the roast?

We work under the assumption that the milk can spread at least up to *kedei netilla*,[6] which is a little less than an inch around

---

1. A mixture of milk and meat.
2. *Rama, Yoreh Deah* 92:1.
3. See *Shulchan Aruch, Yoreh Deah* 92:2,3.
4. *Yoreh Deah* 105:3.
5. The heat of the food on the bottom determines the extent of the transfer of taste.
6. Ibid.:4.

the place where the milk fell, in depth as well as on the top surface. However, when the food(s) is fatty, it is likely that the taste will spread throughout the piece. To make a very long story short,[7] we consider the possibility that the milk taste can spread throughout the roast.

The supposition that the milk taste will spread might appear to create more *issur*, but, in theory, it can be a cause for leniency. If, as likely, the roast is at least sixty times the volume of the milk, the milk taste should be diluted to the point of *bitul*, where it loses its impact on the meat. Thus, a big roast and/or a small spill will allow the roast to remain kosher. However, since it is probable that all or a large portion of the milk will collect near the area where it fell and affect the taste there, a kedei netilla amount around that area must be removed anyway.[8]

If the whole roast does become forbidden, or if some milk rolls onto the pan in which the roast is cooking in a manner that there isn't enough gravy for bitul, then the pan needs to be *kashered*.

---

7. See *Shulchan Aruch* and *Rama, Yoreh Deah* 105:5 and commentators, ad loc.
8. *Rama*, ibid.

E-9: Swallowing Blood From a Cracked Lip

Question: If one has a cracked lip, does he have to be concerned about swallowing blood?

Answer: The prohibition against ingesting blood is a very severe one.[1] However, the full force of the prohibition does not apply to human blood.[2] In fact, according to most opinions, ingesting human blood is forbidden only *mid'rabbanan* (rabbinically).[3] Furthermore, the rabbinic prohibition is not a blanket rule that treats human blood as inherently prohibited. Rather, the prohibition depends on the circumstances, as we shall see.

The *gemara*[4] starts by discussing whether people are permitted to drink mother's milk and brings an apparent contradiction on the matter. The gemara concludes that it is permitted to drink human milk after it has been removed from the body, but not directly from a mother, which is permitted only for babies. It then points out that the opposite is true for human blood, as illustrated by a *baraita*. The baraita says that one may swallow blood that is found in between his teeth, but not if it has found its way onto the piece of bread he is eating. Rashi explains that once it is on the bread, someone might think he is eating animal blood that got on the bread. Following this approach, the Shulchan Aruch[5] calls this a prohibition of *marit ayin* (when the action that people think they are seeing is a forbidden one). In the case of the blood on the bread, it appears that he is ingesting animal blood.

The question then becomes: which situations are included in the marit ayin prohibition? Tosafot[6] says that one is permitted to

---

1. See *Vayikra* 17: 10–14.
2. *Ketubot* 60a.
3. See *Rambam, Ma'achalot Asurot* 6:2.
4. *Ketubot* ibid.
5. *Yoreh Deah* 66:10.
6. *K'ritot* 21b.

lick the blood that drips from a wound on his finger because it is clear, from the fact that the blood is taken directly from the body, that it is human blood. However, the Minchat Yaakov, in his commentary on the Torat Chatat,[7] infers from Rashi in Ketubot[8] that he disagrees. Rashi says that the reason it is permitted to swallow blood from between the teeth is that "there is none who sees it." The Minchat Yaakov reasons that according to this approach, it is forbidden to suck blood from the wound on a finger because it can be readily seen. The Darchei Teshuva[9] cites additional opinions on either side.

What about our case, regarding blood coming from cracked lips? According to Tosafot, it is clearly not a problem for him to swallow the blood. What about according to Rashi? One could claim that if the blood is visible, then it is a problem. However, it is more likely that when Rashi wrote that "there is none who sees *it*," he was referring not to the blood itself but to the ingestion of the blood. While one can notice a person licking the blood off his finger, one cannot usually notice when some blood is licked from the lip into the mouth.

One can make the same calculation with regard to the use of dental floss. (I know there are people who would enjoy a halachic excuse not to floss, but they will have to go elsewhere to find one.) It is true that the floss sometimes picks up some blood, which is noticeable, and that it is not always cleaned before being put back into the mouth, where some may be ingested. According to Tosafot, it is clear that blood found on dental floss comes from a human, and therefore presents no problem. Even according to Rashi, it is not clear to one who sees the flossing that any of the blood will be ingested, and the ingestion will not be visible. Therefore, it is likely that both would agree that it is not necessary to clean the bloodstained dental floss before reinserting it into

---

7. 62:25.
8. Ibid.
9. 66:68.

the mouth. Furthermore, the Kaf HaChayim[10] says that there are more who agree with Tosafot than with Rashi, and one can rely on the lenient opinions in this rabbinic matter.

10. *Yoreh Deah* 66:47.

E-10: What Utensils Require Tevillat Keilim?

Question: Is *tevillat keilim* (immersion in a *mikveh* of utensils that were bought from non-Jews) necessary for all utensils that come in direct contact with food?

Answer: We cannot go into all of the factors that require something to have tevillat keilim, but we will give some guidelines, especially on the issue of direct contact, to which you refer. First, we should point out that only keilim (utensils) made of metal or glass need *tevilla* (immersion). An additional issue, which is important but beyond our present scope, is that disposable items, even if they temporarily have the same function as standard utensils, are not categorized as keilim and do not require tevilla.

The *mitzva* of tevillat keilim is found in the Torah in the context of the mitzva of *hechsher keilim*, removing through heat any taste of a non-kosher food that might be absorbed in the walls of utensils.[1] Rabba bar Avuha states that tevillat keilim applies even to new pots,[2] implying that immersion is necessary regardless of whether anything non-kosher is in the walls. Rav Sheshet asks that if that is the case, then perhaps utensils of all sorts should require tevilla. The answer given is that the Torah was referring only to *klei se'uda* (literally, utensils of a meal).

Understanding the reason why tevillat keilim applies specifically to klei se'uda may help us define this category of utensil. Rashi[3] says that since the Torah describes utensils that are exposed to a flame, it must be talking about utensils that are involved in a meal (apparently, including its preparation). The Pri Chadash[4] asks that there are utensils that are used in connection with heat

---

1. See *Bamidbar* 31:21–24.
2. *Avoda Zara* 75b.
3. Ad loc.
4. *Yoreh Deah* 120:1.

but are unrelated to food. Therefore, he prefers the Rashba's explanation, that these *p'sukim* are dealing with the type of utensil which belongs to the *category* of those things that may require *kashering*, namely, utensils for food preparation and eating.

Taking a very narrow view of the Rashba, one might conclude that the *kli*[5] must come into actual, physical contact with food. However, *poskim* understand that we are talking about the *category* of a utensil, namely, one which is *used directly in connection* with food, whether or not there is actual, physical contact.

This understanding of klei se'uda contains elements of both leniency and stringency. Does a can opener require tevilla? On one hand, if it is being used to open a can of tuna fish, the can opener almost always touches the product. On the other hand, its function is, by design, not connected to the food but to the can. So presumably, incidental contact with food should not make the can opener need to have tevilla. Indeed, the standard *p'sak* is that it does not require tevilla.[6] If, conversely, one covers a baking pan with waxed paper, the food is nevertheless considered to be baking in the pan, despite the fact that it touches only the paper, and the pan requires tevilla.[7]

This is not to say that direct contact between the food and the utensil is not an important factor in determining the requirement of tevilla; it just depends on the nature and the extent of the direct contact. For example, if a pot made of a substance that does not require tevilla is coated in order to improve its function (not just for beautification) with a substance that does require tevilla, then the location of the coating could make a difference. The Shulchan Aruch[8] implies that only when the obligated coating is on the pot's interior is tevilla required (the Rama may argue; see

---

5. Or perhaps even the part of the kli that is made of metal or glass (further detail is beyond our present scope).
6. See *Tevillat Keilim* (Cohen) 11: 171 and footnote, ad loc.
7. Rav Shlomo Zalman Orbach, quoted in *Tevillat Keilim* 1:(7).
8. *Yoreh Deah* 120:1.

commentators). Certainly, if the utensil in question is separated from the food by another kli, then it does not need tevilla. Thus, the Shulchan Aruch[9] says that a tripod that holds a pot over the flame is exempt from tevilla, and the same is true for modern devices for suspending pots.

---

9. Ibid.:4.

E-11: Bishul Akum Regarding Pancakes

Question: I was recently at a hotel in Israel, where I saw an Arab employee making pancakes on the griddle. When I asked him who turned the griddle on, he replied that he had. Why isn't that a problem of *bishul akum*?[1]

Answer: There are two basic exemptions from the rabbinic prohibition of bishul akum:[2] (1) when the food is edible uncooked, (2) when the food is "not fit to be served on the table of kings." In order to be considered edible while still raw, it needs to be readily suitable for eating, not just under pressing circumstances. Thus, considering the state of pancake batter, the first exemption does not apply.

The second exemption is much harder to describe. Does it simply mean that a king must consider the food befitting to him, even if it is not particularly fancy? Alternatively, "the table of kings" may refer to a certain type of very distinguished social/culinary setting. According to the latter approach, the rationale of the exemption is as follows. The reason for the prohibition is to limit the opportunities for a Jew to accept a non-Jew's invitation for a meal since the resulting social closeness between people/families could lead to intermarriage. When people invite each other for meals, they usually serve distinguished foods.[3] Thus, forbidding such foods is sufficient to maintain the necessary social distance.

The consensus of the American rabbinate is that only distinguished foods are a problem. While the practice in Israel, based on several *poskim*, is somewhat more stringent, it is by no means uniform, and people may continue with the lenient approach to which they are accustomed. Although pancakes are popular, one

---

1. The prohibition of eating food cooked by a non-Jew.
2. *Shulchan Aruch, Yoreh Deah* 113:1.
3. *Rambam, Ma'achalot Asurot* 17:16.

does not serve them at fancy affairs. Thus, one has the right to assume that bishul akum does not apply to pancakes.

According to some, there is another strong reason to be lenient regarding bishul akum for pancakes. The laws of bishul akum do not apply, for almost all intents and purposes, to bread that is commercially produced.[4] Some say that pancakes are bread-related and one makes *HaMotzi* on them when he eats a meal that is based upon them.[5] Thus, it is possible that pancakes have the laws of bread in this regard rather than those of cooked food.[6]

The fact that the event took place in an Israeli hotel, which is likely owned by a Jew, can make a difference in some cases. There is a minority opinion, that is not fully rejected, that holds that bishul akum is not forbidden when the cooking is done in the house of the Jew.[7] Rav Ovadya Yosef[8] posits that under the following circumstances, this factor may justify leniency. In general, in circumstances where bishul akum could be a problem, one can solve the problem by having the heat source, whether an oven, stove, griddle, or the like, be lit by a Jew.[9] For Sephardic Jews, this is insufficient. Rather, the Jew must either put the food on the fire, light the fire while the food is underneath, or stir the food while it is cooking. Regarding a case where the cooking is done on Jewish premises, however, Rav Yosef justifies even a Sephardic Jew to rely on the opinion of the Rama[10] that it is sufficient for a Jew to light the fire. This is based on his claim that in a case of *sefek sefeika* (double doubt), a Sephardic Jew can be lenient even if each case of *individual* doubt was forbidden by the Shulchan Aruch.

---

4. See *Shulchan Aruch, Yoreh Deah* 112:2.
5. *V'Zot HaBeracha*, p. 28, based on *Shulchan Aruch, Orach Chayim* 168:8. However, Rav Mordechai Willig told me that the *minhag* in America is to never make *HaMotzi* on pancakes (see *Shulchan Aruch, Orach Chayim* 168:15).
6. See *Tosafot, Beitza* 16b; *Rama, Yoreh Deah* 112:6; *Taz*, ad loc.:6.
7. *Shulchan Aruch* ibid.:4.
8. *Yechaveh Da'at* v, 54.
9. *Rama, Yoreh Deah* 113:7.
10. Ibid.:7.

The laws of bishul akum are such that often a situation that one would have difficulty permitting, based only on one factor, can be permitted based on a combination of factors. Therefore, one can often gain by asking about specific cases that, on the surface, might certainly seem to be forbidden.

Section F:
Tzedaka (Charity) and Ribbit (Usury)

F-1: Pressuring a Business to Contribute

Question: Many schools have charity functions for which the parents solicit gifts from merchants for an auction. Is it wrong to "compel" merchants to contribute by implying that refusal will hurt their business? Shouldn't the parents buy the items for the school?

Answer: Let us first assume that, in effect, the parents are compelling businesses to give the donations. In theory, the *gemara* says that one who pressures others into giving *tzedaka* is greater than the one who actually gives it.[1] However, this is assuming that the donor was obligated to give that tzedaka and was reluctant to do so. It should be noted, though, that one who pressures another who truly cannot afford to give tzedaka into contributing is liable to be Divinely punished.[2]

In any case, parents have no right to compel a storeowner to donate to the institution of their choice. Who says that he doesn't have other causes to which he would like to give his donations? Who says he hasn't given enough tzedaka already? If he is not Jewish, he doesn't have an obligation to give tzedaka at all. What qualifies the parents to make these decisions, especially when they have personal interests in the matter?

Practically speaking, though, it's hard to believe that parents actually have the ability to coerce a merchant to donate. They could impose some type of psychological pressure, but the matter ultimately would remain the merchant's decision. Having said this, any type of significant, negative pressure would be inappropriate, and in some cases, could be forbidden.

However, in the type of scenario you refer to, it appears that the incentive to contribute is usually positive. In other words,

---

1. *Bava Batra* 9a.
2. *Shulchan Aruch, Yoreh Deah* 248:7.

the storeowner is interested in creating or maintaining goodwill and respect with the community of potential customers. Just as customers can ask for courteous treatment, they can also ask for generosity. In either case, the decision remains with the business owner. The contributor often benefits from his donation by being publicly acknowledged. The actual cost to the donor is less than the retail value, and it may be possible for him to get a tax break. If these are the conditions, there should not be any halachic or ethical problems in soliciting the donations. Of course, the solicitor should conduct himself in a manner that preserves the honor of a Torah lifestyle.

Regarding the parents, they have more of an obligation to assist the school that educates their children than others do. However, given the high cost of Jewish education, it is unrealistic for many of them to contribute more than the tuition they already pay.

F-2: Giving Ma'aser Money in a Friend's Name

Question: If you give someone a present for a certain occasion in the form of a donation to charity in his name, can it be taken from *ma'aser kesafim*[1] money?

Answer: This is a fascinating question that we have not found addressed explicitly in halachic literature. There is a related concept found in the *halachot* of sacrifices. One may not take an animal that was set aside for one sacrifice and use it to bring a different, obligatory sacrifice.[2] In other words, at times, one cannot kill two birds with one stone. However, as a halachic source, that concept does not apply to your case.

Let us then analyze the case from a social and halachic perspective. Since the money still is going to charity, there should be no problem, from the standpoint of the laws of *ma'aser*, in giving it in someone's name. The problem, however, is that you are not really giving anything to your friend. The idea of giving a gift in the form of a donation in someone's name/honor is to say, "I know that you care more for the needy than you do about a new tie. Therefore, the money that would have gone for the tie, I'll use for the poor, and it will be as if you gave the donation." However, that is not happening here; rather, the following is occurring. The money, that would in any event be given to charity and could not be used for a friend's tie, is going to the same place it would have even if your friend did not have an occasion. Thus, in effect, one who uses a ma'aser money donation as a present is unknowingly withholding a present and deceiving his friend.

There may be room for leniency in the following cases.

1. A person cannot afford to give ma'aser and, thus, is exempt

---

1. The proper practice of giving one-tenth of one's income to *tzedaka*.
2. *Chagiga* 7b.

from giving *tzedaka* at that rate, but he really wants to give as much as possible to the needy. Therefore, he accepts the praise-worthy practice of giving ma'aser with the condition that it will include presents. In this case, one could argue that he is not really deceiving his friends. This is because more money is going to charity because of the altruism of people like them, who accept donations in their names instead of gifts. Indeed, the alternative is that he, legitimately, would not have adopted the practice of giving ma'aser.

2. If one picks the recipient of the donation to fit his friend's preferences, then, in effect, he is giving a gift to his friend, namely, an element of *tovat hana'a*. Tovat hana'a is the indirect benefit that one receives, in general, by giving a donation. For example, a donor may get special treatment and even specific favors from the recipient. The donor can benefit from the good feeling of knowing that people he cares about are being provided for, and it is fully acceptable for the recipient to be a friend or relative. A receipt that one can use for a tax break is certainly tovat hana'a. Although tovat hana'a is actually worth money, we do not say that its estimated value should be deducted from the sum of tzedaka one is considered to have given. In this specific case, if one chooses a charity that he would not have given to ordinarily because he knows it is beloved to his friend, then he is giving a gift of tovat hana'a. However, the actual value of the present is not the value of the donation; rather, it is its relative tovat hana'a.

F-3: Adoption – Which Child Has Precedence?

Question: Does one who wants to adopt a child have to do so from the closest orphanage or from a Jewish orphanage before a non-Jewish one, as these preferences exist in regard to *tzedaka*? It seems to depend upon whether adoption is a *mitzva* to help the child and, therefore, is governed by the laws of tzedaka or is something that the adopting family does for its own benefit. Which is it?

Answer: Adopting a child is a great mitzva of *chesed* toward the adopted child, whether or not it also benefits the adopting family. There is no contradiction between the two. Let us cite the Talmudic source that lauds adoption. The *gemara*[1] tries to identify the subject of the following *pasuk* in Tehillim:[2] "Praiseworthy are those who… do acts of charity at all times." Who is capable of doing charity at all times? The first opinion is that it is one who raises and supports his own children. The second opinion is that it is one who raises orphans in his home and marries them off. One can use the first opinion to understand the second. Supporting one's own children is certainly a natural thing, which usually includes a significant degree of self-fulfillment. This is not the type of charity reserved for the very pious. Nevertheless, it is still considered a great act of charity. So too, the praise for families who adopt applies even to those who pine for children. On the contrary, if family members prefer not having more children and consider adoption simply out of pity, they should weigh carefully whether they will be capable of seeing the responsibility through, with the necessary self-sacrifice, love, and patience.

All indications are that the laws of *kedimut* (giving precedence to one recipient over others) apply throughout the laws of

---

1. *Ketubot* 50a.
2. 106:3.

chesed. The concept that one gives precedence to those closest to him is hinted in the Torah in the laws of lending.[3] Despite this fact, the Rambam[4] lists the details specifically in the laws of tzedaka and omits them in the laws of lending. Commentaries explain that once it is found in one case, it is assumed in the other.[5] The Chofetz Chayim, in the introduction to his classic work on the laws of chesed, *Ahavat Chesed*, stresses that all of the different forms of chesed share the same underpinnings. Therefore, it appears that there is reason to give precedence to those closest to the adopting family. This would mean adopting Jews before non-Jews, relatives before non-relatives, and neighbors and people from the same city before others.[6] (There are halachic considerations regarding the preference of adopting a Jewish child or converting a non-Jewish child that are not appropriate in this forum and should be discussed with one's personal rabbi if the question arises.)

As far as who is considered a member of the same city, there is a *machloket* among the *Rishonim*. Rav Yitzchak ben Rav Baruch rules that whoever comes to the city is considered in the category of a preferred recipient, whereas the Tur[7] says that only those who are permanent residents of the city are included. The Rama[8] rules like the Tur. However, if a child has moved into a local orphanage on an ongoing basis, he should be considered a local regardless of his place of origin.[9]

The question, though, is to what extent the laws of precedence are binding here. Firstly, even with regard to relatives vs. non-relatives, which is the most serious case,[10] the issue of whom to help is not nearly as crucial as the mitzva itself to give the tze-

---

3. *Shemot* 22:24 and/or *Devarim* 15:11.
4. *Matnot Aniyim* 8:13.
5. See *Lechem Mishneh*, ad loc.; *Minchat Chinuch* #66.
6. *Bava Metzia* 71a.
7. *Yoreh Deah* 251.
8. *Yoreh Deah* 251:3.
9. See *Bi'ur HaGra*, ad loc.
10. See *Rambam*, ibid.

daka.[11] Furthermore, since it is rare for a specific person to have a personal obligation to adopt a child, if he does volunteer, he can do so according to the factors that are important to him.[12] These factors may include cost, reliability of an agency, etc. If one can incorporate the rules of precedence, that is commendable, but the important thing is to succeed in carrying out the tremendous chesed to the benefit of all involved.

---

11. *Ma'aser Kesafim* 10:(299), citing the Chatam Sofer.
12. Based on a parallel case in *Ahavat Chesed* 6:9.

F-4: Spending Tzedaka Money to Visit the Sick

Question: A hospitalized patient who does not get visitors has repeatedly asked me to visit him. The hospital is so far away that travel costs are about $100 a visit. Can I use my *ma'aser kesafim*[1] to defray the costs?

Answer: We will begin with some background information on the uses of ma'aser kesafim before showing how this case differs from much of the classical, halachic discussions.

The Rama,[2] based on the Maharil, rules: "One should not use his ma'aser for matters of *mitzva* like candles for a *beit k'nesset* or other matters of mitzva; rather he should give it to the poor." On the other hand, the Shach[3] and others quote the Maharam, who says that one can use ma'aser for a variety of mitzvot, including making a *brit mila* or wedding for someone else if he couldn't/ wouldn't have done so otherwise.

Some *Acharonim* make distinctions that allow these apparently contradictory rulings to coexist. The B'er Hagola[4] says that the Maharil's opinion applies only when one wants to use the money for a mitzva he is obligated to do; then the rule that one cannot "kill two obligations with one stone"[5] steps in. However, he could use ma'aser to enable a mitzva that is not his personal obligation to be performed. The Chatam Sofer[6] disagrees with this distinction and proves that the Maharil considered using money that was set aside for charity to help someone perform a mitzva to be a form of stealing from the poor. He makes a different distinc-

---

1. The proper practice of giving one-tenth of one's income to *tzedaka*.
2. *Yoreh Deah* 249:1.
3. Ad loc.:3.
4. Ad loc.
5. See *Beitza* 20a.
6. *Shut, Yoreh Deah* 231.

tion, though. If one began the practice of giving ma'aser by giving it only to the poor, then using it for other mitzvot is like stealing. However, if he specified, when adopting the proper practice of ma'aser, that he would use it for other mitzvot, he may do so. The common practice is that people do use ma'aser for a variety of mitzvot. Therefore, the Chatam Sofer should agree that most people can use ma'aser money for mitzvot they are not obligated in. However, it is better to state one's intention clearly when he begins the practice of giving ma'aser.

At first glance, the application of these rules is as follows. If you specifically are required to visit the sick person, then you cannot use ma'aser to fulfill your obligation, unless the expense goes beyond the amount one needs to pay for mitzvot.[7] We do not have enough information to try to determine the extent of your obligation.

However, we learned an important rule from our teacher, Rav Zalman Nechmia Goldberg.[8] The Torah requires one not only to make the effort to perform mitzvot between man and his Maker but also to expend significant money to do so. However, mitzvot involving one's fellow man (other than *tzedaka*) require only effort, not a loss of money. He deduces this idea from the *gemara*'s[9] ruling that one is not required to lose money in order to return a lost item. We are obligated to spend money to help others only to the extent that the expenditure is included in the mitzva of tzedaka. Ma'aser is one of the categories of tzedaka, whereby the average person is expected to give 10% of his earnings for various forms of the mitzva. Therefore, even if you are obligated to visit the person in question, ostensibly the cost may be taken from tzedaka, which includes your ma'aser funds.

There is one question, though, that remains. If the patient can afford it, he should pay for the transportation costs. That is

---

7. See *Rama, Orach Chayim* 656:1.
8. *Shurat HaDin*, vol. VII, pp. 377–444.
9. *Bava Metzia* 30a.

because the ability to use tzedaka money to help someone applies only when the recipient of the help cannot afford to pay for his necessities. What happens if he has the money to pay but does not think of paying or does not want to? Rabbi Yehuda says that when one can support himself but refuses to do so, we give him tzedaka and worry later about getting back the money.[10] However, we accept the opinion that we do not give him tzedaka.[11] Nevertheless, in a case where it is understandable that the patient did not think of offering to pay and asking him for money is likely to reduce the benefit of the visit, ma'aser can be used.[12]

---

10. *Ketubot* 67b.
11. *Shulchan Aruch, Yoreh Deah* 253:10.
12. See *Tzedaka U'Mishpat* 12:(56), who may hint at this.

F-5: Various Ma'aser Kesafim (Tzedaka) Issues

Question: Some people from Israel came to our door collecting for important causes with the blessings of a reputable rabbi. My compassionate wife wrote them checks based on expected, future *ma'aser kesafim*[1] money. Since our account was quite depleted, she post-dated the checks. Unfortunately, the checks were cashed before the date and accepted by our bank, putting our account in overdraft and causing $120 in bank fees. Can these costs, which were incurred by giving *ma'aser kesafim*, count toward future ma'aser or must they be considered a personal loss? Right now, I am not even sure we are obligated to give ma'aser due to our financial situation, but I have always preferred to extend myself to put aside 10% in any case.

Answer: You ask one question but raise others indirectly. We will try to touch upon all of the issues.

Expenses: Money set aside for the purpose of ma'aser kesafim becomes a *tzedaka* fund that you administer. Legitimate expenses related to giving tzedaka may be recovered by the one who outlays them.[2] Complications arise if there is a loss of money due to careless or frivolous actions by the *gabbai tzedaka*, in this case, your wife. However, she seems to have acted extremely generously and responsibly (as opposed to your bank).

Giving money on the account of future ma'aser: In his *sefer*, *Ahavat Chesed*,[3] the Chafetz Chayim raises this issue and cites different opinions on the matter. The Tzedaka U'Mishpat[4] rules

---

1. The proper practice of (calculating and) giving one-tenth of one's income to *tzedaka*.
2. *Tzedaka U'Mishpat* 7:23.
3. 18:2.
4. 5:11.

leniently. They both suggest that, when starting to give ma'aser kesafim, one should stipulate that he plans to, at times, lay out money and deduct it from future ma'aser.

Giving ma'aser under financial hardship: The rule is that dependents' welfare takes precedence over tzedaka to others.[5] On the other hand, even one who receives tzedaka is required to give some tzedaka.[6] It is hard to determine precisely what one's basic needs are, beyond which he should give tzedaka properly. We applaud your generosity and pray that you will be able to maintain it. One suggestion is to continue calculating ma'aser kesafim, but to actually give the money only when you can afford it.[7]

---

5. *Rama, Yoreh De'ah* 251:3.
6. *Shulchan Aruch, Yoreh De'ah* 248:1.
7. *Tzedaka U'Mishpat* 1:(22), in the name of the Chazon Ish.

F-6: Is Buying Israel Bonds Ribbit (Usury)?

Question: What is the rationale for buying Israel Bonds, when it seems to be in clear violation of the prohibition to take interest (*ribbit*) from a fellow Jew (or, in this case, the Jewish government)?

Answer: The answer begins with an explanation of the mechanics of the loan process and its effect on the laws of ribbit. The Torah, in discussing this prohibition, talks about one who lends with interest and then extracts the increased debt from the borrower. Several recent *poskim* view the *obligation* of the borrower to make payment as critical for the existence of the prohibition of ribbit and find this element missing in some modern financial applications.

The most common application is in regard to the modern concept of a corporation. One of the main characteristics of a corporation is that its owners have no personal liability. In other words, no matter how large a corporation's debt is, no one can approach even a principal shareholder and demand payment from his personal assets. Rather, only the resources of the amorphous corporate entity, including the money *already* invested by shareholders, can be taken. Several *poskim*, including Rav Moshe Feinstein,[1] ruled that it is, therefore, permitted to take even fixed interest (*ribbit ketzutza*)[2] from corporations, even those owned primarily by Jews.[3]

The same basic logic applies to a government, which obligates itself as an amorphous institution and does not create personal

---

1. *Igrot Moshe, Yoreh Deah* II, 62–63.
2. Interest that is set at the time of the loan. Only this type of ribbit is forbidden by the Torah. The rest is rabbinic.
3. See a list of opinions on both sides of the issue in *Brit Yehuda* 7:(66). Note that the leniency does not apply to *paying* interest *to* a Jewish owned corporation.

liability for its citizens. However, not all *poskim* accept the corporation leniency; some accept it only on the Torah level, not on the rabbinic level.[4] Therefore, it is preferable to broaden the grounds for leniency in regard to the Israeli government. One distinction is that the shareholders of a corporation are clearly defined. In contrast, the citizens and/or active inhabitants of a country are a fluid group. What is the status of a person who moves to or from the country between the time of the selling of the bond and its payment? Can a citizen cash in on his share of the country's wealth before leaving it? Although one could debate exactly what the legal distinction is, the situation resembles that which the Rashba calls "money without known owners."[5] The Har Tzvi[6] is lenient for this basic reason in regard to loans from a government bank. There are additional grounds for leniency,[7] especially for Israeli citizens who buy the bonds in shekels, as the government has regulatory powers over the currency.

We have already presented sufficient grounds to, at least, seriously consider permitting unrestricted purchase of Israel Bonds. In addition, the Israeli government wisely drew up a *heter iska* for its various financial dealings. Without getting into all of the details of its workings, the heter iska is a widely used document that turns what would have been a loan into a joint investment of the two parties. Although some applications of the heter iska seem to be based on questionable logic, the *minhag ha'olam*[8] is to use the heter iska broadly. Most people who are *machmir* (stringent in practice) on many other halachic issues are lenient regarding heter iska.

In summary, there is very ample reason to allow taking interest from Israel Bonds. Considering the great *mitzvot* of helping

---

4. Ibid.
5. See *Shut HaRashba* I, 669.
6. *Yoreh Deah* 126.
7. See *Torat Ribbit* 17:(59).
8. The standard practice among observant Jews.

to build *Eretz Yisrael*, keeping it in Jewish hands,[9] and address-ing the many security and humanitarian needs of its population (which are so prevalent today), it would be inappropriate to adopt a fringe, stringent opinion to disallow such a practice.

---

9. See *Gittin* 8b.

Section G:
Holy Articles

G-1: Proper Position of Tefillin Shel Rosh

Question: Where is the exact place to put the *tefillin shel rosh*?[1] It appears that many men position it too low in front, and no one says anything!

Answer: There is nothing new under the sun. Rav Kook wrote a pamphlet called *Chevesh P'er* to strengthen the fulfillment of the *mitzva* of tefillin. His main complaint was that men wear the tefillin shel rosh too low (forward) on their heads, and he urged leaders to rectify the matter.

The *gemara*[2] derives that when the Torah instructs us to place the tefillin "*bein einecha* (between your eyes)," it refers to the part of the head that can be shaved, not the forehead (contrary to the *Tzedukim*). Thus, the forward-most part of the tefillin may go no lower than where the *roots* of the hairline are on the scalp.[3] If the front part of the tefillin does not sit directly on the head, but is suspended (which is sometimes a sign that it is too low), one draws an imaginary perpendicular line to the head in order to determine if it is positioned high enough.

There is a *machloket*[4] among *Rishonim* whether the upper part of the tefillin (i.e., where the strap goes through the box) can be placed anywhere on the top of the head or only on the front half. The gemara[5] allows putting tefillin on, or up to and including, the place of a baby's soft spot.[6] The most stringent interpretation of this gemara is that the tefillin must fit within the first four finger-widths (or slightly more) of the head, starting from the

---

1. Of the head.
2. *Menachot* 37a–b.
3. *Shulchan Aruch, Orach Chayim* 27:9.
4. Disagreement.
5. Ibid.
6. See *Beit Yosef, Orach Chayim* 27 and *Bi'ur Halacha* on 27:9.

hairline.[7] This is based on the statement of the gemara that there is room on the head to place two pairs of tefillin[8] (assuming that the minimum size of tefillin is two finger-widths).[9] *Poskim* agree that it is more crucial that the tefillin not be even slightly too low than to be concerned that they not extend too far back.[10]

Why do so many men put their tefillin too low? When large tefillin are fastened (by the part that is furthest back and the knot) so that they feel secure on the head (which is usually when they are relatively forward), they are likely to extend beyond the end of the hairline. (Although it is easier to make *mehudar*[11] tefillin that are large, having large tefillin increases the problems of improper placement.) Even with smaller tefillin, it is common that people are fitted when they get new tefillin or *retzuot*[12] and assume that they are "set for life." However, the retzuot stretch as they are used, causing the tefillin to extend further forward. Few people know how to adjust the knot to compensate for this stretching, and many do not know that this is periodically necessary. Even someone who knows the halacha is likely to assume that "all is well" and that the tefillin look low because the wearer is bald or has a receding hairline. Although we do follow the original hairline, many exaggerate how low it was, and it is difficult to precisely determine to where the roots of one's hair once extended.

It is important to correct people whose tefillin slip down and, certainly, those whose retzuot are so loose that they may not have fulfilled the mitzva in years and make a *beracha l'vatala*[13] daily.[14] However, one must be very careful how he corrects others.[15] It is

---

7. See *Kaf HaChayim, Orach Chayim* 27:41.
8. *Eruvin* 95b.
9. See *Mishna Berura* 32:189.
10. *Chevesh P'er*, 2; *Bi'ur Halacha*, ibid.
11. Of high quality.
12. Straps.
13. A blessing of no value.
14. See Rav Kook's appeal.
15. See *Rashi, Vayikra* 19:17.

best if the rabbi periodically urges men to ask him to check and/or adjust the tefillin. If this isn't done, an individual may have little choice but to gently approach those who need help. For some, it pays to leave an anonymous note. The sensitivity issue is usually more acute for older people, who are more likely to resent being approached by someone much younger. Asking, "Do you want your knot adjusted?" is preferable to saying, "Your tefillin are on wrong."

It takes just a little dexterity and training to adjust the knot, and it does not require undoing it. Therefore, we suggest that readers learn how to do it for themselves and for others.

G-2: Using Holy Scrolls as Art

Question: I want to give as a gift an authentic sacred scroll that is presented in an artistic form. I think that it will add a spiritual touch to the home of the recipient. Is it permitted?

Answer: We have two items to determine: 1) the objective, halachic decision and 2) the subjective outlook on the specific situation, which is much harder to determine.

The *gemara*[1] presents an apparent contradiction. One source says that if one has two *tefillin shel rosh*[2] and no *shel yad*,[3] he can convert one shel rosh into a shel yad. Another source says that one may not turn a shel rosh into a shel yad because one may not lower something from a higher level of *kedusha*[4] (the shel rosh) to a lower one (the shel yad). The gemara answers that the lenient source is talking about a case where the tefillin were not yet used. Based on the rule that *hazmana lav milta* (preparation is not halachically significant), tefillin which were not used do not have the same kedusha as used tefillin. Only the latter may not be lowered in kedusha. According to the opinion that hazmana is significant, says the gemara, the lenient source refers to a case where a stipulation was made during the shel rosh's preparation that it could be used for less holy purposes.

We accept the opinion that hazmana is not binding, and, therefore, one who made a tefillin bag may put coins into it prior to its use for tefillin.[5] However, the Rama[6] rules that a scroll, which is an article of kedusha itself (e.g., *sefer Torah*, tefillin, *mezuza*), in contradistinction to an article intended to serve an article of

---

1. *Menachot* 34b.
2. The tefillin that are worn on the head.
3. The tefillin that are worn on the arm.
4. Sanctity.
5. *Shulchan Aruch, Orach Chayim* 42: 3.
6. Ad loc.

kedusha (e.g., a tefillin bag), is imbued with kedusha by hazmana. Although the Magen Avraham[7] cites those who argue with the Rama, the Bi'ur Halacha[8] says that one should not be lenient contrary to the majority opinion that the Rama presents. However, the stringency is limited to using the scroll for *chol* (mundane use). It may, though, be used for matters of a lower level of kedusha, including for people to learn Torah from it.[9]

After providing the halachic background, let us now address your specific case. If you are talking about a scroll that has already been used for its intended purpose, it is forbidden to use it in an artistic form, which is a lower level of kedusha than the mitzva it was helping fulfill. However, if it was not used, then the matter depends on the context of the use. If the artistic display of the scroll is done in such a way that one can expect it to draw people's attention to its Torah content, then we can say that it is being used for *divrei Torah* in a positive, albeit "off the beaten track," way. Considering its kedusha, one would still need to be careful that it not be permanently displayed in bedrooms or have it pass through bathrooms, but its use would be generally permissible. The content and tone of your description [ed. note – shortened, by necessity, in the published version], gives the impression that the intention is that the kedusha and the specific words of Torah found on the scroll be noticed and have a positive impact on the home. However, it is difficult to judge such matters without direct knowledge of the circumstances.

[*Allow us to comment on a related, recent phenomenon. Happily, Torah themes have gone, in many circles, from being embarrassing to the observant Jew in contemporary society to being acceptable and even popular. As such, different art forms (especially, music) incorporate words of Torah. When we do so properly, we fulfill the laudable practice of "ze keili v'anveihu," of beautifying and adorning*

---

7. 42: 6
8. Ad loc.
9. *Mishna Berura* 42: 19, 23.

Torah and mitzvot. However, when it is done in a manner that ignores or even degrades them (e.g., with grossly inappropriate beats), we run the risk of abusing the kedusha *(see Sanhedrin 101a). The excuse that the intent is to bring Torah to the masses, while legitimate in some cases, can be exaggerated and overused.*]

G-3: Mezuzot at an Office Complex Shared by Jews and Non-Jews

Question: Two Jewish doctors own a medical practice together with a non-Jewish doctor. The premises, which include dozens of rooms and employees, are rented from a hospital group. Do some or all of the doors require *mezuzot*?

Answer: The *gemara*[1] investigates the significance of the Torah's writing that mezuzot are to be put on *"beitecha* (your [singular] house)." It first suggests that beitecha excludes a house owned in partnership (even with a Jew). However, the gemara infers from the plural usage elsewhere in the Torah that the mitzva applies even for partnerships and derives something entirely different from beitecha. The Rashba[2] asks why the gemara did not use the word beitecha to derive that, in a partnership between a Jew and a non-Jew, the Jew does not require mezuzot, as the gemara had done in several similar examples. He learns from this silence that, in such a "mixed" partnership, mezuzot are required. The Rashba also provides a rationale, saying that mezuzot are meant to provide protection, and anywhere that the Jew lives, he is to seek such protection. The Shulchan Aruch does not mention this issue, but in his addendums to the Beit Yosef,[3] he discusses it and writes that the Rashba is correct.

On the other hand, the Mordechai[4] says that in such a partnership, mezuzot are not required, and the Rama accepts his ruling.[5] Commentators disagree as to the reasoning of the exemption, which can be one or more of the following: 1) The area

---

1. *Chulin* 135b.
2. Ad loc.
3. *Bedek HaBayit, Yoreh Deah* 286.
4. *Avoda Zara* 810.
5. *Yoreh Deah* 286:1.

is considered incomplete in regard to mezuzot, as it is partially owned by one who is exempt from the *mitzva*;[6] 2) That is what the analysis of the *p'sukim* indicates;[7] Mareh 3) There is a danger from the possible reaction of non-Jews to a mezuza.[8]

Although how to rule appears to be a dispute between Ashkenazim (like the Rama) and Sephardim (like the Shulchan Aruch / Beit Yosef), that doesn't seem to be the case, as the later *poskim* do not make such a clear break. The Birkei Yosef[9] and Yalkut Yosef[10] are among prominent Sephardic poskim who say that, although one should affix mezuzot in this case, he should do so without a *beracha* because of the doubt. On the other side, the Aruch HaShulchan[11] is followed by recent *sefarim*[12] that say that even Ashkenazim should attach mezuzot without a beracha in the case of a Jewish / non-Jewish partnership where there is no fear of non-Jewish hostility or desecration of the mezuzot.

However, in our case, there are additional grounds for leniency. Firstly, in commercial settings, the obligation of mezuzot, even at a totally Jewish business, is based only on doubt.[13] Secondly, the premises are rented from a hospital group, which, if we understand correctly, is at least primarily non-Jewish. According to many,[14] the obligation of a renter is always only rabbinic, and it is likely that those Ashkenazim who are more stringent than the Rama do so only the case where there likely is a Torah obligation.[15]

We would make the following distinction. In those offices

---

6. *Birkei Yosef, Yoreh Deah* 286:2; *Shach, Yoreh Deah* 286:6.
7. *Taz, Yoreh Deah* 286:2.
8. *Shach* ibid.
9. Ibid.
10. *Sova Semachot, Mezuza* 50.
11. *Yoreh Deah* 286:2.
12. See *Chovat HaDar* 2:2; *Pitchei She'arim* pp. 127–130.
13. See Question G-4.
14. See *Shut Rav Akiva Eiger* I, 66.
15. See language of *Aruch HaShulchan, Yoreh Deah* 286:2.

or rooms that are frequented by Jewish doctors, there is a *hidur* (a favorable but not required practice) to affix mezuzot without a beracha, as well as on the front door, assuming it is not likely to cause animosity or invite vandalism. However, in the other dozens of rooms that Jewish doctors rarely visit (and the Rashba's logic of requiring protection, among other things, is not so applicable), there is little point to place mezuzot.

G-4: Mezuza in the Workplace

Question: Does a place of business require a *mezuza*, and, if so, does one make a *beracha* when affixing it?

Answer: The following answer refers to the situation where the owner of the business is Jewish. Several other permutations exist, but they are beyond our present scope.[1]

The *gemara*[2] says that, in order for a structure to be obligated in having a mezuza, its use must have some connection to that of a *dira* (dwelling). However, it is not always simple to determine what uses meet this criterion.

The Rambam[3] says that a store in a market is not obligated to have a mezuza. It is, therefore, surprising that he rules that storage rooms used for straw or lumber are required to have a mezuza. The Taz[4] explains that storage rooms must have a mezuza since they are used both in the day and at night. Stores, however, are exempt from having a mezuza since the commercial activities of a store are limited to the daytime. Other distinctions can be made. For example, in contrast to a store, a storage room is used as an extension of one's home, which makes it more "dira-like."[5]

Along the lines of the Taz's distinction, the Pitchei Teshuva[6] cites the opinion of the Yad HaKetana, who states that if the store houses the owner's merchandise during the night as well, then it would certainly require a mezuza. Even if one does not agree with the Yad HaKetana, if the business or factory operates well into the night, it is more probable that a mezuza would be required.[7]

---

1. See *Minchat Yitchak* 11, 83.
2. *Yoma* 11b.
3. *Mezuza* 6:9, cited as halacha in the *Shulchan Aruch, Yoreh Deah* 286:11.
4. *Yoreh Deah* 286:10.
5. See *B'er Moshe* 11, 85.
6. *Yoreh Deah* 286:10.
7. *B'er Moshe* ibid.

A further reason to obligate having a mezuza is the approach of the Bach,[8] Perisha,[9] and Yad HaKetana,[10] according to whom, the Rambam (and, likely, the Shulchan Aruch) was misunderstood in his ruling regarding a store. The Rambam,[11] in the aforementioned passage, rules that a *sukka* and living quarters on a ship are not obligated to have a mezuza because they are not *permanent* dwellings. Considering this, the Rambam could be understood to be referring specifically to a store that was part of a market that was open only on special market days. This was a common arrangement in the gemara's time.[12] Accordingly, regular, full-time places of work would be obligated to have a mezuza.

In summary, there is ample justification to affix a mezuza in places of work. Regarding a beracha, several recent *poskim* recommend a safe approach: it is better not to make a beracha because of the doubt in the matter.[13] Yet, we recall that our mentor, Rav Yisraeli, instructed us to make a beracha when affixing the *mezuza* to the doorpost of our office. Still, we cannot say with certainty whether this was a blanket ruling or it depended on the type of activity and the conditions of the specific case.

---

8. *Yoreh Deah* 286:22.
9. Ad loc.:22.
10. Ibid.
11. Ibid.
12. See *Bava Batra* 22a.
13. See *Minchat Yitzchak*, ibid.; *Chovat HaDar* 3:8; *Pitchei She'arim* 286: (132), (133), (138).

G-5: Making a Beracha When Returning a Mezuza

Question: I am going to remove my *mezuza* in order to paint the doorpost. When I put it back, do I make the *beracha* for affixing a mezuza?

Answer: First let us reference a more common discussion among *poskim*, which seems to be almost identical. Then we can see how to apply the conclusions to your question.

The Pitchei Teshuva[1] discusses the case of one who removes a mezuza to check if it is still kosher. His first thought and that of other *Acharonim* (we do not find sources among the *Rishonim*) is to compare this question to an even more well-known one. The Tur[2] says that if one removes his *tallit* with the intention of putting it back on after a relatively short amount of time, he does not make a beracha when he puts it back on. The Beit Yosef[3] disagrees based on a *gemara*[4] that relates that Rava would make a beracha on his *tefillin* every time he returned from the bathroom, despite the fact that he had intended to put the tefillin back on immediately afterward. The Darchei Moshe[5] deflects this proof by distinguishing between the cases based on the nature of the break. When one enters a bathroom, he is not allowed to wear tefillin, so the resulting break is a major interruption. In contrast, one who removes a tallit can put in on again at any time, even in the bathroom. The Shulchan Aruch,[6] based on his comments in

---

1. *Yoreh Deah* 289:1.
2. *Orach Chayim* 8.
3. Ad loc.
4. *Sukka* 46a.
5. *Orach Chayim* 8.
6. *Orach Chayim* 8:14.

Beit Yosef, requires a beracha when putting a tallit on again. The Rama[7] (= Darchei Moshe) says not to make the beracha.

The Admat Kodesh[8] says that those who follow the view of the Shulchan Aruch (classically, Sephardim) should likewise make a beracha when putting back a mezuza, as the *mitzva* was interrupted when he removed it, whereas those who follow the Rama (Ashkenazim) might not. However, on the tallit issue itself, later Sephardic poskim reject the Shulchan Aruch's view and do not require a beracha upon returning a tallit.[9]

The assumed connection between tallit and mezuza is also questionable. One of the most authoritative Sephardic poskim, the Chida, writes[10] that after removing a mezuza to check it, it is possible that one should make a beracha upon reaffixing it. The Pitchei Teshuva[11] explains that the Chida's doubt may be based on the following distinction between the case of tallit and that of checking a mezuza. One who removes the tallit has every reason to expect that he can subsequently put it on without problem or unnecessary delay. However, when one removes the mezuza in order to check it, he should be concerned that it may be found *pasul*. Therefore, it is harder to say that his intention regarding the continued performance of the mitzva is uninterrupted.

Another factor that plays a role is time. The Aruch HaShulchan[12] says that if a day goes by before he puts the mezuza back, he should make a new beracha. It is difficult to summarize all of the opinions among the later poskim. It appears, however, that the majority of poskim say that when one checks the mezuza and puts it back promptly, he does not make a new beracha. To a great degree, this is due to the concept of *safek berachot l'hakel*: if one is unsure whether a beracha is warranted, it is safer to refrain from

---

7. Ad loc.
8. I, *Yoreh Deah* 18.
9. See a summary of opinions in *Yechaveh Da'at* III, 80.
10. *Birkei Yosef, Yoreh Deah*, 286:10.
11. Ibid.
12. *Yoreh Deah* 289:4.

making it. Notably, Rav Ovadya Yosef[13] uncharacteristically requires a beracha where most do not. A logical compromise position is that if one gives the mezuza over to a *sofer* to check, with the matter leaving the owner's control, then a beracha is required, but otherwise not.[14]

When one paints doorposts, he fully expects to put the mezuzot back; thus, at first glance, one would not make a new beracha upon returning them. However, there can be a few reasons to make the beracha, according to our discussion above. Usually one leaves the mezuzot off for a couple of days so the paint will dry. It is also an opportune time to do the required, periodic check (twice in seven years). In addition, if one switches around the mezuza scrolls from different doorposts, even more opinions require a beracha (beyond our scope). If one combines all the factors, the beracha is clearly appropriate.

---

13. *Yechaveh Da'at*, ibid.
14. See *Chovat HaDar* 11:(26).

G-6: Kissing Sefer Torah With a Siddur

Question: Is one allowed to use a *siddur* to kiss a *sefer Torah* as it passes by, or is using it in a manner other than for its intended purpose considered disrespectful?

Answer: We have not been able to find an explicit source on this common practice (although a practice often counts as a source in and of its own right). However, there seems to be a similar case, discussed by the *poskim*, which can serve as a precedent.

The Taz[1] forbids using one *sefer* to raise up another one to make it easier to read, as he is using something holy for a use for which "wood or stone" would work just as well. (It is permitted, according to the Taz, to place one sefer on another if the bottom sefer was initially brought to the place to be used for learning, not as a stand.) It would seem, then, that one should not use the siddur to kiss the sefer Torah, as he can use his hand or *tallit*, etc.

On the other hand, the Magen Avraham[2] disagrees with the Taz and allows one to bring one sefer in order to prop up another. His main source is the *gemara*[3] that states that one may move a *bima* to a place where its presence will prevent *tuma* (impurity) from entering a *beit k'nesset*. One can understand the Magen Avraham in a limited manner: the holy object may be used only if the reason it is moved is not obvious or only if it is in a stationary position when used. However, it appears from the context and language of the Chayei Adam[4] and Mishna Berura[5] that they understood the Magen Avraham in an inclusive manner that would apply to our case as well. In other words, if the use is not, in and

---

1. *Yoreh Deah* 282:13.
2. 154:14.
3. *Megilla* 26b.
4. 31:48.
5. 154:31.

of itself, degrading and, in fact, is intended to aid in a *mitzva*-oriented activity, it would be permitted.

It is also possible that the Taz would agree that his comparison to "wood or stone" is not appropriate in our case. The cogency of the argument may depend on the circumstances. Some may use the siddur as a convenient way to extend the hand and not bother to get closer to the sefer Torah. If so, its use is for human convenience, even though it is within the context of a positive religious experience (showing love for the Torah). However, many use the siddur because they feel it is *more* respectful for the Torah to be touched by something holy, and not by human hands. From that perspective, the siddur is not a replacement of wood or stone but an aid to show respect for the sefer Torah. Moreover, since the sefer Torah is on a higher level than the siddur, the grounds for leniency are stronger than in the Taz's case.

This concept has precedent in a similar case. The Sha'arei Ephraim[6] describes that one who gets an *aliya* kisses the Torah with his tallit or the *me'il* (the cover of the sefer Torah). He does not stipulate that this practice is permissible only if there is no alternative. Thus, considering that the me'il has a higher level of *kedusha* than a talit or even a siddur, it seems that one can freely use holy things for kissing a sefer Torah. Perhaps one could argue that only those items, like a me'il, whose kedusha stems from its use to serve the sefer Torah, may be used to serve the sefer Torah in any way.

In summary, it seems there is a strong basis to permit using a siddur to kiss a sefer Torah, even if alternatives exist. Therefore, one should not criticize or discourage those who have the practice to do so. On the other hand, we cannot totally refute the contention that it is improper to use the siddur for that purpose.

---

6. One of the classic sefarim concerning the laws related to the reading of the Torah – 4:3.

G-7: Fasting if a Sefer Torah Falls

Question: Does halacha require fasting if a *sefer Torah* falls? If so, who fasts and for how long?

Answer: The matter of fasting if a sefer Torah is dropped is mentioned in the Magen Avraham[1] in the name of Mishpetei Shmuel. They describe it as a custom that had been widely accepted, for which they sought a basis. It is fitting, in our view, that because of the emotions involved, practice on this matter has developed in a "beyond-the-letter-of-the-law" and perhaps "grass-roots" manner, rather than through clear halachic dictate. Some *poskim* indicate that the matter is best to be decided by the local rabbi, based on what he deems as an appropriate reaction for his community.[2] We will cite the source for a related practice, which, we believe, is somewhat related to the situation about which you ask.

The *gemara*[3] states that one must rip his garment if he sees a Torah or *tefillin* being destroyed. As destruction is more severe than falling, our *minhag* relates only to fasting, which would be less intense a sign of remorse than ripping one's garment. We will concentrate on a fallen sefer Torah, which, being holier than tefillin, is more serious in several ways, including the effect as regards onlookers.

Most rule that only the one who dropped the Torah must fast.[4] Others say that all who were present when the sefer Torah fell may share a collective negligence and must fast.[5] Some say that the concern at hand is the bad omen for all those who were, for whatever reason, connected to the event. This concern could

---

1. 44:5.
2. See *Tzitz Eliezer* v, 1.
3. *Mo'ed Katan* 26a.
4. See *Tzitz Eliezer* ibid.
5. *Imrei Aish*, quoted ibid.

extend to those who saw the Torah fall[6] or even to the whole community.[7]

As to the number of fast days, most opinions state that one day is sufficient, but others suggest fasting Monday-Thursday-Monday or even forty days. The minimum step to be taken is that the one who dropped the sefer Torah should fast one day. We suggest the following for those who want to take a more stringent yet mainstream approach to deal with the traumatic occurrence. The person who dropped the Torah should fast Monday-Thursday-Monday. If it is difficult for him, he can redeem his fast with *tzedaka* (while trying to fast at least once). It is also nice to donate something to beautify the Torah that fell. Onlookers should fast one day, and, if this is difficult, they can redeem the obligation with tzedaka. These suggestions are consistent with the analysis of the Tzitz Eliezer[8] and Igrot Moshe.[9] If the local rabbi has decided on additional steps, they should be followed.

---

6. *Yad Elazar*, cited ibid.
7. *Divrei Chayim*, quoted in *Igrot Moshe, Orach Chayim* III, 3.
8. V, 1.
9. *Orach Chayim* III, 3.

G-8: A Donor's Name Above HaShem's Name

Question: An *amud*[1] was donated to our *shul*. May the name of the donor be written above HaShem's Name (which appears in the *pasuk* "*Shiviti HaShem l'negdi tamid*")?

Answer: We have several sources in *Chazal* that indicate that HaShem's Name should normally precede other names.

The *gemara*[2] states that on the *tzitz* (the headplate of the *kohen gadol*, upon which was inscribed "*kodesh laHaShem*"), the Name of HaShem was elevated above "*kodesh la.*" This was done out of respect for the Name. This idea was clear even to non-Jews. For this reason, the rabbis who wrote the original Septuagint started the text with HaShem's Name, not with the word for *Bereishit*.[3] Tosafot[4] explains that, since the Greeks understood that it is proper that God's Name appear first, they might have thought that there were two deities, *Bereishit* and *Elokim*[5].

Why, in fact, isn't HaShem's Name mentioned first there and elsewhere?

The last *mishna* of *Masechet Yadayim* records the criticism of the *Tzedukim*[6] concerning the fact that, in a *get*, the name of the king (used to indicate the date) precedes the mention of Moshe. The Rabbis responded that, in the *sefer Torah*, we find the name of Pharaoh before HaShem's Name. Commentaries[7] understand that, when there is a specific need to write another name first, it may be done without being disgraceful to HaShem. In the case

---

1. The podium before which the *chazan* stands.
2. *Shabbat* 63b.
3. *Megilla* 9a.
4. Ad loc.
5. The Name of HaShem, as it appears in the first pasuk of the Torah.
6. Sadducees.
7. See *Tiferet Yisrael*, ad loc.

of the get and the sefer Torah, the need is a matter of textual content. On the tzitz, although it made more sense to have HaShem's Name after *"kodesh la,"* there was apparently a special sensitivity regarding the order of the words since they were on the holiest part of the kohen gadol's garments.

Therefore, normally the name of the donor should be under the pasuk that contains HaShem's Name. (The text would not seem to be adversely affected by having the name of the donor on the bottom.) However, there could be exceptions. One exception would be where the writing is relatively high, and if the pasuk were on the top, it would be difficult for the *chazan* to see it.[8]

---

8. See *Aseh Lecha Rav* IV, 44.4, where he explains the importance of this pasuk, which reminds the one who is praying that the image of HaShem's Presence should always be before him.

G-9: Treatment of Abbreviations of HaShem's Name

Question: Are you allowed to throw out a letter that has on it the abbreviation ב"ה or בס"ד? Is it better not to write them in the first place?

Answer: One should refrain from writing HaShem's name on the types of writings (invitations, newspapers, and letters) that are likely to be thrown out. The *gemara*[1] tells us how the *Chashmona'im* started writing HaShem's Name in documents, in order to reverse the influence of the Greeks. Eventually, the Rabbis abolished the practice out of concern that these documents would be disposed of improperly. The Rama[2] expands and codifies this concept regarding writing in places other than books.

However, abbreviations that are used to refer to HaShem, including ב"ה (which stands for the Hebrew: *B'Ezrat HaShem* – with HaShem's help), have no halachic significance according to several opinions.[3] There is additional reason for leniency when it is not written in *ketav ashuri* (lettering found in a *sefer Torah*).[4] Others rule not to write ב"ה and, if it was written, not to erase it.[5] Regarding י", found often in *siddurim* in place of HaShem's name, the Rama[6] says that it may be erased only if there is a need. He does not go so far as to say that it should not be written. With these opinions in mind, one should weigh whether and when it is productive to write ב"ה. If one has writings with these abbreviations on them, he is not required to put them in *geniza*. It is

---

1. *Rosh Hashana* 18b.
2. *Yoreh Deah* 276:13.
3. See *Yechaveh Da'at* III, 78.
4. See *Shut HaRama* 34.
5. See *Shut Tzafnat Pa'aneach*, quoted in *Yechaveh Da'at* ibid.
6. *Yoreh Deah* 276:10.

sufficient to wrap them in plastic before throwing in the garbage.[7] If one removes the word(s) from the paper, there are no restrictions on the rest.[8]

It is noteworthy that the ה of ב"ה and the י of יי are letters from HaShem's main Name. In contrast, בס"ד (which stands for the Aramaic: *B'Siyata Dishmaya* – with Divine assistance) refers to no part of HaShem's Name and, therefore, does not need to be treated in any special way.[9] This distinction may be why many people use ד as a one-letter abbreviation of His name, instead of ה.

In summary, it is preferable not to dispose of the abbreviations ב"ה and יי in a disgraceful manner. However, בס"ד presents no halachic problem whatsoever, and thus, although it is not required, may ideally adorn our writings with the concept that all of our endeavors are possible only with HaShem's help.

---

7. See *Igrot Moshe, Yoreh Deah* II, 138
8. *Shulchan Aruch, Yoreh Deah* 276:13.
9. *Igrot Moshe,* ibid.

G-10: Berachot for One Who Took the Wrong Tallit and Tefillin

Question: I mixed up my *tallit* and tefillin in *shul* with those belonging to someone else. After a few minutes, I realized my mistake and returned them. When I put on my own tallit and tefillin, should I have recited the *berachot* again, or was it sufficient that I already made the berachot once?

Answer: Every fulfillment of certain *mitzvot*, including tallit and tefillin, must be preceded by a beracha that relates to it. The question is whether the initial beracha you made is able to relate to putting on the second pair of tallit and tefillin.

There are two factors that might prompt one to claim that you did not need new berachot. The Shulchan Aruch and Rama[1] have *machlokot* in equivalent cases, when one takes off tallit or tefillin, intending to put them on again soon thereafter, whether he needs to make a new beracha at that point. The Shulchan Aruch requires a beracha; the Rama does not. In your case, at the time you took off the incorrect tallit and tefillin, you planned to put on another set promptly, so ostensibly the Rama (Ashkenazi) would not require new berachot.[2]

To introduce the second issue, let us start with the "bad news." The mitzva of tzitzit applies only when one *owns* the four-cornered garment.[3] It is true that one can borrow another's tallit without explicit permission, obtain temporary ownership, and make a beracha on it.[4] However, in your case, you did not realize that you needed to acquire ownership of the tallit, which you

---

1. *Orach Chayim* 8:14 and 25:12.
2. Regarding Sephardim, see question G-5.
3. *Shulchan Aruch, Orach Chayim* 14:3 and *Mishna Berura* 14:11.
4. *Shulchan Aruch, Orach Chayim* 14:4.

thought was yours.[5] Thus, the beracha was *l'vatala* (in vain). The matter of the tefillin is less clear. On one hand, one does not need to own the tefillin, and one fulfills the mitzva even with tefillin borrowed without permission, as permission is assumed.[6] However, in this case, when the owner was presumably about to use his tefillin, he did not want you to take them. Thus your action was unintentional thievery, and one does not fulfill the mitzva of tefillin with a stolen pair[7] because it is a mitzva that comes about through an *aveira*.[8]

According to the above, the berachot did not take effect on the first tallit and, perhaps,[9] the tefillin, respectively. Let us consider, though, the following parallel halacha. Regarding one who made a beracha on tefillin and, before putting it on, the knot became undone, the Taz[10] infers from the Beit Yosef that he can fix the knot and put it on without a new beracha. The reason is that the beracha is "waiting" for the opportunity to take effect. Here too, ostensibly, the berachot on the tallit and, perhaps, on the tefillin should be "waiting" to take effect on your own tallit and tefillin.

However, neither of the aforementioned factors applies to your case because of one basic distinction. In both of those areas, the person made the beracha on the same "mitzva object" with which he continued after a delay. In your case, your berachot were on a different set of tallit and tefillin. The Shulchan Aruch[11] says that if one puts on several tallitot, he can make one beracha to cover them all, if he does not "break" between them. However, he says that even without a break, the beracha applies to another tallit only if he had the intention, at the time of the first beracha,

---

5. See *Yevamot* 52b.

6. *Shulchan Aruch, Orach Chayim* 25:12 and *Mishna Berura* 25:53.

7. *Shulchan Aruch*, ibid.

8. See a machloket on the question whether a mitzva performed by an unintentional aveira is disqualified in *S'dei Chemed* IV, pp. 335–336.

9. See previous footnote.

10. 25:12.

11. *Orach Chayim* 8:12.

that it should apply to it. Otherwise, he makes a beracha each time. You had your berachot in mind only for the tallit and tefillin that were in your hands, not on your own set, which you did not realize was elsewhere. We find elsewhere, regarding a case of a beracha on one object that has to be transferred to another object instead (not in addition), that the first beracha is l'vatala, and a new beracha is needed.[12] So, in the final analysis, you should have made new berachot.

---

12. *Shulchan Aruch, Orach Chayim* 206:6; see *Halacha Pesuka* on *Tzitzit* 8:(143).

Section H:
Miscellaneous

H-1: Changing the Name of a Sick Person

Question: Is it a good idea to change the name of a person who is very sick? How does one go about doing it? What are the long-term implications of this change?

Answer: The *minhag* to change the name of a very sick person is an old one that is approved of by the Shulchan Aruch[1] and the Rama.[2] The rationale for it is found in the *gemara*[3] as one of the things that can "tear up" the harsh decree that is upon a person.

However, the step of changing a name should not be taken lightly since a person's name, in addition to having psychological importance to him, could actually be a source of spiritual strength and longevity for him as well. Therefore, great rabbis who have a special expertise in and sensitivity to the more hidden world of the Torah should give approval to such a decision. For this same reason, we also have the practice not to uproot the old name but to add another name to precede it. (The practice of having double names is itself hundreds, not thousands, of years old.)

The name is changed in a "ceremony" done with a minyan, which starts with the recitation of several *perakim* of Tehillim and includes a special *Yehi Ratzon*. The text is found in some complete *siddurim* and books of *Tehillim*. We have cited the order of the ceremony and noted the differences between the Ashkenazic and Sephardic customs in our book, *BeMareh HaBazak*.[4]

The name change is not just ceremonial – it is an actual name change. Although it is not forbidden for a person to use a name other than the one he was given at his *brit* or the one it was changed to, the official Jewish name should be the new one.

---

1. *Even HaEzer* 129:18.
2. *Yoreh Deah* 335:10.
3. *Rosh Hashana* 16b.
4. IV, p. 44.

This has weighty consequences if the person gives or receives a *get*.[5] It also affects how the person is called to the Torah, how a *Mi Shebeirach* will be said on his behalf, and how he should be referred to after his death, whether on a tombstone or in memorial services.[6]

The main requirement to make the change of name permanent is that the sick person become well. (Obviously, we cannot know if his improvement was a result of the name change, but that possibility was the rationale for making the change.) He must recuperate to the point that there was an assumption held for at least thirty days that he recovered.[7] Otherwise, the original name reverts to use at death.

---

5. See *Shulchan Aruch, Even HaEzer* 129:18 and the responsa found in the *Chelkat Mechokek*, ad loc.

6. *Gesher HaChayim* I, p. 31.

7. Ibid.

H-2: Crossing at a Red Light

Question: Is a pedestrian halachically forbidden to cross at a red light when it is safe to do so?

Answer: Although we will discuss halachic elements of this question, we hope that the general merits of following this and other civil laws are sufficient to refrain from crossing at red lights (under normal circumstances). Although we will discuss the situation in Israel, the bottom line is much the same in any country. We will deal with the issues one by one:

Dina d'malchuta (*the law of the land*): According to most authorities, dina d'malchuta is binding not only in the Diaspora, but also in *Eretz Yisrael*.[1] This is certainly the case regarding laws enacted for public welfare, not in order to enrich the king.[2] (We are of the conviction that the Israeli government has a halachic status of *malchut* (kingdom).)[3] There is a halachic dispute whether dina d'malchuta pertains only to matters related to the king's interests or extends even to relationships between individual people. However, the reason of those who limit the king's authority is concern that expanded authority would undermine the role of Torah law in many areas.[4] It certainly is not a threat to Torah authority if the government sets regulations for crossing public streets. Therefore, traffic rules are binding. Secondly, in our times, the government pays, directly and/or indirectly, for much of the expense of accidents (medical, disability, etc.) and it is, therefore, an interested party. It is true that most of the laws of dina d'malchuta discuss monetary payment. Yet, it is illogical to argue that, although the

---

1. See opinions in *Encyclopedia Talmudit* vii, p. 307.
2. *Shut Chatam Sofer, Choshen Mishpat* 44.
3. Rav Yisraeli in *Amud HaY'mini, siman* 7, partially based on Rav Kook in *Mishpat Kohen* 144; see also *Techumin*, iii 238–249.
4. See *Shach, Choshen Mishpat* 73:39.

government may levy fines, the Torah allows us to violate regulations and to take our chances. If the Torah recognizes the government's authority in these matters, then we are bound by the Torah to accept the authority, not to rebel against it. However, there is probably a difference between a regular Torah law and the authority the Torah grants governments, in the following case. If the government would not object were one to violate one of its rules in a specific circumstance where the rule was clearly not intended to apply, then it is permitted to do so. However, this concept should be used sparingly. (After all, in most cases, a pedestrian who deemed it safe to cross at a red light would not do so while being observed by a police officer.)

Endangering one's life: In recent years, one third of traffic fatalities were pedestrians. One must assume that many of them could have been spared had they been careful and followed rules they deemed unnecessary. Nevertheless, it is hard to disqualify a responsible person from judging when it is safe to cross a street. (Let us caution that we have observed that one's ability to cross streets carefully is significantly impaired while speaking on cell phones.) Additionally, there is a concept of *dashu ba rabim*, that it is permitted to enter a situation of potential danger that people regularly ignore.[5]

Chillul Hashem (desecrating HaShem's Name): One should learn the *gemara* in Yoma 86a well. It not only stresses chillul HaShem's severity but also the fact that the more one represents the Torah, the stricter are its parameters. We have heard people comment that religious people are more likely to ignore traffic regulations. Although such generalizations are objectionable, so are actions which encourage such claims to be made.

Example for children: When children, including our own, observe adults ignoring the rules of the road, they learn to follow suit, often with tragic consequences.

Contributing to an atmosphere: We are not individually to

---

5. *Yevamot* 72a.

blame for the atmosphere of disregard for laws, manners, and the value of human life on our streets, nor can we improve it significantly alone. However, since a whole is made up of many parts, each of us is obligated to do his share to push things in the right direction. When pedestrians disregard their rules, motorists are less likely to act courteously or even safely at crosswalks and intersections.

After honestly considering the various factors, we hope that all will agree that it is wrong to cross at red lights. If it that is not enough, we add that it is also halachically forbidden.

H-3: Interests of the Public vs. Those of the Individual

Question: I want a rabbinic teaching regarding how one deals with a clash between an individual's needs and the majority's preferences. Let me illustrate with a hypothetical situation. For a *shul Kiddush*,[1] some people cannot eat *milchig*; some cannot eat *fleishig*. Would the Torah say that the majority's preference overrides the individual's need? I assume that a vegetarian Kiddush, which everyone can eat, is preferable even if the majority prefers fleishig. I recall a teaching that reminds me of this concept. We all give up the right to hear the shofar when Rosh Hashana is on Shabbat lest a single Jew carry it improperly. Can you give me a phrase that sums up this concept?

Answer: We know of no overarching phrase that mandates favoring the more basic needs of the individual at the expense of the preferences of the many. There are numerous specific laws regarding contradictory needs or preferences of neighbors. Examples of cases: one person wants to open a business on a residential street, whereas neighbors don't want to be disturbed by his clientele; a person wants to fertilize his field, whereas others complain that it may attract flies. The basic rabbinic approach is pragmatic and balanced (and, in many cases, similar to modern legal systems).

Particular emphasis is put upon the needs of the community. The apparent rights of the individual are, at times, "compromised" in order to allow the community to lead a normal life.[2] However, the Talmud[3] does use a phrase: "On this condition, Joshua divided up the land [to individuals]." This concept allows one person's *significant* needs to override the rights of another or even mildly

---

1. Refreshments after Shabbat morning services.
2. See *Bava Batra* 97b as but one example.
3. *Bava Kama* 81b.

disrupt the public domain. Nevertheless, balance is "the name of the game."

Let's use your case as an example. A classic Kiddush is fleishig, as the majority prefers. One need not deprive the majority because of a small minority. The minority of vegetarians should be accommodated by having *some* vegetarian food to meet their basic needs. They should be happy that their needs were addressed in a way that did not impose upon others.

The matter of shofar blowing is different. There we suspend one religious law in order that the sanctity of HaShem's Shabbat not be violated, not because of the personal needs of a specific person. Incidentally, when there are competing needs, we, at times, give preference to religious needs. Thus, a neighbor who allows noise to emanate from his house is given more leeway if the noise is from a Torah study hall.[4] Also, although one may not leave a torch outside of his store, lest it burn a passerby's load, one may leave a Chanuka *menora* in a similar position.[5]

---

4. *Bava Batra* 20b.
5. *Bava Kama* 61b.

H-4: Reacting to Bad Dreams

Question: I heard that one is not supposed to share his bad dreams. Is that true?

Answer: Most dreams are insignificant and are generated by one's thoughts during the day.[1] On the other hand, there is a concept that dreams are one-sixtieth of prophecy.[2] Commentators explain that just as full prophecy used to be revealed in a special type of dream, so too, when there is no prophecy, semi-prophetic messages can be conveyed through a dream. In the era of prophecy, it would be clear to a prophet that he was receiving prophecy and what its meaning was. Similarly, a semi-prophetic dream is likely to be more powerful than a regular dream and, if it causes the dreamer to be shaken emotionally, it might be a sign that he should take it seriously.

Although the exact understanding of the Talmud's approach to dreams is elusive, a short excerpt may be instructive: "Rabbi Yochanan said, 'One who had a dream that depressed him should have it interpreted by three people.' Have it interpreted? Didn't Rav Chisda say that an uninterpreted dream is like an unread letter [in other words, it will be less likely to have an effect]? Rather, what was meant is that he should go to three people to 'improve it' (*hatavat chalom*)."[3]

From this and other Talmudic discussions we see our Rabbis' view on four possible reactions to serious, negative dreams: 1. The dream is interpreted negatively – this is potentially dangerous. 2. The dream is suppressed – this is a relatively safe response. 3. A hatavat chalom ceremony (found in some *siddurim*) is performed – a good idea for people who are worried. 4. One fasts on

---

1. *Kohelet* 5:2; *Berachot* 55b-56a.
2. *Berachot* 57b.
3. Ibid. 55b.

the day of the dream to overturn possible negative decrees that were revealed – this may prove especially effective, as the dream might be a warning to the dreamer to repent in order to avert a potential negative decree. One may fast for this purpose even on Shabbat (which is usually forbidden). Nowadays, since we don't always know how to recognize a significant dream, step number four is often extreme.[4]

In summary, there may be reason not to reveal an upsetting bad dream.[5] If one is particularly upset, he can perform a short ceremony and/or fast. The best advice is probably to train one-self not to take dreams too seriously. Nevertheless, if an especially powerful dream or a person's experience causes him to take it as a potential sign of the future, he can consider the aforementioned steps.

---

4. See *Shulchan Aruch, Orach Chayim* 288:5.
5. See *Aruch HaShulchan, Orach Chayim* 220:1.

H-5: Asking Forgiveness When it Hurts the Victim

Question: Someone sinned against his friend, but the victim is unaware of what the sinner did to him and/or will be upset if the episode is raised. Should the sinner raise the issue and ask for forgiveness?

Answer: The *mishna*[1] says that one does not receive atonement on Yom Kippur for sins between man and man until he appeases the victim. Thus, the sinner should go to great lengths to appease him. The question is whether that includes causing further pain to the victim.

This dilemma is said to be a point of disagreement between two of the great teachers of morality of a century ago. The Chafetz Chayim, in the work from which he received his popular name,[2] states that one who caused damage to his friend through speech must ask for his forgiveness even if it requires revealing the story. Rav Yisrael Salanter is reported, in both oral and written records of the exchange, to have protested the ruling. He argues that a sinner may not make efforts to receive atonement at the expense of another, who does not deserve more pain. Rav Avigdor Neventzal is cited[3] as finding it difficult to believe that the Chafetz Chayim is understood correctly. Rav Neventzal understood that it is proper to reveal the offense only if the hurt would result to the sinner alone, not if it would extend to the victim. Whatever version of the Chafetz Chayim's opinion (or Rabbeinu Yona's, upon which it is based) one believes is correct, the accepted approach is that it is wrong to cause new wounds. One should also realize that even if he gets a degree of atonement for the sin (asking for forgiveness

---

1. *Yoma* 85b.
2. *Chafetz Chayim, Hilchot Lashon Hara* 4:12.
3. *Mikraei Kodesh* (Harari), *Yom Kippur* 2:(4).

from man or HaShem does not necessarily assure full removal of every sin), he may increase the grievousness of the damage and, thus, might lose out in the process anyway.

This said, one should realize that sometimes the aforementioned concern is exaggerated. It is true that there are times that even if a victim is aware of the affront, recalling it will cause a painful reopening of the wound. Yet, it is often still worthwhile to ask for forgiveness. In order to heal, wounds often need to be reopened and properly tended to. The offender should not automatically use the initial uneasiness as an excuse to avoid the very difficult task of requesting forgiveness. However, one has to be wise and sensitive about how to proceed. If he makes a quick phone call an hour before Yom Kippur, or the like, it *might* be taken as an insincere effort to get some overly easy atonement. Emotional conversations must be planned, and no two situations are identical or are properly remedied in the same way.

What happens if one decides not to discuss the affront? Firstly, a general request of forgiveness from the party is worth something, certainly when the affront is known but is embarrassing to the victim when brought up.[4] In general, it appears that the mishna that requires appeasing the victim is sometimes taken out of context. Indeed, it is futile to attempt to do *teshuva* for sins between people by addressing only HaShem without receiving forgiveness from his friend. However, it can be illustrated from the mishna's context and from related sources that this is because one cannot be sincere about his repentance if he has the ability to remedy the situation and refuses to do so. Therefore, for example, the Rambam[5] talks in one breath about not making necessary monetary payments and not appeasing. The Pri Chadash[6] and Minchat Chinuch[7] write

---

4. See *Mishna Berura* (written by the Chafetz Chayim) 606: 3, who agrees in this case.
5. *Teshuva* 2:9.
6. *Orach Chayim* 606:1
7. #364.

about not getting atonement even for the element of the sin of the affront to HaShem in these cases. These and other sources describe a process that fulfills one's duties to seek forgiveness from victims who are not willing to forgive. The implication is that if one does all that he should for his counterpart, then HaShem will grant him at least partial atonement. Thus, if one refrains from revealing details only in order to spare his friend pain (as Rav Salanter requires), he can expect to receive partial atonement, according to his sincerity.

H-6: Our Approach to the Gray Areas of Halacha

Question: Sometimes your published responses from your internet Ask the Rabbi service end off without clear guidelines as to how one should act but offer a few possibilities. Why is that?

Answer: Although we usually give clear guidelines, we acknowledge the truth of your observation and will take this opportunity to explain our thinking on how to present halacha to the public.

Just as in most fields of scholarship, matters are not always clear-cut, so too the answers to pertinent halachic issues classically fall into different categories. Some cases are clearly forbidden. Some cases are clearly permitted. There is almost always a gray area where it is difficult to give an unequivocal answer. This can occur, mainly, for two reasons. First, the various opinions may be very similar in strength, making the options almost equivalent in the eyes of the respondent. Additionally, a myriad of subjective factors can affect the advisability of various approaches in subtle, complex and sometimes unanticipated ways.

Almost all of our responses include elements that fall into each of these categories, and we try to briefly explain the underpinnings of the topic and the logic behind the different approaches within the gray areas. By doing so, we hope to present a clearer picture of the issue as a whole, which we could not do if we rendered guidelines in the form of ABC.

What is one to do in those cases where no conclusion is given? Firstly, it is important for everyone to have a personal halachic authority with whom to discuss such questions. Such a *rav* will be aware of some of the subjective factors that relate to the person and his circumstances and will be able to inquire about additional factors that he needs in order to *pasken*.[1] There

---

1. Render a halachic ruling.

have been times when we gave the questioner a more specific answer, based on information specific to him, but published the question in a more general form with a more general answer. Furthermore, there are times when the person who receives the halachic information has to choose for himself. We try to describe the gray areas carefully because they contain different shades of gray. We often use carefully chosen language to indicate that we lean in a certain direction but don't close the door on another approach. Whether one wants to take the more lenient or stricter approach can legitimately be the reader's decision. The wise decision may depend on factors that change according to one's setting or circumstances. (How many times does the Rama end off that something is permitted only in a case of significant loss, and who can give an absolute dollar sum for such a loss?) If we would always give a clear decision, we would deprive the serious reader of the legitimacy of sometimes deciding for himself.

We also are well aware that those who read our publications comprise a broad spectrum of society, varying one from another in regard to community, personal background and/or philosophy. This makes it prudent to, at times, report the various legitimate approaches taken. Why should someone who is legitimately lenient feel deficient because the respondent favors the more stringent opinion? Why should we tempt a member of a family or a community where the approach is stricter or just different to change to the *minhag* that we think is slightly more justified? Let him ask his personal rav what he should do with his new understanding of the matter.

One of our main purposes in bringing contradictory opinions and approaches as (equally) viable options is to promote harmony within and between communities. Human nature causes some to look down upon those who are more lenient than they are. Others are hostile to those who are stricter. Most of us have a tendency to do both, depending on the issue. We hope to educate as many people as possible that often "these and those are the words of the living God."[2] We are unrepentant but apologize for any frustration this at times may cause.

---

2. *Gittin* 6b.

H-7: Standing for Memorial Siren

Question: I am disturbed by the refusal of some religious Jews to stand for the siren on *Yom HaZikaron* (Israel's Memorial Day). Someone told me that it is forbidden to do so. If true, why doesn't the rabbinate come out against it? If not, shouldn't all religious Jews stand?

Answer: Those who say that it is forbidden to stand for the minute of silence on Yom HaZikaron claim that it is a problem of *chukot hagoyim* (following practices of gentile nations), a prohibition that is derived from *Vayikra* 18:3. Indeed, the practice of standing for the siren was learned from non-Jews. However, we have not found a published, scholarly *p'sak* that rules that it is forbidden (it is possible that one exists). Furthermore, based on the classical sources on the subject, it is difficult to forbid the practice on halachic grounds, as we will see.

There is an apparent contradiction between two *gemarot* regarding the parameters of chukot hagoyim. It was once customary for both Jews and non-Jews to burn objects after their king's death. The gemarot agree that the practice is permitted but give different justifications. Avoda Zara 11a says that the activity does not fall under the category of *chuka* (singular of chukot) but is an act of *chashivuta* (showing importance). Sanhedrin 52b says that it is a chuka and is permitted only because there is a *pasuk*[1] that mentions the practice in a Jewsh context, which allows us to view it as a practice that was learned from Jews, not gentiles.

Tosafot[2] explains that these gemarot are complementary. The chuka discussed in Avoda Zara refers to a practice connected to actual idol worship. In such a case, a preceding Jewish source for the custom is insufficient grounds for leniency. However, says the

---

1. *Yirmiya* 34:5.
2. *Avoda Zara* 11a.

gemara, the burning after a king's death was not an idolatrous act and is permitted if there is Jewish precedent. Chuka in Sanhedrin, though, speaks about a non-idolatrous gentile practice, which is permitted if there is a Jewish precedent.

We need to define what constitutes the latter category of chuka, because, if we go to an extreme, many things, such as wearing a suit and tie,[3] would be forbidden. The Maharik[4] explains that practices that are initiated by non-Jews for logical reasons and are not negative in nature are not considered chukot at all. The Rama[5] *paskens* like the Maharik, as do a predominant majority of *poskim*,[6] despite the Gra's[7] protestations.[8]

It is not always simple to apply the rules to contemporary situations. For example, in three responsa, Rav Moshe Feinstein wrestles from different perspectives with the issue of whether elements of the American holiday of Thanksgiving are chukot hagoyim.[9] In our case, however, the Maharik's requirements are clearly met. Anyone who has experienced standing at the sound of the siren as the whole country *together* stops everything, silently contemplating the sacrifices and contributions of the fallen *kedoshim*, knows how effective a remembrance it is. It is, therefore, fully logical and permitted.

So why can't we all agree? Some within the religious community frown upon almost anything that symbolizes the Israeli government or general society. Although we share many of their complaints, our approach is to be thankful to HaShem and to the people who have sacrificed to enable all the good that comes

---

3. See *Igrot Moshe, Yoreh Deah* I, 81, which explains why this is not so.

4. #88.

5. *Yoreh Deah* 178:1.

6. See *Maharam Shick, Yoreh Deah* 165, *Yabia Omer* III, *Yoreh Deah* 24, and many others.

7. *Yoreh Deah* 178:7.

8. See Rav Yehuda Henkin's article in *Techumin* IV, in which he tries to prove that the Gra would agree in our case.

9. *Igrot Moshe, Yoreh Deah* IV, 12 deals with the contradiction.

with our Jewish state. Although it is a *chillul HaShem* not to stand (especially in public), publicizing the fact that people don't stand, which applies only to a minority of the religious community, causes even more chillul HaShem. We feel that one most effectively deals with conflicts among our people with love, and not, for example, by yelling "Shabbos!" For the sake of consistency and a desire to make things better, not worse, we urge that this disagreement be handled with love and understanding, not with mud-slinging.

H-8: Building a Proper Guardrail

Question: How complete does a guardrail on a staircase have to be? How big may the gaps be? Does it matter if, technically, a baby might be able to fall through?

Answer: This question is hard to answer in detail, but understanding the concept should give you a pretty good idea how to approach the matter.

The Torah writes, "When you build a new house, you shall make a fence for your roof, and you shall not place blood in your house, should the one who falls fall from it."[1] Although the *pasuk* mentions just a roof, *Chazal*[2] extended this law to a variety of dangerous places (such as a pit) in one's property. You refer to a guardrail for a staircase, which can be a dangerous place, especially for small children.

If the halacha applies to all places where a person can fall, then why is the roof singled out? There are a few basic approaches one can take to answer this question. The Sefer HaChinuch[3] says that the Torah just gave a common example of a place that requires a fence. However, there is another, not necessarily contradictory, approach found in several *Acharonim*, which seems logically appealing according to classical halachic analysis.

Let us employ an analytical tool that some of us like to call "*tzvei dinim*" (Yiddish), two elements to the halacha. The requirement of a fence for a roof is quite objective and formalistic. The requirement elsewhere is more subjective, and it depends on the specifics of the situation. This distinction makes the case of a roof often stricter but, at times, more lenient than other cases. For example, a dwelling that doesn't meet a house's size requirements

---

1. *Devarim* 22:8.
2. *Sifrei*, ad loc.
3. # 546.

is exempt from having a fence for its roof even if it is used in the
same manner as other roofs.[4] Additionally, the minimum height
of the fence is ten *tefachim* (roughly two and a half feet), hardly
enough to totally prevent someone from falling.[5] Rather, this
height is the classic one for a halachic wall in a variety of contexts,
from the laws of *sukka* to the laws of *eiruv* and elsewhere. Thus,
the maximum space in between the vertical bars of a roof's fence
is probably three tefachim (approximately nine inches), the normal size for a gap to be considered halachically significant.

That is in regard to the more formalistic and defined application of these *halachot*. Nevertheless, by extending the concept to
a wide range of dangers (including raising a "bad" dog[6]), Chazal
were telling us that, beyond the formalistic element of the *mitzva*,
the spirit of the law is binding as well. Thus, where there is palpa-
ble danger, further steps may need to be taken. This requirement
is derived not from the positive commandment to "build a fence"
but from the negative commandment not to "place blood in your
house" and the more general commandment to "be careful and
safeguard your life."[7] One difference that stems from the distinction between the more defined and less defined applications of the
halacha is that even those who require a *beracha* when building
a fence[8] do so only for a fence on a roof.[9] Another distinction is
that, in other cases, one first must determine whether a potentially dangerous area is actually used.[10] This is unlike the law in
the case of a straight roof, which needs a fence as long as it can,
in theory, be used.[11]

Thus, in your case, one has to consider what the actual dan-

---

4. *Shulchan Aruch, Choshen Mishpat* 427:2.
5. Ibid., 5.
6. See *Bava Kama* 15b.
7. *Shulchan Aruch, Choshen Mishpat* 427:8.
8. *Rambam, Berachot* 11: 12.
9. *Ha'amek She'ala* 145:17; *Chayei Adam* 15:24.
10. *Minchat Yitzchak* v, 122.
11. *Aruch HaShulchan, Choshen Mishpat* 427:5.

gers are. If there is reasonable danger for children, then you have to ask a technical expert what the maximum width between bars should be. Although halacha does not expect one to spend all of his money removing the most remote danger, it is, in general, better to err on the side of caution.

H-9: Netilat Yadayim – Must it be Done Near Bed?

Question: Some people do *netilat yadayim* in the morning immediately upon waking up, using water and a basin they had placed near their bed. Is this necessary or may one wash his hands at a sink outside of his bedroom? If this leniency is acceptable, please cite sources and the rabbinic authorities who sanction it.

Answer: The requirement to wash one's hands upon arising and make the appropriate *beracha* is mentioned in the *gemara*.[1] The reasons offered by the *Rishonim* are 1) to remove before *davening* residue from things he may have touched while sleeping and 2) upon awakening as a "new creation," we should thank HaShem, Who created us to serve and bless Him.[2] However, the practice of being careful not to walk four *amot*[3] in the morning before washing one's hands is not mentioned in the gemara or by other early, classical *halachic* sources. The source is a statement of the Zohar,[4] which is cited by several *Acharonim*.

The Shevut Yaakov[5] rules that one need not be stringent in this matter. He and others cite a statement made by Rabbi Shimon ben Elazar (admittedly, in a different context) that whatever is in a house is considered within four amot.[6] Note that this logic would not apply when sleeping outdoors or in other instances when one has to walk more than four amot outside of his dwelling before washing. On the other hand, the Mishna Berura,[7] based

---

1. *Berachot* 60b.
2. See *Mishna Berura* 4:1.
3. Approximately six feet.
4. The primary source of the mystical teachings of the Kabbala, which we respect but do not delve into ourselves.
5. III, 1.
6. *Berachot* 25b.
7. 1:2.

on the Zohar, is stringent in this matter, except in pressing circumstances.

It is important to correct the misconception that *walking* four amot, in and of itself, is the main halachic problem. The bigger problem is delaying the removal of the spirit of impurity that rests on the hands during the night's sleep. Thus, to lie awake in bed until someone can bring water within four amot or to walk more than four amot in small increments makes the matter worse, not better.[8] One should also not postpone going to the bathroom, if it is difficult to wait, in order to wash his hands first. This is because it is forbidden to delay going to the bathroom when one has an acute need.[9]

The more prevalent practice is not to be meticulous about having netilat yadayim at one's bedside. Our mentor and teacher, Rav Shaul Yisraeli, taught that even *bnei yeshiva* may rely on the lenient opinion.

---

8. *Mishna Berura*, ibid.
9. Ibid.

H-10: Cutting Down Fruit Trees

Question: May one cut down a fruit tree that is more bother than it is of value?

Answer: The Torah forbids cutting down fruit trees.[1] This is the most formal and strict application of the concept of the *mitzva* not to be destructive and wasteful, and it is the only application for which one can be punished with *malkot* (flogging).[2] Since the prohibition of cutting is not absolute but applies specifically to destructive activity,[3] the *gemara* and *poskim* cite examples of where it is permitted to cut down fruit trees.

The gemara[4] grants permission in the following cases: 1. The tree no longer produces a *kav* (around 1.5 liters) of fruit. (One may not take steps to cause a healthy tree to deteriorate to this point.[5]) 2. The tree is worth more for wood than for fruit.[6] 3. One tree is damaging a more valuable tree in a significant way.[7] 4. The tree is damaging someone else's property.[8]

We must know how broadly we can apply these rules. We cannot properly deal with all the different possible cases or cite all of the opinions and will need to be satisfied with a discussion of some of the main issues. The Rosh[9] derives from the gemara above[10] that one may cut down a tree if he needs to use its loca-

---

1. *Devarim* 20:19.
2. *Rambam, Melachim* 6:8.
3. Ibid.
4. Primarily, *Bava Kama* 91b–92a.
5. *Rambam* ibid.
6. See *Rashi* ad loc.
7. See *Tosafot* ad loc.
8. *Bava Batra* 26a.
9. *Bava Kama* 8:15.
10. *Bava Kama* ibid., specifically in regard to case #3.

tion. The Taz[11] applies the Rosh's rule to building a home on the site. Most poskim understand that the Taz is referring even to expanding a home, at least when the addition is significant and objectively more valuable than the tree.[12] The gemara tells of the son of an *Amora* who died because he cut down a fruit tree prematurely. Rav Yehuda HaChasid also warned about the consequences of violating this mitzva. Therefore, because of the potential severity of the matter, some prefer that the work be done by a non-Jew[13] or that an effort be made to uproot the tree with earth and to replant it.[14]

Questions sometimes arise in regard to cutting off branches. The gemara[15] forbids using wood from fruit trees to burn on the altar, but for a different reason. The Mishne LaMelech[16] says that our prohibition doesn't apply in that case because he is only cutting branches and leaving the tree. The Be'er Sheva[17] says it could have been permitted in order to fulfill a mitzva (as it is, therefore, not in a destructive context). According to both explanations, it would be permitted to cut branches to use as *s'chach*.[18] One should keep in mind here that pruning is healthful for trees,[19] but, of course, not all cutting is healthful pruning.

Many practical cases combine a variety of factors (lenient or strict) and should be considered by a *rav* on an individual basis.

---

11. *Yoreh Deah* 116:6.
12. See *Chayim Sha'al* I, 22; *Yabia Omer* V, *Yoreh Deah* 12.
13. Ibid. Note that non-Jews are not commanded on the matter and should not be subject to negative consequences.
14. *Chatam Sofer, Yoreh Deah* 102.
15. *Tamid* 29b.
16. *Issurei Mizbei'ach* 7:3.
17. Cited ibid.
18. *Yechaveh Da'at* V, 46.
19. *Har Tzvi, Orach Chayim* 101.

H-11: Marketing Orla[1]

Question: We bought land in a tropical region to plant noni trees. Someone told us that *orla* applies even outside *Eretz Yisrael* and that we cannot benefit from the fruit. If this is true, we will have a tremendous loss. Can we work around the problem by having a non-Jewish partner? We are putting a non-Jew in charge of growing and harvesting the noni (for a 25-percent share of the sales); we plan to process and market it.

Interim Response: Orla does apply outside Eretz Yisrael, as a *halacha l'Moshe miSinai* (oral tradition given to Moshe).[2] Many people don't know about it because, in *chutz la'aretz*, it applies only when one *knows* the fruit is *orla*.[3] In your case, you do know!

The *gemara*[4] compares and contrasts a partnership with a non-Jew in a new orchard to a partnership with a non-Jew in a business which is open on Shabbat. If done *in the proper way*, your non-Jewish partner can buy a share in the land, whereby he will get control and ownership of all of the fruit for the first three years, and you will get them after that. If this is feasible and you would like to explore this option, we will send more details.

Question (Part II): Your suggestion will not help us. We need to get the business going under our control (machinery, marketing, etc.) and to start selling. There is a shortage of noni fruit worldwide, and we need to ensure our market position now. We are willing to give all profits to *tzedaka* for the first three years! By the way, noni fruits taste and smell horrible. They are extremely healthful

---

1. Prohibition on using fruit grown during the first three years of a tree's existence.
2. *Kiddushin* 39a.
3. Ibid.
4. *Avoda Zara* 22a.

and can be used only for vitamins and for no more than 10% of a juice drink. Does that make a difference?

Answer (Part II): Your last piece of information is crucial. Rav S.Z. Orbach[5] writes that he believes that orla applies only to edible fruits, not to those that can be used only for their extract, as the Torah refers to the fruit of "food-producing trees."[6] It is true that orla applies even to benefits from uses of the fruit other than eating (e.g., burning, making paint[7]). However, if the fruit is inedible and is used only for its extract, then it is not included in the prohibition. Although Rav Orbach is not fully decisive in his ruling, there is a rule concerning doubts on the matter of orla that one should be stringent with Israeli fruit and lenient with others.[8] Therefore, you can rely on the approach that orla does not apply to noni fruit, as you describe them.

Had we been discussing an edible fruit, the situation would be as follows. A partnership with a non-Jew, which the gemara[9] mentions as helping in connection to an orchard of orla, does not make the fruit permitted. It simply creates a situation where the Jew has no benefit from the fruit during those years. Even orla fruit which is fully owned by non-Jews is forbidden for Jewish benefit. Thus, you could not sell the fruit, in spite of your intention to give the money to tzedaka. Plans to give away the profits in the future do not remove the status of benefit from the sale in immediate terms. Besides benefiting by receiving money, there are other problems. Commerce with forbidden foods is prohibited (details are beyond our present scope[10]). Also, use of the fruit to obtain a market share itself would be considered benefit. The

---

5. *Minchat Shlomo* 71.4.
6. *Vayikra* 19:23.
7. *Pesachim* 22b.
8. *Berachot* 36a.
9. *Avoda Zara* 22a.
10. See *Yoreh Deah* 117 and see Question E-6.

Rama[11] rules that one cannot even help pick a non-Jew's orla fruit free of charge because of the benefit accrued from the favor the non-Jew now owes.

---

11. *Yoreh Deah* 294:8.

H-12: Following a Father's Practices on Halachic Matters

Question: Regarding a halachic issue about which there is a *machloket* (disagreement), do older children, at least those living at home, have to follow the decision that their father follows?

Answer: In this response, we assume that the father is following a legitimate opinion and that the family is not bound by a local ruling. We can address only a few principles and applications.

The topic begins with a *gemara*.[1] The people of Beishan had the practice not to travel to Tzidon on Fridays. Their sons approached Rabbi Yochanan, hoping to end this practice, which they found difficult. Rabbi Yochanan said that since their fathers had already accepted the stringency, the *pasuk* "… do not forsake your mother's Torah"[2] applied, and they had to continue the practice.

The Rivash,[3] Chavot Yair[4] and others say that the fathers of Beishan did not have the authority to obligate their sons individually, but, as a community, they could create a *minhag hamakom* (local practice). The Chavot Yair reasons that people raised in Beishan who moved elsewhere could have ceased keeping the minhag, whereas newcomers to Beishan were obligated by it. The Zichron Yosef[5] makes the following distinction. A stringency that a father accepts is binding on his son only if the son began keeping the minhag, which was the situation in Beishan. Of what significance, then, was the fathers' acceptance, if the sons were, anyway, bound by their own actions? The Korban Netanel[6] cites an opinion that states that since the minhag stemmed from the fathers'

---

1. *Pesachim* 50b.
2. *Mishlei* 1:8.
3. 399.
4. 126.
5. Cited by the *Pitchei Teshuva, Yoreh Deah* 214:5 and many others.
6. *Pesachim* iv, 3:5.

acceptance, it was not possible to stop the practice by using *hatarat nedarim* (absolution of oaths). Other answers are given as well.

We have discussed cases where a father accepted stringencies that exceeded halachic requirements. Do the same rules apply to our case in which the father's practice follows one side of a machloket concerning whether something is objectively permitted or forbidden? Recent *poskim* discuss a parallel case that includes both types of practices – a marriage between an Ashkenazi and a Sephardi who are unsure whose practice they should adopt on matters where there is no established local practice in their community. (The question was rare centuries ago because couples followed the minhagim and rulings of the place they lived; now, most cities have separate communities based on *edah* [ethnic subgroup]). The Tashbetz[7] and most recent poskim,[8] who say that the wife adopts the practices of her husband's edah, make little or no distinction between minhag and halachic rulings.

Is the wife's following of her husband's practices a valid precedent for children living at home? We cannot delve into a full explanation, but it appears that the level of interconnectedness, the potential for conflict, and the prospect of staying under one roof for many decades are issues that are qualitatively more significant for spouses than for children. Thus, one cannot conclude that children are automatically "drawn after" their father's practices. On the other hand, numerous sources assume that children follow their father's lead under normal circumstances, even in the absence of a community-wide practice. For example, the Maharam Shick[9] says that the fact that a young adult living with his father refrains from the same things as his father is not a sign that he has accepted these practices indefinitely. Actually, one is expected to conform when possible, for leniency or stringency, even to the halachic practices of one's unrelated host in order to

---

7. III, 179.
8. See *Yabia Omer* v, *Orach Chayim* 37; *Noam*, vol. 23.
9. *Orach Chayim* 249.

avoid acrimony. This is all the more so regarding a father who not only links the child to the chain of tradition, but whom the child is obligated to honor. Yet, there are times that children may act differently from their father even in his presence.[10] Much depends on the father's tolerance and on other circumstances.[11]

In summary, a father's practice need not determine halachic rulings for his child who is mature enough to choose his own path. However, his approach is the assumed point of departure, and his feelings should be considered, especially in his presence.

---

10. Compare *Rama, Yoreh Deah* 112:15 and *Shulchan Aruch, Orach Chayim* 168:5.
11. See *V'Aleihu Lo Yibol* I, p. 64.

H-13: Use of Permanent Cosmetics

Question: There is an excellent cosmetic system whereby an injection in the eyebrow lasts for at least three years. Is this included in the prohibition of tattooing (*k'tovet ka'aka*)?

Answer: It is forbidden to make a mark on one's body by means of piercing the skin with a needle and inserting any type of coloring. There are opinions that hold that, since the Torah refers to this prohibition as "writing,"[1] one violates the *mitzva* only if he writes a letter of the alphabet. However, the Ra'avad and Rash Mishantz[2] state that the Torah prohibition applies to any sort of marking. In the works of several other *poskim*,[3] there are implications that they agree to this approach. Additionally, even those who rule out a Torah prohibition in the case where only markings are made seem to agree that there still is a rabbinic prohibition.

Rav Ezra Basri[4] suggests that there may not be an absolute rabbinic prohibition regarding non-writing markings, but only a lower level, subjective concern of *marit ayin*,[5] which might not apply in our case.[6] Based on additional leniencies related to minority opinions, he allowed a woman who had no eyebrows to undergo the treatment. In justifying his opinion, he refers to the halachic weight given to steps to avoid embarrassment, as it allows us, in certain instances, to push aside rabbinic laws and to rely upon minority opinions. The analysis of our mentor, Rav Shaul Yisraeli, is not as lenient as Rav Basri's. Additionally, one should

---

1. *Vayikra* 19:28.
2. Referenced by the *Acharonim* cited below.
3. See *Minchat Chinuch* #253; *Pitchei Teshuva, Yoreh Deah* 180:1; *BeMareh HaBazak* II, p. 81.
4. *Techumin* X, pp. 282–287.
5. Onlookers may confuse an action with a prohibition.
6. See article, *Techumin* ibid.

note that even Rav Basri does not seem to permit the practice for the average woman.

Some *Rishonim*[7] define the prohibited act of tattooing as something that remains on the body *kol hayamim* (literally, all the days). Thus, one might claim that eyeliner that lasts for "only" a few years would be halachically different. However, the Nimukei Yosef[8] describes k'tovet ka'aka as lasting "a long time." No one explicitly takes issue with the Nimukei Yosef, and one might say that something that remains for three years is sufficiently permanent to be called *kol hayamim*. Even if there is no Torah level prohibition, there likely is a rabbinic one. Therefore, one should not be lenient regarding such sub-dermal marking unless it can be classified as lasting "a short time."

---

7. *Ritva* on *Makkot* 21a and *Sefer HaChinuch* #253.
8. *Makkot* 21a.

H-14: Hatarat Nedarim to Suspend a Good Practice[1]

Question: I have always been careful not to eat or drink anything prior to *davening*, even on Shabbat. Now that I'm serving as a rabbi on *shelichut* (an emissary from Israel), giving a *shiur* before davening and often serving as *chazan*, it is quite difficult for me to concentrate without having eaten. Do I need *hatarat nedarim* (nullification of vows) before following the standard halacha? As I understand it, I can drink water, tea or coffee. May I put sugar in the tea and coffee?

Answer: One may drink water, tea and coffee before davening, especially if it enables him to function properly during davening. Regarding sugar in the tea and coffee, the Mishna Berura[2] generally objects, but Rav Ovadya Yosef justifies the common practice of adding sugar.[3]

The question of hatarat nedarim is quite interesting. The Rama[4] says that even those who have the custom to fast on the day before Rosh Hashana may eat at a *brit mila* that day. The Magen Avraham[5] says that hatarat nedarim is not needed[6] and that this leniency can be extended to one who is mildly sick.[7] However, the Shulchan Aruch[8] states that one who wants to forgo this fast because he is not healthy needs hatarat nedarim, and the Rama's silence implies that he agrees. Why does the Rama require hatarat

---

1. Based on *BeMareh HaBazak* II, p. 12–13
2. 89:22.
3. *Yabia Omer* IV, *Orach Chayim* 11.
4. *Orach Chayim* 581:2.
5. 581:12.
6. See parallel case in *Rama, Orach Chayim* 568:2.
7. See also *Mishna Berura* 581:19.
8. *Yoreh Deah* 214:1.

nedarim for sickness but not for a brit mila? The Shach[9] claims that when people adopt the custom of fasting, they mentally exclude cases of brit mila but do not anticipate sickness.

The Dagul Merevavah[10] argues with the Shach's explanation, as he considers it based on a difficult set of assumptions. He reconciles the apparently contradictory sources with the following distinction. One does not require hatarat nedarim to *temporarily* suspend a good *minhag* under specific circumstances, such as the case of the brit mila. He claims that the situation of the Shulchan Aruch[11] is different, as it concerns one who plans to stop his practice of fasting permanently because of a weakened constitution. The Dagul Merevavah implies that his thesis goes along the lines of the aforementioned Magen Avraham. The simple understanding of the Magen Avraham, however, is not identical with that of the Dagul Merevavah. The Magen Avraham differentiates between one who fasts due to a widespread practice and one who goes out of his way to accept a stringent practice. In the latter case, one requires hatarat nedarim, and the simple implication is that this applies even if he wants to stop the minhag temporarily.[12]

Based on the Dagul Merevavah, Rav Mordechai Eliyahu ruled that if you want to drink before davening only during the period of your shelichut, which presents a special situation, you would not require hatarat nedarim.

---

9. Ad loc.::2.
10. Ad loc.
11. Ibid.
12. See *L'vushei Srad*, ad loc.

Section I:
Family Law

I-1 Public Sanctions Against One Refusing to Give a Get

Question: A man in our *shul*, who has been instrumental in the shul's operations and finances for some time, divorced his wife a few years ago. For whatever reasons (I never asked) he did not give his wife a *get*. This man is never given an *aliya* and is shunned by our rabbi. Although I understand that it is proper to give a get, I question whether our rabbi has the halachic right to treat him so harshly.

Answer: We cannot discuss the specific case to which you refer, as we do not know its particulars. However, we must speak strongly about the phenomenon you describe.

One of the people whom we are most required to help, by searching for a legitimate halachic remedy and otherwise, is an *aguna*. An aguna[1] is a woman who is unable to live with her husband, either because he is missing or because they are incompatible, but to whom she is halachically "chained" because she lacks a get or evidence of his death. Although her main, practical problem is that she is unable to remarry, the feeling of helplessness from which she suffers creates one of the most tragic situations that exist. Only someone who has been personally involved in such a situation can fully appreciate its severity.

At times, a woman can be an aguna without anyone being at fault (e.g., the husband is in an irreversible coma). However, some women are in this horrible predicament because their husbands are spiteful or have monetary or other demands. This behavior is unacceptable! It is as morally wrong as the behavior of one who stalks his ex-wife because of his animosity toward her! If a husband has grievances against his wife, he may raise them in court, preferably a *beit din*. The beit din may side with him; it may side

---

1. From the Hebrew root *ogen* – anchor.

against him. However, the Jewish community should not tolerate a husband taking the law into his own hands by withholding a get.

At different times and places in history, religious courts had the ability to physically coerce a stubborn husband to give a get, when a get was mandated in the most clear-cut manner. (There are husbands in Israel who are in jail for that purpose.) In cases that are a little less clear-cut, a *harchaka d'Rabbeinu Tam* can be employed. This is a painful form of publicly shunning the husband, not only in shul, but also in commercial and personal settings.[2] Withholding *aliyot* is only a simple means of pressure. Nowadays, outside of Israel, the main recourse is usually moral and (moderate) public pressure. Tragically, weak public response often results in the husband feeling only mild or, in some cases, no pressure.

Again, we cannot comment on the specific case that you raise. However, if the rabbinical courts have instructed your acquaintance to give a get and your rabbi has been asked to ensure some form of communal disapproval, then that is the *very least* that should be done. Others should follow the rabbi's lead, not question it, and should not allow their good intentions to be misdirected.

---

2. See *Even HaEzer* 154.

I-2: Giving a Wedding Band Before the Wedding

Question: Usually a man gives his fiancée a nice, expensive engagement ring well before their wedding. I understand that it has no religious significance. The wedding band, though, is traditionally standardized (no stones or engraving, etc.). May I give the eventual wedding band, which will be used in the ceremony, as an engagement ring? I would buy the nicer, more expensive ring with a stone after the wedding.

Answer: First of all, mazal tov. Allow us to give some halachic advice, not a halachic ruling. (Of course, there is also the important issue of how your fiancée will feel about not getting the nicer ring right away, but since we do not know you and that is not our field, we'll leave that issue out.) Let us deal with two surmountable halachic issues that your suggestion would cause.

To effect the marriage, the groom has to present the bride with something that *he owns* that is of value.[1] At first glance, if you will have already given the wedding band as a present, it's your fiancée's, not yours. It is true that she could transfer ownership back to you before the wedding. However, since she expects to receive it back soon thereafter, we must deal with the question,[2] when one gives an object to another with the understanding that it will be returned soon, whether or not he has intent for a full *kinyan* (transfer of ownership). In the final analysis, almost all agree that the transfer is effective.[3] It would be even better if your fiancée would state explicitly that she is aware of the issue and intends to give you the band as a full present or would sell it to you. Since

---

1. *Even HaEzer* 28.
2. *Gittin* 20b.
3. See *Pitchei Teshuva* 28:28; *Otzar HaPoskim* ad loc.

this needs to be done with halachic care, this could be "asking for trouble" and is frowned upon by some *poskim*.[4]

One could also raise questions about the impression given by a single woman wearing a classic wedding band, which is usually a sign of marriage. This situation touches on a halachic topic known as *sivlonot*. The details are both complicated and fluid, depending on local practice,[5] but here is the basic idea. In some situations where a fiancé gives his fiancée gifts, there is concern that they may be married already by the time the present was given. This can be for one or both of the following reasons. The giving of the gifts itself can serve as *kiddushin* (initial stage of the marriage process), which does not need specifically a *chupa* or an officiating rabbi to take effect. It can, alternatively, be a sign that at some time in the past, there must have been kiddushin (or else he wouldn't have given her those presents). Based on a variety of factors, as reported already many hundreds of years ago,[6] this concern basically doesn't apply in modern-day society. However, one could raise the issue that, in our days in many places, a certain type of ring, which we call a wedding band, is indeed a very strong sign of marriage. It is possible that the almost forgotten laws of sivlonot should apply to such a case. So again, it may be "asking for trouble" for an engaged woman to receive from her fiancé something which is normally a sign that she is married.

In truth, we feel that both issues are surmountable, and it is the job of a rabbi to solve problems. However, it is also the responsibility of a rabbi to have things run smoothly so that problems are kept to a minimum and there are no grounds to cast aspersions. Everyone rightfully prefers that his or her wedding process be valid without any questions. So, unless there is some type of unusually pressing situation that we are not aware of, we strongly

---

4. See *HaNisu'in K'Hilchatam* 7:18.
5. See *Kiddushin* 50b and *Even HaEzer* 45.
6. See *Shulchan Aruch, Even HaEzer* 45:2.

suggest that you not give a wedding band until the wedding. In case of need, you can discuss the matter with your officiating rabbi, who can decide what to do based on the circumstances.

I-3: A Woman Performing a Brit Mila

Question: Does halacha permit a Jewish woman to perform a *brit mila*?[1]

Answer: The Shulchan Aruch[2] rules that a woman may perform a brit mila, although it is preferable that an adult male do so. The Rama (which is the primary source for Ashkenazic practical halacha) cites an opinion that holds that women may not perform the brit, and he states that the custom follows this position.

This disagreement stems from the *gemara*,[3] which mentions varied views of *Tanna'im* regarding whether a brit mila done by a non-Jew is valid. Rav and Rabbi Yochanan argue concerning the reason why a non-Jew's brit mila would be disqualified. Rav said it is because they do not belong to the group that was specifically commanded to have a brit. Rabbi Yochanan said that only one who is circumcised may circumcise others.

The gemara points out that, according to Rav, a woman is disqualified because brit mila doesn't apply to her. However, according to Rabbi Yochanan, a Jewish woman, as a member of the covenantal nation, is considered as if she is circumcised and, therefore, is qualified. Interestingly, a circumcised non-Jew is considered uncircumcised because he is not part of the covenant of which the brit mila is a sign. (Note that "brit" means covenant.) The *Rishonim* disagree as to which opinion should be accepted as halacha, as do the aforementioned Shulchan Aruch and Rama.

We conclude with the gemara's attempted proof that a woman may perform a brit mila. After all, Tziporah circumcised Eliezer to save Moshe's life.[4] The gemara, however, deflects the proof by

---

1. Circumcision.
2. *Yoreh Deah* 264:1.
3. *Avoda Zara* 27a.
4. *Shemot* 4:25

noting that it is possible that she gave the rock to someone else to do the brit or that she only started the mila, but Moshe completed the job.

I-4: Which Relatives Are Invalid Witnesses?

Question: What are the general rules of distant relatives serving as witnesses on a *ketuba*?[1] In particular, I want to know about the bride's mother's sister's husband (uncle through marriage).

Answer: We will start with the background and some basic rules. The laws of people being invalid to testify about their relatives are derived from the following *pasuk*: "Fathers shall not be killed because of sons, and sons shall not be killed because of fathers."[2] The *gemara* determines that "because of" refers to testimony by relatives and that these laws apply to all forms of testimony.[3] It also derives the degree of relationship that is disqualified by analyzing linguistic nuances. The Shulchan Aruch presents the details in the section regarding monetary law.[4] Let us note that a ketuba is primarily a monetary document and does not effectuate the marriage. The requirements for witnesses for the marriage are basically the same.[5]

The basic halachic terminology follows. A first-level relationship (parent/child; siblings) is called *rishon b'rishon*. The next generation relationship (first cousins) is called *sheni b'sheni*. Members of these first groups may not testify for one another (or together). Second cousins are *shlishi b'shlishi* and are valid witnesses. Halacha also deals with mixed generations. Using your case as an example, an uncle is a *rishon b'sheni*, which is a closer relationship than cousins are, and is certainly an invalid witness.

What about the fact that the uncle in question is only an uncle through marriage? The Torah, in forbidding relations with

---

1. Marriage contract.
2. *Devarim* 24:16.
3. *Sanhedrin* 28a.
4. *Choshen Mishpat* 33.
5. *Even HaEzer* 42:5.

an uncle's wife, calls her an aunt.[6] The gemara[7] derives from this that relationships through marriage are *much the same* as those of blood relatives. There are two areas of practical difference, however. Consider a borderline relation such as a great-uncle (*shlishi b'rishon*). If the relationship is through marriage, then the relatives can testify for or with each other.[8] Additionally, if cousins (sheni b'sheni) are double in-laws, then they can testify. In other words, husbands of two female first cousins may testify together,[9] although this too should be avoided.[10] Regarding double in-laws of uncles and nephews (rishon b'sheni), who are closer, there are two opinions in the Shulchan Aruch,[11] and the Rama is lenient *b'd'ieved* (after the fact). Although the *uncle in question* has this type of relationship with the groom, *everyone* would agree that he *is invalid* because he is a single in-law of the bride. After all, a witness may not be related to either the bride or the groom, as, at the wedding, he is testifying about both of them. Thus, the question of a double in-law of the couple will never arise at a wedding.[12]

Valid witnesses are required to effectuate a marriage or, in this case, ensure a valid ketuba [which is (rabbinically) required for the couple to live together]. Witnesses for a ketuba should preferably have a working knowledge of its language and basic laws. In addition to the laws of relatives, witnesses should be beyond suspicion of sins that could render them invalid. Decisions regarding witnesses are the domain of the *mesader kiddushin* (officiating rabbi). As he is responsible to ensure that everything is done properly, he should be allowed the opportunity to make calm, informed decisions and not be pressured to accept someone as

---

6. *Vayikra* 18:14.
7. *Sanhedrin* 28b.
8. *Shulchan Aruch, Choshen Mishpat* 33:3.
9. Ibid.:4.
10. *Rama* ad loc.
11. Ibid.
12. The question of double in-laws is possible at weddings where two relatives, who are not related to the bride or the groom, testify together.

a witness just because the family feels close or obligated to him. The rabbi can make a decision concerning how "distant" a relative is only after full disclosure of the relationship, which people sometimes forget to make. In your case, halachically, this uncle (by marriage) is not distant at all, and it is good that you had the foresight to determine this with time to spare.

I-5: Pidyon HaBen for an Adult – Still His Father's Mitzva?

Question: I am my parents' firstborn son, and my father recently told me that my planned *pidyon haben* was delayed because of my illness and was never done. (My parents were not fully observant.) Is there something I should do now?

Answer: At first glance, it sounds like you require a pidyon haben, as the *mitzva* does not expire. However, first we have to try to determine if you definitely require it, and then we can discuss how to proceed.

Not every firstborn male needs a pidyon haben. The main exemptions are as follows: if either of your parents is the child of a male *kohen* or *levi*, if your mother had a miscarriage prior to your birth, or if you were born in a caesarean delivery. Also ascertain from your father if, after all these years, he is sure that there was no pidyon haben. It is possible that the rabbi/kohen who was to have done the pidyon did so in a quick, halachic procedure that your father may have forgotten about, while he remembers that the party was canceled. If there is uncertainty, please contact us again, as we cannot give a blanket rule in advance.

Assuming that you need a pidyon haben, we have to deal with an interesting, relevant dispute among halachic authorities. A father is required to redeem his son. However, if he fails to do so, the son becomes obligated to redeem himself once he is *bar mitzva*.[1] The question, though, is whether, at that point, only the son is obligated or if the father's obligation remains. If a grown son does his own pidyon haben, the halachic obligation has certainly been discharged. However, differing opinions arise in a situation where the father is now willing to do this mitzva, which, for whatever reason, was delayed.

---

1. *Kiddushin* 29a.

347

The Rashba[2] contends that since the mitzva of pidyon haben creates a monetary obligation upon the father's property from the outset and nothing was done to remove it, the father's obligation remains. The *gemara*[3] states that if one has enough money to redeem only himself *or* his son, he should redeem himself because the mitzva that relates directly to himself has precedence. From this, the Rivash[4] infers that the son's obligation to redeem himself is the primary obligation, and the father's practical responsibility to redeem his baby is due only to the fact that a small child is incapable of performing the pidyon haben himself. When the child grows up, he alone is obligated. Many later authorities have debated the matter, and it is difficult to say that one approach is more accepted or acceptable than the other.[5] How then should you proceed? Should you or your father do your pidyon haben?

We suggest the following. As you know your father better than we do, try to determine if he would want to be involved in the pidyon haben. If you think he wouldn't mind, there is no problem doing it yourself. If he wants to do it, it is possible to ensure that the right person will end up doing the mitzva. One such halachic method is as follows: Your father gives you the money and says that if the mitzva is his, then you should be his agent to do the pidyon on his behalf.[6] You prepare another sum of your own money and physically give the two sums of money to the kohen with the appropriate blessings and statements. You just state that it is being done on condition that the halachic redemption should relate to the person who should rightfully be doing it and to his money. The process is slightly complicated. Since few kohanim have done a pidyon haben in a case where a person is doing it for himself, you will anyway need a learned kohen and/or a rabbi to

---

2. *Shut* II, 321.
3. *Kiddushin* 29a.
4. *Shut* 131.
5. See *Pidyon HaBen K'Hilchato* 1:(16).
6. See *Pidyon HaBen K'Hilchato* 1:15–17 regarding pidyon haben by means of an agent.

make the appropriate adjustments in the text of the blessings and statements. We would be happy to provide an explanation to the kohen should he desire it.

In any case, it is both important (a full Torah law) and not as complicated as it might sound to do the pidyon haben. While it is customary to have a *minyan* present,[7] it can be done privately to avoid embarrassing your father.

---

7. *Otzar Pidyon HaBen* 18:2.

I-6: A Delayed Pidyon HaBen at Night

Question: Our son's *pidyon haben* (redemption of the firstborn) falls on Shabbat, so it is pushed off until after Shabbat. Must we do it on *Motzaei Shabbat*, which is late this time of year, or may we do it the next day (before nightfall), when it is easier for our guests and us?

Answer: Mazal tov! You seem to assume that Motzaei Shabbat is the halachically preferable time. Let's first check that assumption, and then we will be more equipped to deal with your specific question.

The Torah says that pidyon haben is to be done from the time the child is a month old.[1] The Talmud is replete with references to its being carried out after 30 days. There are two basic ways to determine when this time has come. The Shach[2] says that pidyon haben should take place after an astronomical month (which is slightly more than 29½ days). The Magen Avraham[3] says it is performed on the 31st day of the child's life, which, depending on the time of birth and the time of the pidyon haben, could be anywhere from just over 29 full days after birth to just under 31. Our clear *minhag* is to never do a pidyon haben before day 31. However, it is less clear whether this is sufficient or whether we must also ensure that an astronomical month is complete.

If we require both the 31st day and an astronomical month, then we can understand the rationale for the Shach's[4] minhag not to do a pidyon haben at night. This is because it is common that the night of the 31st precedes the passing of an astronomical

---

1. *Bamidbar* 18:16.
2. *Yoreh Deah* 305:19.
3. 339:8.
4. Ibid.:12.

month.[5] Although most Ashkenazim follow the Shach's *minhag*,[6] the reason behind it is less accepted. This is crucial for our case. The Sha'arei Teshuva[7] says that we do a pidyon haben during the day in order to better publicize the *mitzva*. This factor is less applicable today since people are more available to take part in such mitzva events at night than they are during the day. Other more esoteric reasons are proposed as well.[8] One practical application that highlights the difference between the reasons for doing a pidyon haben during the day is when a pidyon haben is delayed until Motzaei Shabbat. In this case, as the month is undoubtedly over, the first reason does not apply, and it becomes appropriate to do the pidyon haben at night.[9] According to the other explanations, however, a delayed pidyon haben is no different from a regular one.

Assuming that it is acceptable to do the pidyon haben on Motzaei Shabbat, is it preferable, and, if so, how preferable? Although the prompt performance of a *brit mila* is more pressing than that of a pidyon haben, the Shulchan Aruch[10] does say to do a pidyon haben "*miyad* (right away) and not let the mitzva be delayed." His source[11] seems to base the need for such diligence on the general recommendation not to delay mitzvot. While we do not want to underestimate this factor, general diligence does not get most of us up by sunrise to do the various mitzvot of the day. Additionally, the importance of doing a pidyon haben "right away" when it has already been delayed may be diminished.[12]

After learning some of the sources, let us put things in

---

5. See *Dagul Merevava* on *Magen Avraham* 568:10.

6. *Pidyon HaBen K'Hilchato* 6:7.

7. 568:8.

8. *See Pidyon HaBen K'Hilchato* ibid.:(23).

9. *Dagul Merevava*, ibid.; *Mishna Berura* 568:20 – see their context. It may be preferable in some special cases.

10. *Yoreh Deah* 305:11.

11. See *Beit Yosef, Yoreh Deah* 305 in the name of the Rosh.

12. *Tosafot, Mo'ed Katan* 8b; *Magen Avraham* 568:10.

perspective. Any time from Motzaei Shabbat till nightfall on Sunday is valid. It is unclear whether, all things being equal, it is preferable to have a delayed pidyon haben on Motzaei Shabbat or the next day.[13] Either way, the halachic difference is not great. Note that it is prevalent nowadays to schedule a standard pidyon haben during the afternoon. Although there is a delay of a few hours, there is an advantage regarding the number of participants who celebrate the mitzva.[14] Therefore, feel free to do what works best for you, based on religious and/or personal considerations. As you have probably learned, the birth of a firstborn brings much elation but also a fair share of fatigue and even emotional stress. May you enjoy the mitzva of pidyon haben with peace of mind.

---

13. *Otzar Pidyon HaBen* 17:2 claims that the minhag is to do it on Motzaei Shabbat.
14. See ibid. 16:(9).

Section J:
Monetary Law

J-1: When is Compromise Appropriate?

Question: I am a student who has sold a product to friends on behalf of a businessman for a percentage of the sales. I mentioned to the owner my concern about a safe place to keep the sales money until I would find time to give him the money, but we decided "it would be okay." I thought that if something happened to the money, it would be his loss. It turns out that a significant amount of the money was stolen, and the owner expects me to pay. I told him that I didn't think I had to pay, and that we could go to a *din Torah* (rabbinical court case). Then the idea arose that instead of having a din Torah, we would make a *p'shara* (compromise). Which way am I better off with?

Answer: First of all, we have a problem giving advice that could afford you a monetary advantage at someone else's expense. The *mishna* in Pirkei Avot warns us to avoid being like *orchei hadayanim* (translated, in modern Hebrew, as lawyers). There are different opinions exactly when this applies.[1] Our policy, as a service dedicated to helping Jews further their Jewish knowledge and practice, is to not take sides in disputes between litigants, as honorable as either side might be.

The next thing you need to understand is what "I am better off" should mean. While society, in general, concentrates on how to get every penny one can, the Torah teaches that it is at least as important to pay every penny he owes. Now, it is true that when one is not sure whether he owes money, the halacha often is that "the burden of proof is upon the one who wants to extract money," and the one who is "holding on" need not volunteer to pay. However, if the defendant knows he owes the money, he is obligated to pay everything he owes unless the plaintiff relinquishes his rights.

---

1. See *Shulchan Aruch, Choshen Mishpat* 17:9.

P'shara, whether by means of arbitration or mediation, is the best way to solve a conflict.[2] Even a *beit din* (rabbinical court) that is requested to adjudicate should try to convince the parties to agree to a compromise.[3] However, that is the case as long as each of the litigants believes that he is (or, at least, is likely to be) correct. The Shulchan Aruch[4] rules: "Someone who has been demanded to pay money is forbidden to search for means to avoid paying in order that the other party will agree to make a p'shara with him and relinquish his rights to the rest of the money."

Realize that if you want us to look into the facts, as you present them, we cannot assure you that you deserve to win the case, as we do not know how the other party would respond to your claims. We might, though, determine that, even according to your version of the story, you are responsible for some or all of the disputed funds. Then you would be bound to pay what you owe, and a p'shara would not be possible for that portion of the money. You would be responsible to inform the other side how much you concede, so that any money he would relinquish through compromise would be based on informed consent, not ignorance.

Although, as mentioned, one must normally pay that which he knows the beit din would require to pay were it to adjudicate, there are exceptions. For example, if you are correct, in principle, but are unable to prove your claims, then you could take *certain* steps to pressure the other side to a p'shara rather than simply lose the din Torah.[5] Other circumstances and steps are discussed[6] but not all are clearly permitted. You are permitted to appeal to your counterpart's sense of fair play and to encourage him to go beyond the letter of the law. This would justify telling your counterpart that, although halachically you have to pay (if that is the

---

2. See ibid. 12:2.
3. Ibid.
4. Ibid.:6.
5. *Tumim* 12:5.
6. See *Pitchei Teshuva, Choshen Mishpat* 12:8.

case), you have claims that strengthen your side morally. This is permitted even after a formal verdict of the beit din has been handed down.[7]

OUTCOME: The student requested that we try to determine his status. Based on his story alone, he seemed to owe at least most of the money [details beyond our present scope]. He informed the other side of this and appealed to him with a variety of claims; they reached a gentlemanly compromise somewhere in the middle, to the satisfaction of each.

---

7. See *Shach, Choshen Mishpat* 12:6.

J-2: A Matchmaker's Demand for a Non-Standard Fee

Question: I was, *baruch HaShem*, successful in making a *shidduch*.[1] I don't want *shadchanus gelt*[2] in the form of money or a present. Rather, I want the couple to agree to (try their absolute hardest to) make a shidduch within two years. I know that there are people who really need to be set up and are not getting the help they need and that, often, married couples forget their friends after they are fortunate enough to find each other. If this couple pays me, they may not work as hard as I feel they should. On the other hand, do they need to give a monetary payment in order to get the *segula*[3] of *sholom bayis*[4] and children? Also, if they don't succeed in two years, can I get the money?

Answer: The rules of a *shadchan's*[5] pay depend on the local custom.[6] (In many communities, no formal payment is customary.) A shadchan may forgo her right to payment without negative repercussions.[7] Thus, you need not receive monetary payment. However, after the shidduch has been made without prior stipulation, the shadchan cannot demand more or a different type of payment than is customary.

Even if the couple were to agree to work on shiduchim as payment, problems may arise. First, how will you decide on the amount of effort they must exert? Success does not always depend

---

1. Matrimonial match.
2. Pay due to a successful matchmaker.
3. A situation or act that helps bring Divine assistance in a certain area.
4. Domestic harmony.
5. Matchmaker; a female should grammatically be called a *shadchanit*, but in a mix of English and Yiddish, the speaker usually uses shadchan for a woman as well.
6. *Rama, Choshen Mishpat* 185:10; *Pitchei Teshuva, Even HaEzer* 50:16; others.
7. *Pitchei Teshuva* ibid; *Pitchei Choshen* III, 14:3.

upon energy expended, nor is failure a proof of laziness. Thus, if they did not succeed within two years, they would not be obligated to pay you.

One possibility is for you to forgo your fee on the condition that the couple will succeed in a shidduch within two years. The couple does not have to accept your condition and may either pay you immediately or agree to try their luck.

Be careful to present your ideas peacefully and not to cause unpleasantness. Even though your intent is very noble, it does not justify quarreling. Hopefully, your dedication will spread to others.

Let us conclude with a *beracha* that you will succeed in many more shidduchim.

J-3: If and How to Make Children Pay for Household Damage

Question: Two of my children (who are above *bar mitzva*) caused damage in the house, entirely by their recklessness. I think they should cover the cost of the repairs, which is significant. Each child works around the house and gets paid for it. May I dock their pay and in that way receive payment for the damage?

Answer: There are three possible approaches to take to solve your dilemma. One approach is to figure out how you could get the money from the children in a legal, halachic manner. Without knowing the particulars, we would note that the great majority of families spend enough on their children that they can find ways to withhold funds to make up for the damage. Another approach is to come to a totally informal agreement. This could entail appealing to the children's sense of fair play to see if they are willing to volunteer (partial) payment or deciding to forgo the money altogether as one more act of love. The third approach is to present the children with what the consequences should be according to the Torah and to allow that information to serve as the basis for a *p'shara hakerova ladin* (compromise that resembles the law) at which you Can arrive. It is difficult to imagine cases where the first, harshest approach would be educationally appropriate. Between the second and third approaches, it depends very much on the dynamics of the case, the relationships, and the personalities involved. It is, of course, up to your discretion to educate your children as you decide. We will share with you some basic, halachic guidelines to discuss with them. Certainly, we cannot give a halachic ruling after receiving only a brief description from one party.

Whereas children under bar mitzva are exempt from paying for the damage they cause,[1] those above bar mitzva are ob-

---

1. *Shulchan Aruch, Choshen Mishpat* 424:8.

ligated. The fact that parents support them has some halachic ramifications that classify children above bar mitzva in the same category as those below bar mitzva, but not in this regard. There is a rabbinic institution to exempt a wife from paying for damage she causes to her husband's property in order to maintain family tranquility.[2] There is some question how far-reaching this rule is,[3] including whether it applies only to a wife or to other members of the household.[4] However, in the case of damage caused by recklessness, clearly no exemption applies. Thus, in theory, one could sue his children for such damage. Of course, the potential emotional damage that insensitive handling of the situation could cause generally precludes that option.

Let us assume that you will assure your children that you will not take away money, even in a legal form, but will just withhold certain gratuities. Can you withhold money for jobs that the children perform around the house? Many parents expect their children to do significant chores without pay. Although your children are not used to that arrangement, you could implement that policy until the damage is worked off. The question then becomes: what if your children (respectfully?) refuse to do the work if they are not getting paid? Children, certainly at that age, are required to perform the *mitzva* of *kibud av va'em*,[5] which includes helping out their parents, as long as they don't have to lay out money to do so.[6] On the other hand, it is hard to define the exact limits of what a child is required to do without payment to help healthy parents. It is also hard to predict how the process will affect relationships.

We hope and pray that you find the right balance between accommodating your children by understanding that damage

---

2. *Shulchan Aruch, Even HaEzer* 80:17.
3. See *Chelkat Mechokek*, ad loc.:29.
4. See *Shai LaMorah*, ad loc.
5. Respecting one's parents.
6. *Shulchan Aruch, Yoreh Deah* 240: 4, 5.

does occur and teaching them about responsibility for inexcusable mistakes. Remember that the halachic information is only one factor to help arrive at that balance.

J-4: Non-Refundable Enrollment Fee

Question: Our daughter was accepted by a seminary, and we paid $1,500 as a non-refundable registration fee to hold a spot. She decided to attend a different institution. When we informed the first seminary, they refused to return the money. Given that another girl has already replaced our daughter, do they have the right to retain the money?

Answer: We wish you in advance *nachas* from your daughter's spiritual gains during her studies in whatever fine institution she will attend. The willingness of people like you to part with their children for a while and to spend much hard-earned money has revolutionized our community. We will address both the halachic and moral elements of the question, as Torah institutions should be concerned about both. We will start with institutions' rationale for this common policy, which is important regarding both elements. (We cannot say anything authoritative without hearing both sides' claims in *beit din*.)

Firstly, these institutions incur heavy expenses well before students arrive. These include transportation for recruitment teams and tens of hours of administrative work in addition to various other costs, which, in total, reach tens of thousands of dollars. It is logical that applicants should help defray these costs and that those who complete the process should pay more. However, $1,500 seems too much just to defray costs.

The main logic of the payments' non-refundable nature is that it is preventative. Often institutions will end up with fewer students (and less money to cover expenses) if students can freely change their minds. In addition, a student's change of decision can have a domino effect on her friends, which can severely damage an institution. Even if they can be replaced numerically, in the meantime the "top" wait-listed students usually commit elsewhere. Replacing a few top students with others who are marginally suitable can affect the character of a school's student body and its reputation in the short and even the long term.

The fact that the money is non-refundable also puts the student and parents in a mind-set of certainty about their choice. Then, like an engaged couple, one does not consider changing her mind, unless a serious mistake surfaces. This mind-set usually benefits all concerned. Students remain positive, and seminaries can hire a staff that suits the incoming student body. While $1,500 sounds high (and might be so), were it much lower, it would not sufficiently deter cancellations.

Now we can examine the halachic issues. You hired a seminary to teach your daughter. Usually, an employer can break an employment agreement and not pay the agreed-upon wages, even if a *kinyan*[1] was done, as long as the worker can find alternative employment (i.e. another student).[2] However, there is a halachic rule that states that conditions that are made to change standard, financial arrangements are binding.[3] You agreed to the stipulation of non-refundable payment and made the agreement final by transferring the money unconditionally.

Your only claim is that an *asmachta*, an exaggerated obligation that one accepted because he did not think it would come to fruition, is not binding.[4] However, the Shulchan Aruch[5] says that, even regarding asmachta, if one already gave money as a guarantee, he cannot demand it back. Although the Rama[6] argues, one cannot extract money from a *muchzak*[7] when there is a serious contending position. The seminary may have additional claims to

---

1. An act of finalization.
2. *Shulchan Aruch, Choshen Mishpat* 333:2; see *Pitchei Choshen* III, 10:7.
3. *Ketubot* 56a.
4. *Choshen Mishpat* 207.
5. Ad loc.:11.
6. Ad loc.
7. One who has possession of the matter in dispute.

justify its position.[8] At the risk of over-simplifying a complicated matter, it does not appear, based on what we know, that you can halachically *demand* the money back.

Just as it is a *mitzva* for you to see the seminary's side of the matter, so it is for the seminary to see your side. If you can convince the administrators that: 1) you were confident that your daughter would attend, 2) something came up which caused you to change that decision, and 3) it turns out that the seminary was not seriously damaged by the withdrawal, then we hope they will return much of the deposit.

---

8. See ibid.:16, regarding penalty clauses to prevent damage, and *Tosafot, Bava Metzia* 66a regarding accepted practices.

J-5: Charging a Fixed Rate Which May Prove Inaccurate

Question: I do editing work for papers that are being presented for acceptance by scholarly publications. I am trying to work out a system for charging that is fair both to my clients and to me. The problem is that it is very difficult to anticipate how long a given paper will take to edit. The most equitable system is to charge by the hour, but most clients demand a fixed rate in advance. Therefore, I usually charge according to a system I have developed for estimates. However, sometimes I receive significantly less than I deserve because the work was more difficult than anticipated, while, at other times, the opposite is true. I feel bad taking more than I deserve, but if I return money when I come out ahead and don't ask for more when I estimate to my detriment, I'll be losing out. What should I do?

Answer: Our favorite questions are monetary ones that are asked not to try to gain money but to make sure that the money a person gets is deserved.

The halachic issue involved is *onaah* (overcharging or underpaying), a Torah prohibition with monetary consequences, including returning the extra money or voiding the transaction when the ona'ah is significant enough. Among the cases where the totality of these laws does not apply are the sale of land[1] and the wages of a worker, which are indirectly compared to land.[2] However, regarding cases where one is paid by the job (as you usually are) and not by time, the Shulchan Aruch[3] rules that the regular laws apply. Actually, even regarding land, the *prohibition* of overpricing applies, with the difference being in the monetary ramifications

---

1. *Bava Metzia* 56a.
2. *Shulchan Aruch, Choshen Mishpat* 227:33.
3. Ibid.:36.

once the prohibition has occurred. In any case, since you want to do the right thing, such a loophole would not be fitting.

You imply that one might look at the fairness of pricing on average over the course of the business, in general, as opposed to the appropriateness of each, individual fee. Of course, if a certain price is unfairly high, it doesn't help that someone else got the better of you a different time. Even if the same person got a good deal in the past because you decided not to demand compensation at the time (thus relinquishing any possible rights), you cannot make up for it by charging too much later. However, the fact that you often undercharge is a relevant factor for the following reason.

Overpricing is forbidden when one goes beyond the accepted range of prices. Several factors help determine what the range is. One of them is the chance that the work will be much greater than average. Consider this example. A taxi driver's meter *usually* reads $40 for a trip to midtown Manhattan. If he takes someone at a fixed rate, he has a right to ask for more than the median rate because he sometimes sits in traffic for a long time. His set price of $50 represents the market rate, which takes both opportunities and risks into account. Thus, as long as your estimates are within the market range and your clients agree in advance, you need not worry about fluctuations in either direction and can accept payment as agreed.

You should, though, consider the root of your occasional overestimation of the work. If you find a given paper easier than expected, you may have been concentrating extra well or it is your good fortune that you received a relatively easy paper.[4] However, if you realize that your estimate was *inherently flawed* (e.g., you miscounted the number of pages or you used your price list for non-native English speakers instead of a native one), it is appropriate to adjust the fee downward. The fact that you also make mistakes to your detriment does not morally justify keeping a flawed estimate in your favor. (One could argue that the flawed price *might*

---

4. See an analogous but not identical case, ibid. 334:3.

still be within the range of market value or cite after-the-fact reasons not to have to change an estimate. However, that approach does not befit the level of integrity you so laudably strive for). Your willingness to forgo questionably deserved money should help you continue to find favor in the eyes of HaShem – and present and future clients.

J-6: Damage Payment on an Already Damaged Object

Question: My car got a deep scratch in the door when it was parked. The offender drove off without leaving a note. We decided to leave the door as is because it was expensive to fix it. Some time later, a similar damage occurred, but this time the person responsible left a note. He is willing to pay to have it fixed if he is obligated. Once the door is removed, there is little difference in price between fixing one scratch or two. Can I make the second person pay for the repair of the door, including the first scratch, or do I figure out the further damage he caused after the first accident?

Answer: We want to commend you and the person who caused the accident for wanting to do the right thing regardless of personal loss or gain. (The question ignores any involvement of insurance companies, and the answer follows accordingly.)

In general, there are two possible approaches concerning how one must compensate for damage he has caused. One approach is to pay for the property's depreciation in value that was a result of the damage. The other approach is to see to it that the damage is repaired. At times the former is more expensive, and at times the latter is. These two approaches are likely the basis of the following dispute. The Rambam[1] writes: If Reuven demands payment from Shimon for the damage he caused by digging two holes in his field and Shimon claims that he dug only one hole, there is a rabbinic requirement for Shimon to swear that he didn't dig the second hole. The Rambam explains that even though, in general, a partial admission creates a Torah-level requirement to make an oath, here the subject is land, and as the Talmud states, Torah-level oaths are not required for disputes over land. The Ra'avad[2]

---

1. *To'ein V'Nitan* 5:2.
2. Ad loc.

contends that despite the fact that the subject is a field, the nature of the claim is a monetary one, and therefore the requirement to make an oath is on a Torah-level. The Rambam may view payments for damage as a means of repairing the object, which in this case is land, whereas the Ra'avad views them as monetary compensation for the loss. The Shach[3] and Chazon Ish[4] imply that the Ra'avad agrees that when the normal course of action is to fix the damaged object, then the payment is geared to that need.

It appears that according to either approach concerning this fundamental issue, you are not entitled to demand payment to fix the door entirely. This is because the second driver is only responsible for the damage *he* caused, not for previous damage that you incurred. Regarding depreciation of the car's (re-sale) value, there is probably little difference between a car with one scratch on the door and a car with two. The possibility that the same, second scratch would have made a bigger difference in the price had it been the car's only blemish is not relevant. If one severely damages a luxury car and a second person subsequently "totals" it, the second person is responsible to pay only the value of a severely damaged car.

In terms of having him pay to fix the door, you probably do not have a claim. The fact that you decided not to fix the door after the first scratch seems to indicate that the damage does not warrant fixing, given the cost of repair and relatively minimal benefit. In such a case, even the Rambam should agree that one does not pay to have it fixed, and his financial obligation would be only for the diminished value of the car. Is it logical to require an exorbitant price to fix something of little value or to improve it only slightly?

Under two circumstances, however, you could demand the second damager to pay to fix the scratch he made. If the average person would have paid to have the car fixed the first time but you

---

3. *Choshen Mishpat* 95:18.
4. *Bava Kama* 6:3.

decided not to do so for whatever personal reason, you can now decide to have it repaired. However, you can charge the second damager only for the added cost of fixing the second scratch. In the following scenario, the second damager would have to pay more. The added damage from the second accident is that which causes the car to be in such a state that the average person would fix it despite the expense. In this case, the second person would have to pay the whole price of fixing the scratch he made, not just part of it. The rationale is the same as above: we compare the situation before and after the accident and require the damager to make up the difference.

Responsibly figuring out the car's depreciation and whether fixing it is warranted calls for an experienced appraiser. Hiring one is probably expensive enough to encourage a compromise that all can live with as the best option for two honest people.

J-7: Receiving Full Pay for Reduced Work

Question: I was hired by a school to work as a speech therapist. They promised that I would be paid for a minimum of twelve hours weekly. During the course of the year, some students left the school, and now there are a couple of hours a week during which I have nothing to do. The school continues to pay me in full. Is it right for me to take the full pay?

Answer: It is challenging to answer questions of what is best to do, as most of *Choshen Mishpat* (monetary law) deals with rulings of one's rights and outright obligations. However, we cannot ignore such a noble question. We will present halachic background, and you should know better than we how to act best in your case. Should a disagreement arise in the future, this response, which is based on partial information from one side, cannot be used to bolster either side.

There are a few Talmudic precedents that deal with a worker who was hired for a job that became (partially) superfluous. If, based on the case's particulars, one side can anticipate the change, he is responsible to stipulate what to do should that occur. If he fails to do so, he is at a legal disadvantage.[1] In this case, it seems that it was stipulated that the school would pay you even if there was no longer a need for twelve hours of work, as has happened and they are doing. However, in the *gemara*'s parallel cases, there are two things the employer can do to minimize the loss of having to pay for work he does not receive. We will now discuss for your consideration whether either is appropriate for you.

Halacha recognizes that part of a worker's pay corresponds to the toil he has to put into the job. Consequently, in a case where a person gets paid without having to work, his salary is reduced corresponding to the toil, and he is paid as a *po'el batel* (an idle

---

1. See *Bava Metzia* 77a.

worker). The gemara[2] points out that some people do not like being idle, in which case there is no salary reduction.

The gemara,[3] discussing a worker who is paid daily and who finished the job before day's end, says that the employer can instruct him to do other work during the remaining time if such work is not more difficult than the work for which he was hired. There is even an opinion that he can give the worker harder work if he pays for the extra effort.[4] Another option for the employer is to give him work on someone else's behalf, thereby obtaining some compensation.[5]

Thus, the school could plausibly ask to reduce your salary to that of a po'el batel or ask you to do other jobs in your spare time if they are not more difficult. (Difficulty may not be limited to exertion but could include factors like embarrassment about doing things which people of your professional standing are not accustomed to do.[6]) The proviso of being paid for twelve hours of therapy *might* preclude these possibilities, as might the standard professional practice, which is a crucial factor in commercial agreements. You are in a better position to ascertain the matter than we are.

It is likely that by having remained silent and having paid you normally, the school has relinquished its rights (*mechilla*) to the above remedies up to this point.[7] (In order to use the logic of mechilla, you need to know that someone of sufficient authority is aware of the situation and accepts it.) However, if you want to be particularly noble, you could consider volunteering to either reduce your wages a little or help the school in other ways.

It is logical to say that this case is different from the gemara's discussion of uncompleted work. Here, you continue to work at

---

2. Ibid.
3. Ibid.
4. *Rama, Choshen Mishpat* 335:1.
5. Ibid.
6. See ibid. and *Bava Metzia* 30b.
7. See *Rama, Choshen Mishpat* 333:8.

your job, just that you have more free time than expected.[8] There is reason to suggest that under such circumstances, the legal, and perhaps the moral, obligation to take a cut in salary or take on additional responsibilities is diminished. Much depends on the extent of the reduction of your workload.

8. See *Tosafot HaRosh, Bava Metzia* 77a.

Section K:
Hashkafa
(Jewish Outlook)

K-1: Special Remedies for Sick People

Question: I heard that there is a written manual in the Jewish holy books that lists remedies for various illnesses. My husband is currently on the waiting list for an organ transplant. May HaShem bless you in perhaps directing us to the path to a *refuah shleima* (full recovery)!

Answer: There are some medical remedies mentioned in the Talmud, as well as in other, later works, such as the Rambam's books on medicine (he was also a physician). However, these are not special, secret remedies. The Torah tells us that he who injures is responsible to see to the healing of the injured.[1] The Talmud derives from this verse that it is proper and mandatory to seek medical help to deal with illness,[2] and this refers to the conventional medicine of the time.

The remedies mentioned in ancient sources are based on the best medical information available to the rabbis in their time. When modern medicine agrees, that is wonderful. When it does not, one should follow present-day experts. We hope and assume that your husband is receiving the best medical care available to you.

We, of course, do not rely exclusively upon medical help. We are instructed to turn to HaShem for help, for He is the true Healer. However, as with medical remedies, there are different, complementary religious approaches. We should rededicate ourselves to the proper service of HaShem, which is the purpose of our being put in this world. Each weekday *Shemoneh Esrei* includes a prayer for health, in general; it is an appropriate place to insert our requests regarding specific people who need refuah. We can say Tehillim (Psalms) on behalf of the ill. We can go to holy places to

---

1. *Shemot* 21:19.
2. *Bava Kama* 85a.

pray and ask holy people to join us in prayer. *Tzedaka* (charity) is a particularly powerful *mitzva* in this regard.

Will these things bring health? In any given case, we have no way of knowing. However, the good deeds will be remembered above and will manifest themselves in ways we may never know. The ancient "remedies" of prayers and good deeds, along with the best in modern medicine, are the best we can do. We extend our sincere wishes for your husband's full and speedy recovery. If you would like to send us his name (Jewish name and mother's Jewish name), we will, God willing, include him in the list of the sick for whom we pray.

K-2: Jewish Education as a Profession

Question: The *gemara* in *Berachot*[1] quotes a *baraita* in the name of Hillel that states the following, as explained by Rashi. During an era of *machnisim* (Torah is not being taught sufficiently by *talmidei chachamim*[2]), one should take it upon himself to teach Torah. In contrast, during a time of *mefazrim* (when many scholars are teaching), it is best to refrain from public teaching. Rashi explains that this latter course promotes *k'vod HaShem*[3] since it displays avoiding assuming a position of authority unnecessarily. Is today a time of machnisim or a time of mefazrim? Is it appropriate, nowadays, to aspire to a career in teaching Torah?

Answer: Today is a time of both. There are circles where, *baruch HaShem*, the ranks of *mechanchim*[4] are saturated. Even in those circles, there still is a purpose for one to go into a career in *chinuch*.[5] It is possible that *A* is more talented and/or dedicated than *B*, who would get the position were *A* to go into a different field. Rashi seems to stress that it is appropriate to refrain from teaching only when the most qualified are already doing so. Furthermore, if *A* gets the position, it may force *B* to find a position outside of his natural community, where there may be a bigger need for mechanchim.

There are sectors of communities and, certainly, regions throughout the world (including Israel) where the need for all sorts of religious help is great. Much of the help can be provided by non-rabbis. However, we need many, many people, including "Torah professionals," to go out and to reach out. It is mainly a

---

1. 63a.
2. Torah scholars.
3. Honor of HaShem.
4. Jewish educators.
5. Jewish education.

question of whether you (if, indeed, this is a personal question) and those who know both you and "the field" feel that you have "what it takes" to contribute. "What it takes" is not monolithic; it depends on the specific nature of a given position, your God-given abilities, your level of idealism and perseverance, etc.

In general, if you have the desire to contribute, you probably are suitable. Chovot HaLevavot[6] says that if one feels an inclination toward a certain profession, he should consider it a sign from HaShem. Presumably, this is all the more so in the area of teaching Torah, even if one falls short of the highest level of motivation described by the Rambam at the end of *Hilchot Shemitta V'Yovel.*

---

6. *Sha'ar HaBitachon* 3.

K-3: Tzedaka From Money Earned in a Prohibited Manner

Question: If one works on Shabbat and gives some of his earnings to *tzedaka* (charity), is that money tainted because of the way in which it was earned? Is the *mitzva* of tzedaka compromised?

Answer: It is difficult to answer this question because the word "tainted" is hard to employ in a precise manner. Let us divide the discussion into two parts, halacha and philosophy.

Halachically, there is a concept that a mitzva can be nullified if it is linked directly to the violation of a prohibition. One example: if one steals an *etrog* and then uses it on Sukkot as the Torah commands, he has not fulfilled his mitzva. However, this rule does not apply here because the linkage between the sin and the mitzva is not direct enough. (If you like, we can present a Talmudic discourse to explain the distinction, but this is the bottom line). Thus, the tzedaka is not halachically tainted.

The mitzva of tzedaka, like, perhaps, all other mitzvot, is not just a perfunctory act where the only factor is how much a person gives. Notably, Maimonides goes into much detail about eight different levels of giving tzedaka (he concentrates on levels of avoiding the pauper's embarrassment). Part of the philosophy behind giving away a portion of one's earnings is that he thereby demonstrates that he realizes that HaShem ordains all of his blessings (including his earnings).[1] If one earns a portion of the money that he donates in a manner in which he transgresses HaShem's commandments (e.g., by violating Shabbat), that element of giving tzedaka is incomplete. Sometimes, one does realize that it is HaShem who controls a person's successes and failures and is remorseful that he has not succeeded in fulfilling His will. If he thus sees his tzedaka as a way of saying "thank you" and "sorry,"

---

1. See *Beitza* 16a.

respectively, then we have a mixed bag. On one hand, that is wonderful, as this mitzva, with the proper intention, can bring him closer to his Maker and Provider. On the other hand, he should not see it as a reasonable trade-off ("I'll continue to work on Shabbat, but it is okay because part of my money goes to tzedaka"). If he does, then the tzedaka could be considered an "accomplice" to the continued violation.

Leaders of Torah institutions have been torn over similar issues. On one hand, one cannot "dismiss" Jews because of their shortcomings in the performance of some mitzvot, even crucial ones, especially in light of the very weak religious climate by which most Jews are surrounded. Shouldn't all Jews be wholeheartedly encouraged to perform good deeds (tzedaka is a great one) and be praised for doing so? Additionally, the connection to HaShem and the spiritual elevation that so often accompany sincere, heartfelt donations to worthy institutions can often bring the person closer to Him. A small minority take the opposite approach, claiming that the responsibility to rebuke those who sin precludes our embracing those who are still in the midst of sinning. Otherwise, they believe, we encourage wrongdoers to continue without correcting their ways.

As spiritual disciples of the great Rav Kook (our mentor, Rav Shaul Yisraeli, was a close student), we believe in embracing all Jews, regardless of their level of religious observance. Certainly, we believe in encouraging the fulfillment of any mitzva and will not say to someone, "All or nothing." Nevertheless, one should not mislead a Jew by telling him or implying that "as long as you give money to institutions or people we deem worthy, you are fine in HaShem's book." We don't have access to HaShem's book of the righteous and His book of the sinners. If we did, I am sure we would find many surprises. We do have access to HaShem's book of instructions for a proper Jewish life – that is the Torah. It is the responsibility of all of us to both fulfill those instructions ourselves and to help others do so. It is not easy to do that perfectly, but we need to try our best.

K-4: Why Certain Halachic Issues Seem to be Overly Stressed

Question: I am very confused about a certain attitude among Orthodox people. Many people place a lot of importance on how long you wait between eating meat and milk. However, let us look at the source for waiting between meat and milk. It is just a rabbinic *seyag* (fence) not to eat them together (when cooked separately) and a further seyag not to eat them in the same meal. As a result, people in different cultures who had a meat meal would end up waiting the amount of time until the next meal before having dairy products. The whole "six-hour/three-hour thing" doesn't seem to be so important, yet people make you feel so guilty if you adopt a more lenient *minhag*.

Answer: We understand your confusion and frustration. Let us try to put things somewhat in perspective. [*Further insight on the matter can be gained by reading the introduction, The History and Process of Halacha.*]

There is an underlying system that has guided the development of halacha and minhag over the centuries. However, some fluidity allows for Divine intervention, rabbinic ingenuity, and socio-religious developments. It is sometimes difficult to ascertain how certain rulings/minhagim have evolved, although there has been substantial research on the topic. Indeed, the importance of certain issues *seems* to have been "blown out of proportion" in comparison to others that appear more crucial. In certain areas, stringency has been added onto stringency, while in others, leniency has been added onto leniency.

At times, it is appropriate for rabbinic leaders to step in and restore things to their proper proportion. However, most of the time, the rabbinic community has a basic trust in the dynamics of the development of normative practice and allows things to progress as long as they do not contradict halacha and are not religiously dangerous. There are two, divergent statements in *Chazal* on the issue, which happen to start with the same words. One source says: "Leave [the people of] Israel alone; if they are not prophets, they are sons of prophets."[1] The other says: "Leave Israel alone; it is better that they sin unintentionally than intentionally."[2] (In fact, there is a responsum of the Terumat HaDeshen[3] where he ends off with the words, "Leave Israel alone, etc." The *poskim* attempt to determine to which of the two quotes he is alluding and, thus, how enthusiastic he is about the discussed practice). The first quote refers to a confidence in the Divine approval of the development of a given minhag. The other refers to a degree of fatalism, that even when a minhag is regrettable, it is difficult, and often unwise, to attempt to alter it.

Regarding your specific issue, we agree that we seem to be very stringent, and we discourage people from being overly judgmental of others. However, we also remind you that just as sometimes a minhag (or the weight given to it) is particularly stringent, other minhagim can be surprisingly lenient. As traditional Jews, we *usually* take the phenomenon as a whole, and we follow the stream in most cases, following the accepted stringencies along with the leniencies. Passing on family traditions and community minhagim is an important part of our tradition and spiritual survival. It should not be taken lightly.

---

1. *Pesachim* 66a.
2. *Beitza* 30a.
3. II, 78.

K-5: Choosing the Most Appropriate Mitzvot

Question: I am confused about how I am to choose the right things to do with my time. I want to do the biggest *mitzvot* I can, yet it seems that most of one's time is spent on mundane matters. Are things like making a living or caring for a family really the biggest mitzvot one can be doing?

Answer: It is difficult to know what the biggest mitzva is in a given situation. Furthermore, the question of a mitzva's "size," although asked with beautiful intentions, is not the right one. The real question is: what does HaShem want us to do?

People spend a large part of their days attending to such mundane needs as sleeping, eating, etc. These may not be the most uplifting activities, but HaShem created us in such a way that they are necessary and expected. Although it is best not to spend more time than necessary on these activities, it is wrong to neglect them significantly over time. One needs to learn how to properly allocate her time.

Just as there are basic bodily needs, there are also other needs and responsibilities that, as HaShem created humanity, need to be addressed. Such time-consuming activities as earning a living, tending to a house and a myriad of other family needs have *both* mundane and spiritual elements to them. (When one performs mundane tasks with the intention of advancing important matters in life, the tasks take on a spiritual quality.) A husband is required by halacha[1] to support his wife in a respectable manner, and, under normal circumstances, should not forsake this obligation with the excuse that he is too busy doing some other "bigger mitzva." A wife is usually required to take care of several

---

1. See *Ketubot* 46b.

household needs.[2] She should not, under normal circumstances, neglect them with the logical sounding excuse that she is so busy with *chesed*[3] that she has no time to take care of her familial obligations.

Even when involved in chesed, one should not seek only the chesed that is, objectively, the "biggest." For example, one is required to give *tzedaka* to one's needy relatives before giving to non-relatives,[4] even if the latter are needier.[5] Similarly, learning Torah, which is the most prominent of all mitzvot, is, nevertheless, pushed aside by "smaller" mitzvot that are incumbent upon a person at given times.

The critical element here is having the proper balance between "more mundane" activities (which would even include *mitzvot* that are one's personal *obligations*) and the fulfillment of some special chesed or mitzva *opportunities* that require putting normal activities on hold. To a great extent, it is halacha's job to instruct a person how to achieve a balance between conflicting, positive activities. (For example, the Aruch HaShulchan[6] rules that, although relatives have precedence regarding tzedaka, it is clear that one who can afford it must set aside funds for poor people who are not his relatives). However, halacha cannot address every scenario that may arise in a person's life. Additionally, different people who are trying to ascertain the best way to serve HaShem may require different answers based on their different abilities and circumstances. Therefore, many decisions are left to the individual. One must be aware of the great value of family and professional obligations, as well as the critical importance of

---

2. See *Ketubot* 59b.
3. Acts of kindness.
4. *Shulchan Aruch, Yoreh Deah* 251:3.
5. *Shut Chatam Sofer, Yoreh Deah* 231.
6. *Yoreh Deah* 251:5.

Torah study, chesed, and other mitzvot. Then she has tools to try to implement the sage advice: "It is good that you seize this, but also from the other do not withdraw your hand."[7]

---

7. *Kohelet* 7:18.

Glossary/Index

A

Acharei Mot A-14 – the name of one of the Torah portions

Acharonim – the Talmudic and halachic scholars who lived from the 16th century until our days

afikoman D-14 – the matza eaten toward the end of the Pesach (Passover) *seder*

aguna I-1 – see referenced question

Akeidat Yitzchak D-1 – the Biblical event in which Abraham bound Isaac upon an altar to be brought as a sacrifice (see Bereishit 22)

Aleinu A-6 – a prayer recited at the end of each of the daily prayers

Al HaEtz B-3 – the blessing recited after eating grapes, figs, pomegranate, olives, or dates

Al HaMichya B-5 – the blessing recited after eating grains not prepared as bread

aliya A-2, A-12, G-6, I-1 – when a man is called up the Torah to bless before and after a section of its public reading

aliya laregel D-6 – the mitzva to come to the Holy Temple in Jerusalem for three festivals (Pesach, Shavuot, and Sukkot) during the year

alot hashachar A-9 – the halachic beginning of the morning, somewhat more than an hour before sunrise

amen A-2, B-1 – the response to a blessing, which indicates agreement with its contents

amira l'nochri D-8 – a Jew telling a non-Jew to do something that is forbidden for the Jew to do. This is often rabbinically forbidden.

Amora – a rabbinic scholar of the Amoraic period, from approximately 200–500 CE

amot A-1, A-4, C-2 – cubits; a measurement with applications in several halachic contexts. The standard opinion is that it is approximately a foot and a half (45 centimeters).

amud G-8 – the podium in the front of the synagogue from which the cantor leads the services

arba'at haminim D-7 – the four species of vegetation that one is obligated to take in his hands during the holiday of Sukkot

aron A-14 – the ark in which the Torah scrolls are stored

Ashkenazi – a Jew of Central or Eastern European origin

asmachta J-4 – see referenced question

Ata Chonantanu C-10 – the prayer added to the fourth blessing of *Shemoneh Esrei* to indicate the end of Shabbat and usher in the week

Av D-22 – month in the Jewish calendar, in which we commemorate the destruction of the Holy Temple

aveilut D-23 – the atmosphere and/or laws of a period of mourning

aveira (plural – **aveirot**) D-1, G-10 – sin

Avraham A-1, D-1 – Abraham

B

ba'al koreh A-8 – one who publicly reads the Torah for the congregation

Bamidbar I-6 – *Numbers*, the fourth of the books of the Pentateuch

baraita – a Talmudic text from the time of the *Tannaim* that was not incorporated into the *mishna* or the *tosefta*

bar/bat mitzva B-2, D-7, I-5, J-3 – one who is old enough and competent enough to be obligated to perform *mitzvot*. It also refers to the point at which one reaches that stage and the celebration that accompanies it.

Barchu A-1 – an important part of the prayers toward the beginning of the morning service

baruch HaShem – thank God

basar b'chalav E-8 – milk and meat mixed together in such a way that the combination is forbidden

batel C-4, D-15 – the status of a [forbidden] object being nullified and thereby losing its halachic status

b'di'eved A-13, C-5, C-6, D-13, E-7, I-4 – after the fact; a situation that one is supposed to avoid, but after the situation has already occurred, it may be halachically acceptable under the circumstances

bedikat chametz D-16, D-17 – the mitzva to check one's house for *chametz* before the Pesach holiday

be'ein D-15 – an object which is intact and not "swallowed up" by something else

beit din D-21, I-1, J-1, J-4 – a rabbinical court, which may rule on a variety of matters, often on monetary disputes

Beit HaMikdash D-6, D-23 – the Holy Temple in Jerusalem. The first one was destroyed some 2,600 years ago; the second one, some 2,000 years ago. We pray for the building of the third and final one.

beit k'nesset (plural – **batei k'nesset**) A-2, F-4 – Hebrew for the Yiddish, shul – a synagogue, where Jews assemble to pray

ben Torah A-5 – a Jewish man who takes the laws and ideals of the Torah very seriously

bentch B-7 – Yiddish for reciting *Birkat HaMazon*

beracha (plural – **berachot**) (see table of contents for section B on berachot) A-9, A-11, A-12, C-5, C-6, C-11, C-13, D-2, D-6, D-11, D-12, D-18, D-22, G-3, G-4, G-5, G-10 – a blessing. There are a few categories of berachot; some are recited periodically and some under certain circumstances.

beracha achrona B-3 – a blessing recited after one eats

beracha l'vatala G-1, G-10 – a blessing that was recited in such a manner that it was of no value. It is forbidden to do so.

beracha rishona B-3 – a blessing recited before one eats

Bereishit A-14, G-8 – *Genesis*, the first of the books of the Pentateuch

besamim C-5 – fragrant herbs or branches. One smells them, with a blessing, after Shabbat to "revive" the soul after the passing of Shabbat.

b'hidur G-3 – in a manner of *hidur* (see *hidur*)

Bilam A-1 – Balaam

bima A-14, G-6 – the platform in the middle of the synagogue upon which the Torah is read

Birkat HaMazon B-1, B-5, B-7 – the series of blessings recited after eating a meal that includes bread

birkat haTorah (plural – **birkot** ...) A-12 – a blessing recited before the study of Torah each new day or before and after the formal public reading of the Torah

birkon C-9 – a book(let) containing certain standard blessings

bishul akum E-11 – food that is forbidden because it was cooked by a non-Jew

bitul E-8 – the concept of something being *batel* (see batel)

bitul chametz D-16 – the nullification, performed before Pesach, of *chametz* that may not have been sold or destroyed

b'li neder C-10 – a statement that conveys the idea that some good action or oral commitment should not be construed as a binding vow

bnei yeshiva H-9 – students in a Torah academy

boneh C-3 – the prohibition of building on Shabbat

borer C-12, C-17, C-19 – the prohibition of selecting on Shabbat

Borei Pri HaGefen – see HaGefen

Borei Nefashot B-3 – the blessing recited after eating a food that does not belong to a food group that has a more specified blessing

brit – see brit mila

brit mila F-4, H-1, H-14, I-3, I-6 – the mitzva of circumcision of Jewish males

C

chag (plural – **chagim**) D-21 – a holiday or festival

challa (plural – **challot**) A-12, C-11, C-21 – a traditional type of bread that is eaten on Shabbat or holidays

chametz C-18, D-15, D-16, D-17, E-4 – leavened bread or other grain-based food, forbidden on the holiday of Pesach (Passover)

chametz she'avar alav haPesach D-16 – *chametz* that was in Jewish possession over the Pesach (Passover) holiday and, thereby, became forbidden.

Chanuka D-10, D-11, H-3 – the eight-day holiday in the early winter that commemorates the Hasmoneans' triumph over the Greeks, over 2,000 years ago, and the subsequent miracle that a small amount of oil lasted eight days

chanukiya (plural – **chanukiyot**) D-10 – the candelabrum used for the mitzva of lighting lights on the Chanuka holiday. It is often called a *menora*.

Chashmona'im G-9 – Hasmoneans. Jewish family that defeated the Greeks and subsequently ruled the Jewish kingdom over 2,000 years ago.

chatzot A-9, C-11, D-14 – the astronomical middle of either the day or the night. It has halachic significance in a number of contexts.

Chazal – a generic term for the rabbis at the time of the Talmud (approximately 1–500 CE)

chazarat hashatz A-2, A-3, D-18 – the repetition of the *Shemoneh Esrei* prayer by the cantor

chazan A-4, A-6, A-10, A-14, G-8, H-14 – cantor

chesed D-12, F-3 – act or attribute of kindness

chillul HaShem A-3, H-2, H-7 – the desecration of the Divine Name, often by the improper behavior of those who are seen to represent Jews or Judaism and thus shame it

chillul Shabbat D-1 – the desecration of the sanctity of Shabbat by violating its negative commandments. This is one of the most serious violations of halacha.

chinuch c-14, d-4, d-7, k-2 – the obligation to educate a child; the field of Jewish education

chiyuvim a-11 – obligations; sometimes, those who are supposed to receive an honor in the synagogue

Chol HaMo'ed d-6, d-8, d-9 – literally, the mundane of the festival; the intermediate days of the holidays of Pesach and Sukkot. These days contain some, but not all, of the halachic elements of the main days of the festival (*Yom Tov*).

chukat hagoyim (plural – **chukot** ...) h-7 – the prohibition of copying the distinctive practices of non-Jews

Chumash d-5 – the Five Books of Moses (Pentateuch)

chupa i-2 – the bridal canopy; part of the ceremony that effectuates a Jewish marriage.

chutz la'aretz d-7, d-13, d-21, h-11 – the Diaspora (lands outside the Land of Israel)

D

davar gush c-20 – a solid piece of food. According to some, the fact that it is likely to maintain a high temperature for a relatively long time gives it a unique status regarding certain halachot.

daven(ing) a-7, a-9, a-10, a-11, a-13, c-11, d-2, h-14 – Yiddish for either the act of *tefilla* (prayer) or for the body of the prayers

derech eretz a-2 – literally, the way of the world; the proper behavior expected of a refined person

Devarim i-4 – *Deuteronomy*, the fifth of the books of the Pentateuch

devarim shebekedusha a-10 – those particularly holy prayers that require a quorum of ten men in order to be recited

dina d'malchuta h-2 – the concept that the law of the land, even though it is neither Divine nor rabbinic in origin, is halachically binding

din Torah j-1 – a monetary court case that is held before a rabbinical court

d'orayta D-14 – a law whose source and authority is from the Torah, and not merely a rabbinical injunction

d'rabbanan B-7 – see mid'rabbanan

duchen A-8 – Yiddish for the act of the *Kohanim* (priestly tribe) blessing the assembled congregation

d'var Torah (plural – **divrei** ...) A-2, G-2 – an idea of Torah that is shared, formally or informally, between Jews

E

edah H-12 – an ethnic grouping within the Jewish people, based on the country of origin

eiruv C-2, D-1, H-8 – a series of walls, poles, and strings that encloses an area and enables those within to carry on Shabbat

Eliezer I-3 – Moses' second son

Elokim G-8 – one of the Names of God

Emet V'Yatziv A-9 – the blessing after *Kri'at Shema* in the morning prayers

Eretz Yisrael D-7, H-2, H-11 – the Land of Israel. This can refer to the boundaries at various times in Jewish history, from Biblical times till today. It is noteworthy that the current boundaries of the State of Israel are similar to the boundaries described in the Bible.

Erev D-17 – eve of ...

etrog D-6, K-3 – a specific citrus fruit (citron), which one is obligated to hold in his hands during the holiday of Sukkot

F

fleishig E-3, E-7, H-3 – Yiddish for a food that comes from or has absorbed taste from meat. It is forbidden to eat such a food together with milk products.

G

Ga'al Yisrael A-9 – a blessing recited after *Kri'at Shema*

gabbai (plural – **gabba'im**) A-1, A-11, A-14, F-5 – person in charge of something (e.g. synagogue services, charitable funds)

gemara (plural – **gemarot**) – the section of the Babylonian Talmud that contains the discussions of the *Amora'im*. See Introduction, chapter 4, B

gematria D-19 – the numerical value of Hebrew letters and words. These values are used as hints of various concepts.

geniza G-9 – the burial of sacred scrolls and objects

get G-8, H-1, I-1 – a religious bill of divorce

H

HaAdama B-6 – the blessing recited before eating vegetables and other foods that grow from the ground (excluding processed grains and tree fruits)

hachana C-9 – the rabbinic prohibition of preparing on a holy day for the needs of a different day

hachnasat orchim A-1 – welcoming guests into one's home

HaEtz B-6 – the blessing recited before eating tree fruit

HaGefen C-6 – the blessing recited before drinking wine

halacha (plural – **halachot**) – the field of Jewish law (see Introduction, chap. 1); an operative Jewish law; the halachic opinion that is accepted as practically binding in the case of a rabbinic dispute

halacha l'ma'aseh C-2 – the halacha as expected to be practiced, as opposed to a theoretical halacha that is unlikely to be implemented

Hallel D-7 – several psalms that are recited joyously on festivals

HaMavdil C-10 – the short, semi-formal declaration made after Shabbat that allows one to do actions that are forbidden on Shabbat

HaMotzi B-1, E-11 – the blessing recited before eating bread

Har Sinai D-5 – Mount Sinai

hashgacha (plural – **hashgachot**) C-6 – rabbinic supervision, usually to ensure the *kashrut* of food

HaShem – literally, the name. Common practice is to use this word to refer to God in order to avoid using His Name in inappropriate settings.

hatarat nedarim H-12, H-14 – the process of annulling oaths, also used by those who want to stop adhering to a commendable religious practice that they accepted explicitly or implicitly

hatavat chalom H-4 – the ceremony to pray that a bad dream should be transformed into one that signals good things

hatmana C-20, C-21 – the rabbinic prohibition of insulating hot food on Shabbat

Havdala C-5, C-10 – the blessing recited over wine at the end of Shabbat, which acknowledges God's part in the transition from Shabbat to the weekdays

hazmana G-2 – preparation of an object to be used as a holy article

hechsher keilim E-10 – literally, making utensils fit. See meaning in context in referenced question.

hefsed merubeh E-2 – a case where a stringent ruling will cause a significant monetary loss

hefsek A-2 – an interruption, often in the performance of a *mitzva*

heter iska F-6 – see referenced question

hidur G-3 – literally, an adornment (of a mitzva); a manner of performing a mitzva that beautifies it or is halachically preferable

hosafa (plural – **hosafot**) A-11 – when an additional person is called to read from the Torah

I

issur E-8 – a prohibition

issur hana'a D-17 – a prohibition to benefit from something

itchazek issura E-4 – Aramaic for "the matter was once definitely forbidden"

K

Kabbala D-1 – esoteric, mystical Jewish teachings and the literature related to them

Kaddish (plural – **Kaddeishim**) A-2, A-6, A-8 – a prayer (in which we sanctify God's Name) that is recited by a member or members of the congregation (often by mourners)

Kaddish D'Rabbanan A-6 – a Kaddish that is recited after the study of Torah

kashering (verb – **kasher**) E-2, E-3, E-8, E-10 – popular term for *hechsher keilim* (see entry)

kashrut (see table of contents for section E on kashrut) B-1, C-4, C-6, D-10 – the field dealing with keeping kosher

katan (feminine – **ketana**) B-7 – a minor, as defined by halacha, generally under thirteen for a boy or under twelve for a girl

kavod [k'vod] K-2 – honor [of]

k'vod haberiyot C-16 – [maintaining] human dignity

kedoshim H-7 – literally, the holy; those whose lives were taken because they were Jewish.

Kedusha A-2, A-9, D-6, G-6 – a prayer recited during the repetition of *Shmoneh Esrei*; in lower case – sanctity

ketav ashuri G-9 – see referenced question

ketuba I-4 – a formal marriage contract that, among other things, ensures a Jewish wife that her husband will support her financially

kibud av va'em J-3 – see referenced question

Kiddush A-12, C-1, C-6, C-11, H-3 – the blessing through which we sanctify Shabbat. It is recited over wine before the Shabbat meal both at night and in the daytime. It can also refer to the food eaten after the blessing.

kinyan D-7, I-2, J-4 – an act of acquisition; see contexts in referenced questions

kitniyot D-15 – legumes and other foods that are not *chametz* but have some similarity to grains that can become chametz. Ashkenazic custom forbids eating these foods on Pesach out of concern that they will be confused with or contain chametz.

kli C-15, E-10 (plural – **keilim / klei** – keilim of) – utensil

kli rishon C-12, C-20 – a utensil in which food was heated

kli se'uda E-10 – a utensil used in connection with a meal

kli sheini C-12, C-20, E-2 – a utensil into which food was transferred from a *kli rishon*

kli shemelachto l'issur (plural – **keilim shemelachtam l'issur**) C-3, C-15 – a utensil whose normal use is forbidden on Shabbat or *Yom Tov*

kli shlishi C-12 – a utensil into which food was transferred from a *kli sheini*

kohen (plural – **kohanim**) A-8, I-5 – a member of the priestly tribe (who descend from Aaron). Members of this tribe have special religious obligations, roles, and privileges.

Kohen Gadol A-14, G-8 – the High Priest

Korban Pesach D-14 – the Paschal Lamb. The sacrifice that, in Temple times, was offered on the afternoon before Passover and was eaten as a central part of the *seder* on the first night of Passover.

korei'a C-16 – the prohibition of tearing on Shabbat

Kotel D-6 – The Western Wall, remnant of the Holy Temple in Jerusalem

kri'at haTorah A-7, A-14 – the reading of the Torah during services in the synagogue

Kri'at Shema A-2, A-4, A-8, A-9, A-13, A-15 – three sections of the Torah containing basic elements of our faith. The Torah commanded us to recite these sections every morning and evening.

k'zayit B-3 – the size of an olive. This measurement has many halachic ramifications.

L

Lag BaOmer D-20 – minor holiday in the middle of the period of semi-mourning in between Pesach and Shavuot

l'chatchila C-6, E-7 – literally, in the first place. The proper way to go about doing something. This term is often used in contrast with *b'di'eved*, which is what to do after one did something in a less than optimum way.

levi I-5 – a member of the tribe of Levi, who has a special standing, but less than a *kohen's*

libun (kal) E-7 – heating a utensil to a very high temperature, a method used to *kasher* a utensil

lifnei iver C-4 – the prohibition of being responsible for the sin of another person

limud z'chut A-8 – see referenced question

l'minyanam D-1 – using the secular date

l'vatala – see beracha l'vatala

lo itchazek issura E-4 – not *itchazek issura* (see entry).

lulav D-6, D-7 – a branch of a palm tree, which is one of four species that a Jewish man is obligated to hold daily during the festival of Sukkot (Tabernacles)

M

Ma'ariv C-10, D-18 – the evening prayer

ma'aser kesafim F-2, F-5 – the recommended practice of giving one-tenth of one's earnings to charity

machloket (plural – **machlokot**) – disagreement, in our context, concerning matters of scholarship

machmir (plural – **machmirim**) F-6 – rules strictly; he who is strict (see also Introduction, chap. 4, section 4.1)

maftir A-14 – the last portion of the public Torah reading

marit ayin C-18, H-13 – onlookers may confuse an action with a prohibition

matanot la'evyonim D-13 – the *mitzva* on Purim of giving a donation to the poor

matza D-14 – unleavened bread. We are commanded to eat matza on Pesach (Passover).

mechallel Shabbat C-4, D-1 – violating the negative commandments of Shabbat; one who desecrates Shabbat

mechilla J-7 – relinquishing monetary rights; forgiveness

mechirat yud gimmel D-17 – a sale of *chametz* done earlier than usual, on the 13th of Nisan

megilla, Megillat Esther D-12, D-18 – *The Book of Esther*, read on Purim

melacha (plural – **melachot**) C-8, C-14, C-16, D-8, D-9 – an activity that the Torah prohibits on Shabbat

menora D-10, H-3 – candelabrum

Mezonot B-6 – the blessing one recites before eating cake or certain grain products (not on bread)

mezuza (plural – **mezuzot**) G-2, G-3, G-4, G-5 – a scroll containing certain fundamental Torah passages. There is a mitzva to attach mezuzot to the doorposts of one's house.

middot A-8 – literally, attributes; manners

mid'oraita B-7 – [a law that was] Divinely ordained (see Introduction, chap. 2)

mid'rabbanan B-7, E-9 – [a law that was] instituted by the rabbis (see Introduction, chap. 3)

midrash (plural – *midrashim*) D-1 – the homiletic writings of the Rabbis of Talmudic and post-Talmudic times

mikveh E-10 – a specially constructed pool that removes ritual impurity from people and objects

milchig E-3, H-3 – Yiddish for a food that comes from or has absorbed taste from milk. It is forbidden to eat such a food together with meat products.

Mincha A-7, A-9 – the afternoon prayer

minhag (plural – **minhagim**) A-3, A-10, A-11, A-15, B-2, B-4, C-2, C-3, C-10, D-1, D-2, D-11, D-20, D-21, D-22, D-23, E-3, E-7, E-11, G-7, H-1, H-6, H-12, H-14, I-6, K-4 (see also Introduction, chap. 4, section 4.3) – custom

minhag hamakom H-12 – the custom as practiced in a specific place

minim B-3 – species, including in the context of species in regard to which the Torah praises the Land of Israel

minyan (plural – **minyanim**) A-3, A-6, A-7, A-10, A-13, D-12,

D-18, I-5 – a quorum of ten men who pray together. A minyan is required in order to say certain prayers.

Mi Shebeirach H-1 – literally, He who blessed …; a blessing for someone's success or recovery

Mishlei H-12 – Proverbs

mishlo'ach manot D-13 – the *mitzva* to send food goods to a friend on Purim

mishna – the most authoritative teachings of the Tanna'im (1–200 CE – see Introduction chap. 4, A)

mitzva (plural – **mitzvot**) – a commandment; a good deed

mo'ed (plural – **mo'adim**) (see table of contents for section D on mo'adim) – one of the festive periods during the course of the year with special remembrances and/or practices.

Moshe A-7, D-5, G-8, H-11, I-3 – Moses

Motzaei Shabbat C-5, C-10, I-6 – Saturday night, after the conclusion of Shabbat

motzi B-7, D-18 – perform a *mitzva* in a manner that enables another person to fulfill the mitzva

muktzeh C-3, C-7, C-9, C-15, C-16, D-8, D-16 – something that does not have a function on Shabbat and, therefore, may not be moved

muktzeh l'mitzvato D-8 – the idea that an object that is set aside for a certain mitzva is off limits to other use during the time that the mitzva applies

N

nachas (In Hebrew, pronounced nachat) J-4 – Yiddish for a good feeling, especially in regard to the accomplishments of a child

ner (plural – **nerot**) C-5, D-10 – candle or oil bowl which is lit

netilat lulav D-6 – the mitzva to take in hand the four species [of which the lulav (= palm branch) is the largest] during the holiday of Sukkot

netilat yadayim H-9 – the mitzva to wash one's hands in a certain way under certain circumstances

Nevi'im C-11 – the [books of the] Prophets

Nine Days D-22 – the period of national mourning leading up to and including the anniversary of the destruction of the Holy Temple in Jerusalem

Nisan D-21 – the month in the Jewish calendar in which the holiday of Pesach falls

O

ochel C-17, C-19 – literally, a food; a halachic classification of something as a desired object.

ona'ah J-5 – the prohibited practice of overcharging or underpaying

oness D-16 – extenuating circumstances that prevent a person from acting in the manner halacha normally requires

orla H-11 – fruit from a tree that is less than three years old. One may not eat or derive benefit from these fruits.

P

parasha A-2 – the weekly Torah portion read on Shabbat; a specific Shabbat day or that which relates to it

pareve E-7 – Yiddish for a food which is neither a milk product nor a meat product and, thus, may be eaten with either

pasken – Yiddish for rendering a halachic ruling

pasuk (plural – **p'sukim**) – a Biblical verse

pasul A-14, G-5 – unfit

pat haba'a b'kisnin B-5 – explained in referenced question

perek (plural – **perakim**) H-1 – chapter

Pesach A-11, D-15, D-16, D-17, D-21 – Passover, the festival that celebrates the liberation of the young Jewish Nation from slavery in Egypt

pesolet C-17, C-19 – a halachic classification of something as an undesired object

peticha A-14 – opening of the ark that contains the Torah scrolls

pidyon haben D-22, I-5, I-6 – the mitzva to "redeem" a firstborn son "from" a *kohen*

pikuach nefesh B-1 – danger to one's life

Pinchas A-14 – the name of one of the Torah portions

po'el C-18 – a worker who is paid based upon the amount of time that he works

posek (plural – **poskim**) – scholars who regularly render halachic rulings

p'sak – a halachic ruling

P'sukei D'Zimra A-2, A-4, A-13 – the psalms and other Biblical passages that are recited toward the beginning of the morning prayers

p'sukim – see *pasuk*

Purim D-12, D-13 – the holiday celebrating the salvation of the Jews of the Persian Empire from a cruel oppressor

Purim Meshulash D-12 – the situation that arises where the celebration of Purim must be broken up over three days

R

rabbeim – rabbis / teachers

Rav – Rabbi

refuah C-13 – healing

refuah sheleima K-1 – a full recovery; a standard blessing for recovery

ribbit F-6 – usury, which the Torah prohibits

ribbit ketzutza F-6 – lending money with a rate of interest that is set from the outset

Rishon (plural – **Rishonim**) – the Talmudic and halachic scholars from approximately 1000–1500 CE (see Introduction 4, D)

Rosh Chodesh D-21 – the beginning of a Jewish month (lunar)

Rosh Hashana D-1, D-2 – the holiday that is both the Jewish New Year and the Day of Judgment

S

s'chach H-10 – the special roof that one puts on his *sukka* (booth) for the festival of Sukkot

seder A-15, D-14 – the "order" of religious observances and feast on the first night(s) of Passover

sefek sefeika E-11 – doubt of a doubt; two *possible* reasons that both indicate the same halachic conclusion

sefer (plural – **sefarim**) C-9, F-5, G-3, G-6 – books, in our context, those that deal with Torah topics

sefer Torah A-7, A-12, A-14, G-2, G-6, G-7, G-8, G-9 – Torah scroll

sefira D-18, D-20, D-21 – short for *sefirat ha'omer*

sefirat ha'omer D-18, D-19 – the daily counting of forty-nine days from the second day of Pesach (Passover) until Shavuot; the aforementioned period of time itself

seminary J-4 – a school of intensive Torah study for young women

Sephardim – Jews who originated in the communities of North Africa, the Middle East and the Near East

se'uda shlishit C-9, C-11 – the third meal of Shabbat

seyag K-4 – a rabbinic injunction designed to distance a person from the possibility of violating the Torah

Shabbat (plural – Shabbatot) (see table of contents for section C on Shabbat) A-7, A-11, H-11, H-14, K-3 – the Sabbath; the time from sundown Friday until Saturday night. This day is hallmarked by its special observances, prayers, and many restrictions on different types of work.

Shacharit A-6, A-9 – the morning prayer

shadchanus gelt J-2 – Yiddish for the money due to a matchmaker when a couple decides to marry

shaliach C-18 – an agent whose actions are halachically considered as if they were done by the person who appointed him

shalosh regalim D-5 – the three holidays (Pesach, Shavuot, Sukkot) during the year when, in the times of the Temple, Jews made pilgrimages to Jerusalem

Shavuot D-21 – Pentecost; the holiday during which we celebrate the giving of the Torah on Mount Sinai

Shechina A-4, A-8 – the Divine Presence

Shehakol B-6 – the blessing recited before eating any of many foods that do not fit into a special category. Animal products and most drinks are included.

Shehecheyanu B-2, D-22 – a blessing made upon certain happy and/or cyclical events

Shemoneh Esrei A-2, A-3, A-4, A-8, A-9, A-10, A-13, K-1 – the main section of the daily prayers, during which one "stands directly before God" to praise him and make important requests

Shemot I-3, K-1 – *Exodus*, the second of the books of the Pentateuch

sheini C-12, C-20, I-4 – second [level]

Shemini Atzeret D-5 – a holiday at the end of Sukkot

shevarim D-2 – the triple blast that is part of the shofar blowing on Rosh Hashana.

shiur H-14 – a Torah class; an amount that meets a certain halachic standard

shlishi C-12, I-4 – third [level]

Shlomo HaMelech D-5 – King Solomon

shofar B-7, D-2, H-3 – the ritual "musical instrument" made of a ram's horn that is used to blow certain types of blasts on Rosh Hashana.

shomer Shabbat C-4 – one who observes the Sabbath according to its restrictions

shul – A-2, A-4, A-7, A-12, C-10, C-11, D-2, D-12, G-8, G-10, H-3, I-1 – Yiddish for synagogue, house of prayer

siddur (plural – **siddurim**) – A-4, A-14, C-9, D-1, D-16, G-6, G-9, H-1, H-4 – prayer book

siman – a chapter in some books

Simchat Torah A-11, D-5 – the holiday at the end of the holiday of Sukkot in which congregations celebrate the completion of the yearly Torah-reading cycle

Sivan D-21 – one of the months in the Jewish calendar, in which Shavuot falls

sofer G-5 – a scribe who writes Torah scrolls, tefillin and me-zuzot

sugyot D-8 – sections of Talmudic discussion

sukka B-4, G-4, H-8 – the booth that we sit in during Sukkot (Tabernacles) in commemoration of the period after the Exodus when the Israelites lived in the wilderness

Sukkot D-5, D-6, D-7, D-21 – Tabernacles, the holiday during which we celebrate the Divine protection of the Jewish people during their sojourns in the wilderness as well as the yearly harvest

T

takana A-12 – a practice of rabbinic origin intended to improve a certain element of life within the Jewish community (see Introduction, chap. 3)

tallit A-8, G-5, G-6, G-10 – a four-cornered garment that is worn during prayers. As required by the Torah, it has special fringes.

Tammuz D-22 – one of the months in the Jewish calendar, in which the fast of 17 Tammuz falls

talmidei chachamim A-7, C-10, K-2 – literally, the students of the wise; Torah scholars

Tannai'm – a rabbinic scholar of the Tannaic period, approximately 1–200 CE

tarat D-2 – an acronym for one of the sets of *shofar* blasts (*tekiah, teruah, tekiah*)

tashat D-2 – an acronym for one of the sets of *shofar* blasts (*tekiah, shevarim, tekiah*)

Tashlich D-1 – a prayer recited on Rosh Hashana (Jewish New Year) next to a body of water

tashlumin A-9, C-5 – see referenced questions

tashrat D-2 – an acronym for one of the sets of shofar blasts (*tekiah, shevarim, teruah, tekiah*)

tefach (plural – **tefachim**) H-8 – a measure used in halachic matters, approximately three inches (eight centimeters)

tefilla (see table of contents for section A on tefilla) C-11, D-1 – prayer

tefillin B-2, G-1, G-2, G-5, G-7, G-10 – phylacteries, specially made boxes containing hand-written scrolls upon which four sections of the Torah are written. Jewish men wear them during weekday morning prayers.

tefillin shel rosh G-1, G-2 – the tefillin placed upon the head

tefillin shel yad G-2 – the tefillin that are placed upon the arm.

Tehillim H-1, K-1 – Psalms

teki'a D-2 – a long blast of the shofar that is part of the shofar blowing on Rosh Hashana

teru'a D-2 – a long series of short shofar blasts that is part of the shofar blowing on Rosh Hashana

teshuva H-5 – repentance; responsum

tevilla E-10 – immersion of a person or an object in a specially constructed ritual bath known as a *mikveh* as part of a process of purification

tevillat keilim E-10 – immersion of certain newly acquired utensils in a *mikveh* (see tevilla)

Three Weeks D-22 – the period of time between Shiva Asar B'Tammuz and Tisha B'Av, two fasts that mark stages in the destruction of the Holy Temple in Jerusalem

Tisha B'Av D-23 – the fast day that marks the destruction of the first and second Holy Temples in Jerusalem

Tishrei D-21 – one of the months in the Jewish calendar, in which Rosh Hashana, Yom Kippur and Sukkot fall

Torah D-8 – teachings of Jewish law, Bible, and ethics; The Five Books of Moses (see Introduction chap. 1, 2)

tosefta (plural – toseftot) compilation of halachic rulings from the period of the *Tanna'im* (see Introduction 4, A)

treif E-2, E-3 – Yiddish for non-kosher

tzedaka D-13, G-7, H-11, K-1, K-3 (see table of contents for section F on tzedaka) – charity

Tzedukim G-1, G-8 – Sadducees, a group of Jews who deviated from certain basic tenets of belief

tzeit hakochavim A-9 – literally, the emergence of stars; the halachic beginning of the night, and a new Jewish calendar day

tzibbur A-7 – a community (it can refer to different sizes, depending on the context)

Tziporah I-3 – Moses' wife

tzitzit G-10 – the special fringes that are attached to the corners of four-cornered garments. Commonly, it refers to the garments that have the fringes attached, as well.

U

uvdin d'chol C-7 – activity on Shabbat or a festival that is characteristic of weekday activity

V

Vayikra H-7, H-11, H-13, I-4 – *Leviticus*, the third of the books of the Pentateuch

V'Zot HaBeracha D-5 – The final portion of the Torah

Y

yayin migito C-6 – literally, wine coming from the wine press; the Talmudic equivalent of grape juice

Yehi Ratzon H-1 – A type of prayer beginning with the words "May it be Your Will"

Yerushalmim D-6 – residents of Jerusalem

Yerushalayim D-6 – Jerusalem

Yitzchak D-1 – Isaac

Yom HaAtzma'ut D-20 – Israel Independence Day (5 Iyar)

Yom Kippur D-3, D-4 – The Day of Atonement; the fast day, which is the holiest day of the year

Yom Tov (plural – **Yamim Tovim**) A-11, C-1, C-2, D-8, D-16 – the main day(s) of Jewish festivals, during which it is forbidden to engage in most of the activities that are forbidden on Shabbat

Yom Yerushalayim D-20 – Jerusalem Liberation Day (28 Iyar)

yotzei D-18 – fulfill a positive commandment

Yotzer Or A-9 – the first blessing before *Kri'at Shema* in the morning

Z

zei'ah E-7 – giving off moisture

zimun B-1, B-7 – the introduction to *Birkat HaMazon*, recited when three men eat together

z'maniyot C-11 – proportional [hours], $\frac{1}{12}$th of day or night period, which fluctuate in length depending upon the season

Others

17 Tammuz D-22 – the date of the fast that commemorates when the Romans breached the walls of Jerusalem, which led to the destruction of the Holy Temple

9 Av – D-22 – see Tisha B'Av